Postdramatic Theatre

Hans-Thies Lehmann's groundbreaking study of the new theatre forms that have developed since the late 1960s has become a key reference point in international discussions of contemporary theatre. *Postdramatic Theatre* refers to theatre after drama. Despite their diversity, the new forms and aesthetics that have evolved have one essential quality in common: they no longer focus on the dramatic text.

Lehmann offers a historical survey combined with a unique theoretical approach, illustrated by a wealth of practical examples, to guide the reader through this new theatre landscape. He considers these developments in relation to dramatic theory and theatre history, and as an inventive response to the emergence of new technologies and a historical shift from a text-based culture to a new media age of image and sound. Engaging with theoreticians of drama and theatre from Aristotle, Hegel, Szondi and Brecht to Barthes, Lyotard and Schechner, the book analyses the work of recent experimental theatre practitioners such as Robert Wilson, Tadeusz Kantor, Heiner Müller, The Wooster Group, Needcompany and Societas Raffaello Sanzio.

This excellent translation is newly adapted for the Anglophone reader, including an introduction by Karen Jürs-Munby which provides useful theoretical and artistic contexts for the book.

Hans-Thies Lehmann is Professor of Theatre Studies at the Johann Wolfgang Goethe Universität, Frankfurt am Main, Germany. His numerous publications include *Theater und Mythos* (1991) on the constitution of the subject in ancient Greek tragedy, *Writing the Political* (2002) and, with Patrick Primavesi, *Heiner Müller Handbuch* (2004).

Karen Jürs-Munby is Senior Lecturer in Drama, Theatre and Performance at the University of Huddersfield.

Postdramatic Theatre

Hans-Thies Lehmann

Translated and with an Introduction by
Karen Jürs-Munby

Routledge
Taylor & Francis Group

LONDON AND NEW YORK

For Eleni Varopoulou

First published 2006 by Routledge
2 Park Square, Milton Park, Abingdon, Oxon OX14 4RN

Simultaneously published in the USA and Canada by Routledge
270 Madison Ave, New York, NY 10016

Routledge is an imprint of the Taylor & Francis Group

German edition © Verlag der Autoren, D-Frankfurt am Main 1999;
English edition © Routledge 2006

**The publication of this work was supported by a grant from
the Goethe-Institut.**

Typeset in Baskerville by The Running Head Limited, Cambridge
Printed and bound in Great Britain
by The Cromwell Press, Trowbridge, Wiltshire

British Library Cataloguing in Publication Data
A catalogue record for this book is available from the British Library

Library of Congress Cataloging in Publication Data
Lehmann, Hans-Thies.
  [Postdramatisches Theater. English]
  Postdramatic theatre / Hans-Thies Lehmann; translated and with an
introduction by Karen Jürs-Munby.
    p. cm.
  Includes bibliographical references and index.
1. Theater—Germany—History—20th century. 2. Experimental
theater—Germany—History—20th century. 3. German drama—
20th century—History and criticism. I. Title.
  PN2654.L35 2006
  792.02'23'09430904—dc22

ISBN10: 0–415–26812–5 (hbk)
ISBN10: 0–415–26813–3 (pbk)

ISBN13: 9–78–0–415–26812–7 (hbk)
ISBN13: 9–78–0–415–26813–4 (pbk)

Contents

Preface to the English edition

In presenting this study to the Anglophone readership (with a certain delay due to adverse circumstances), I would like to express my gratitude to Karen Jürs-Munby who carried out the translation not only in an impressively short time but with admirable precision and competence. In addition, she contributed many a valuable reference. Her introduction will facilitate the access for the interested Anglophone readership and offer the possibility to relate the analyses and theses of the book to other theatre works especially in Britain and the USA.

Wherever possible I have placed importance on discussing only performances I have been able to see myself. Consequently, the occasional imbalance has been unavoidable due to my personal reception or the accidental nature of circumstances. Otherwise, there would have been more of an emphasis, for example, on British fringe theatre and performance. The American avant-garde has left deep marks on international theatre and thus it comes as no surprise that a number of American artists and companies are acknowledged and discussed in the present study (Wilson, Foreman, Schechner, Jesurun, The Living Theatre and The Wooster Group to name but a few). The case is objectively somewhat different with respect to British theatre and here the introduction by Karen Jürs-Munby will add to the picture.

It should be mentioned that a (roughly speaking) neo-realist wave in the new German theatre of the 1990s has frequently been considered as having been inspired by the British 'movement' of 'in-yer-face' theatre. Indeed the 'attack' on the spectator in such plays is a trait that would have to be theorized as a tension between dramatic and postdramatic theatre; and *4.48 Psychosis* by Sarah Kane would almost have to be invented as one of the great texts in analogy to postdramatic theatre if it did not already exist. But as is explained in the book, it is not the text but the theatrical means that are the focus of this study. The investigation is aimed at theatre, in as much as it problematizes the constitution of a dramatic fiction and world in general and with it also an immediate reference to social reality.

The book intends to give prominence to an aesthetic logic within the development of theatre towards the postdramatic. The analyses do not aim at a comprehensive review of the discussed productions and artists but are rather designed for the reader to transfer and translate *mutatis mutandis* what is developed here to other work in the theatre. The international resonance of the book makes me hopeful that this will also be the case for Anglophone theoreticians, students and practitioners of theatre.

Hans-Thies Lehmann
Frankfurt am Main, January 2005

Introduction

Karen Jürs-Munby

What's in the 'post'?

Due to the delayed English translation of this book (published in German in 1999 and already translated into several other languages[1]), we are faced with the curious situation that, ahead of its publication in English, *Postdramatic Theatre* has already become a key reference point in international discussions of contemporary theatre. An increasing number of English publications engage with the concept in their own studies of new theatre texts and productions.[2] Hans-Thies Lehmann's study has obviously answered a vital need for a comprehensive and accessible theory articulating the relationship between drama and the 'no longer dramatic' forms of theatre that have emerged since the 1970s. This relationship has often been neglected, or at least under-explored, by approaches that have preferred to call these new theatre forms 'postmodern' or more neutrally 'contemporary experimental' or 'contemporary alternative'. A notable exception is Elinor Fuchs' *The Death of Character* (1996), which focuses on the deconstruction of dramatic character in contemporary American theatre in relation to postmodern theories of subjectivity and which in this context also examines new work in its relation to the breakdown of dramatic conventions. Like Fuchs and other critics who relate theatre and performance to postmodernism, Lehmann sets out to find a language for the new theatre forms but does so by systematically considering their relation to dramatic theory and theatre history, including their resonances with (and divergences from) the historical theatre avant-gardes. Unlike Fuchs, he systematically considers the new theatre aesthetics in terms of their aesthetics of space, time and the body, as well as their use of text. Throughout, he also explores theatre's relationship to the changing media constellation in the twentieth century, in particular the historical shift out of a textual culture and into a 'mediatized' image and sound culture. His approach here draws on a wide range of media analyses and aesthetic theories from Benjamin and Adorno to Barthes, Kittler and McLuhan, as well as perhaps less familiar thinkers, such as film theorist Vivian Sobchak and image theorist Gottfried Boehm. The middle chapters, 'Panorama of postdramatic theatre', 'Performance', and 'Aspects: text – space – time – body – media', develop positive analytical categories for a description of the new theatre aesthetics. The focus on the relationship between drama and new theatre and performance leads Lehmann to consider a wide range of international examples from hetero-geneous theatre and performance 'genres' that are often treated separately under different names: 'devised' experimental performance work, physical theatre and dance, multimedia theatre, performance art and 'new writing', as well as innovative stagings of classical drama that push this drama into the post-dramatic (by directors such as Einar Schleef, Robert Wilson and Klaus-Michael Grüber).

In the following, I would like to indicate some of the critical, artistic and institutional contexts that inform this book. I shall contextualize Lehmann's study by way of exploring the overdetermined and complex meaning of the prefix 'post' in *Postdramatic Theatre*. In his Prologue, Lehmann expresses his own wariness of the prefix 'post' by quoting Heiner Müller's corny joke that he only knew of one postmodern author – namely August Stramm, a poet who worked at the post office. (I could retort that since I used to work as a postwoman as a student I must therefore be qualified to talk about all thing 'post'-al.) On a more serious note, I would like to argue here that the 'post' in postdramatic is prone to similar misunderstandings as the 'post' in postmodernism and can be under-stood to function analogously to its working as explained by Lyotard.[3] Thus, it will hopefully become clear that 'post' here is to be understood neither as an epochal category, nor simply as a chronological 'after' drama, a 'forgetting' of the dramatic 'past', but rather as a rupture and a beyond that continue to enter-tain relationships with drama and are in many ways an analysis and 'anamnesis' of drama. To call theatre 'postdramatic' involves subjecting the traditional rela-tionship of theatre to drama to deconstruction and takes account of the numerous ways in which this relationship has been refigured in contemporary practice since the 1970s.

Working closely with this book in the intimate 'reading' of translation has caused me to reflect differently on many of the performances I have seen over the years. As with Lehmann's writing, a personal theatre-going journey is thus inscribed in the performance examples I shall draw on during the course of this introduction. Forced Entertainment, for instance, feature heavily as I have been following their work closely since the early 1990s. These examples – mostly British and American – are, however, neither a complete account of my own journey, nor in any way an exhaustive or representative 'overview' of all Anglo-phone theatre that could be considered postdramatic. Rather I hope they can function as further postdramatic 'landmarks' in the theatre landscape of recent decades to complement Lehmann's own international 'panorama'.

(Post)dramatic theory 'post' Szondi and Hegel

Lehmann's theory of postdramatic theatre is in part a response to Peter Szondi's seminal *Theory of the Modern Drama*, which read plays from Ibsen and Strindberg through to O'Neill and Arthur Miller in terms of a 'crisis of drama'.[4] This 'crisis', according to Szondi, manifested itself in an increasing tension between the

formal requirements of Aristotelian drama and the demands of modern 'epic'
social themes which could no longer be contained by this form. Arguing against
traditional normative Aristotelian dramatic theory, which conceived of dramatic
form as timeless, 'as existing outside history', Szondi theorized the history of
drama in terms of a historical dialectic of form and content. 'Drama', he argued,
was a 'time-bound concept' that 'stands for a specific literary-historical event –
namely, the drama as it arose in Elizabethan England and, above all, as it came
into being in seventeenth-century France and was perpetuated in the German
classical period'.[5] Its aesthetics sprang from the need of 'a newly self-conscious
being who, after the collapse of the medieval world, sought to create an artistic
reality within which he could fix and mirror himself on the basis of interpersonal
relationships alone'.[6] This resulted in a self-contained form he calls 'absolute
drama', which is characterized by the following: the dominance of dialogue and
interpersonal communication; the exclusion of anything external to the dramatic
world (including the dramatist and the spectators, who are condemned to silent
observation); the unfolding of time as a linear sequence in the present; and the
adherence to the three unities of time, place and action. According to Szondi,
this ideal came under increasing pressure at the end of the nineteenth century in
the dramatic works of Ibsen, Chekhov, Strindberg, Maeterlinck and Hauptmann
when the 'crisis of drama' manifests itself as a discrepancy between the self-
contained absolute form of drama with its interpersonal emphasis and the new
social, politico-economic and philosophical subject matter which transcends it.
Szondi goes on to read twentieth-century drama as responses to this 'crisis'.
Naturalist, Expressionist and Existentialist works are analysed as various 'rescue
attempts' that still seek to adhere to dramatic form whilst exploring new content,
whereas works by Piscator, Brecht, Bruckner, Pirandello, O'Neill, Wilder and
Miller are discussed in terms of 'tentative solutions' that introduce what Szondi
calls an 'Epic I' into drama.

Lehmann's study of postdramatic theatre, as Markus Wessendorf states, is in
many ways 'a continuation of Szondi's project, but a continuation that is at the
same time based on a major revision and reassessment of Szondi's predominantly Hegelian model'.[7] Lehmann contends that Szondi's Hegelian understanding of twentieth-century theatre development – rooted as it is in the
opposition between Aristotelian drama on the one hand and epic tendencies on
the other – is conceptually limiting. Such an approach privileges Brechtian epic
theatre as the major break with tradition – when, from the perspective of postdramatic theatre, Brecht's innovations are considered precisely as *part of* the dramatic tradition. Consequently, Szondi remains blind to theatrical and critical
developments other than those structured by the Aristotelian/epic dialectic.
Lehmann argues that this model ultimately does not allow Szondi to imagine
theatre *without* drama, i.e. without the representation of a closed-off fictional
cosmos, the mimetic staging of a fable. By systematically paying attention to
theatre as performance (unlike Szondi who reads drama predominantly as literature[8]), Lehmann can show that theatre and drama as such have drifted apart in
the second half of the twentieth century.

Through a close deconstructive analysis of Hegel's own theory of drama, Lehmann traces not only how the idea of drama could have become historically so powerful, but also how the seeds of an eventual crisis of dramatic theatre are already harboured in the contradictions and tensions within this model of drama as the reconciliation of beauty and ethics. The 'exclusion of the real' is an essential principle of drama, and its performance through particular real individuals always already constitutes a constant latent threat to its abstract ethical content. If read against the grain, Hegel's *Aesthetics*, as Lehmann demonstrates, can thus be read as pointing the way towards the dissolution of the dramatic concept of theatre *within* drama.

The turn to performance

Lehmann's theory of postdramatic theatre is testament to a new emphasis on performance in European and North American theatre and art from the 1960s onwards, which consequently led to a paradigm shift in the study of theatre and to the emergence of Performance Studies as a discipline.[9] The emergence of neo-avant-garde art forms such as happenings, environments, Fluxus events and performance art or live art all resulted in a renewed attention to the materiality of performance in theatre and in renewed challenges to the dominance of the text, challenges that had previously been championed by the historical avant-garde, most prominently by Antonin Artaud. The text was to become just one element in the scenography and general 'performance writing' of theatre.

The theatre that Lehmann identifies as postdramatic often focuses on exploring the usually unacknowledged anxieties, pressures, pleasures, paradoxes and perversities that surround the performance situation as such. Thus, to cite some of my own examples, in 1989 the Australian theatre company Sydney Front toured to Europe with a piece called *The Pornography of Performance*, which confronted the audience with their voyeuristic desires. Entering the performance space in semi-darkness, we were invited to reach through the holes of large vertical cylinders. Feeling up the naked performers inside the cylinder, we were suddenly 'caught red-handed' when bright lights came up, the 'grope tubes' rose to the ceiling and we were confronted with the now clothed and masked performers glaring back at us. Other acts of the performance included what looked like a mother–daughter heart-to-heart from a Naturalist kitchen sink drama turning into a spitting match between the performers (Andrea Aloise and Elise Ahamnos); a performer speaking a monologue from Oscar Wilde while eating dog food out of a can; the same performer (Chris Ryan) singing 'You make me feel like a natural woman' while dressed in a seventeenth-century shepherdess outfit with the front panel missing (thus exposing his genitals); and another performer (Nigel Kellaway) having cake stuffed up his bum.[10]

Similar concerns with audience expectations, stage fright, exposure, compulsory gender performance and other performance pressures are already announced in the very name of the Sheffield-based company Forced Entertainment – which significantly leaves it open whether it is us or them who are being 'forced' to entertain or be entertained. Pieces like *First Night* (2001), which can be read as a contemporary reworking of Peter Handke's already postdramatic text *Publikumsbeschimpfung* (*Offending the Audience*, 1966), explored the imperative to perform in a vaudeville theatre setting. Dressed in glamorous but uncomfortable suits/dresses and wearing grotesque make-up and painfully forced smiles, the performers greeted the audience with barely hidden contempt and proceeded to put themselves through various 'acts' that inevitably failed. At other points, the audience – usually expected to forget about their own bodies while watching a performance – were verbally reminded of their repressed need to blink, drink, salivate or go to the toilet, while the performers did just that and took a break. In a poignant clairvoyance act, spectators were reminded of their own mortality when the performer Cathy Naden pointed at audience members and seemed to be making predictions about how people were going to die. The turn to performance is thus at the same time always a turn towards the audience, as well.

Feminist theory, queer theory and postcolonial theatre scholarship, as well as the more recent analyses of disability and performance and age and performance, have all pointed out that performance has the power to question and destabilize the spectator's construction of identity and the 'other' – more so than realist mimetic drama, which remains caught in representation and thus often reproduces prevailing ideologies.[11] For example, Ursula Martinez' recent show, *O.A.P.*, based on interviewing old people in the community, investigated her own fear of growing old while also exploring gender as performance. At one point, the early middle-aged Ursula re-emerged from under a covered table (where she had been confessing her fears to us via a live video link) having morphed into 'old Ursula' (played by one of her senior collaborators dressed in the same slinky dress). In a memorable scene, 'old Ursula' donned high heels and make-up and turned to the audience asking whether anybody would like to kiss her. During the embarrassed silence that followed, we were left to decide whether it was just the distance to the performer on stage or the image of old people as non-sexual beings that prevented us from volunteering to kiss her. Similarly, Graeae Theatre Company, Britain's foremost company of performers with physical and sensory impairments, addresses theatre's collusion in the marginalization and 'othering' of disabled performers through their performance aesthetic. In *Peeling*, a play written by Kaite O'Reilly, three actresses (Lisa Hammond, Caroline Parker and Sophie Partridge), who are stuck in enormous tent-like frocks, turn out to be 'extras' in the chorus in an otherwise unseen performance of the *The Trojan Women*. The performance switches between the actresses speaking their bit parts in this play-within-a-play and them chatting and arguing as they pass the long time when they there are not 'on'; as they gradually peel off the layers of their frocks/tents they reveal devastating stories about their reproductive 'choices' which connect them to those of the Trojan women. Throughout the performance, the actresses use sign language and speak about each other in the third person to describe actions, the text of which is also visually displayed on video. While this particular piece arguably still has a dramatic structure, its main effects, I would contend, are created through an alternative dramaturgy that fully incorporates (rather than adds on) the use of sign language and audio description into the performance writing – effectively combining both inclusivity/accessibility and gestic defamiliarization. There is also a deliberate blurring between the characters of the actresses and the disabled performers themselves as they address the spectators and let them know they know they are being stared at and are returning the gaze.

As this example shows, the notion of postdramatic theatre and its valorization of the performance dimension does not imply that texts written for the theatre are no longer relevant or cannot be considered in this context. Yet, in new writing for the theatre, too, a 'turn to performance' can be observed. As Malgorzata Sugiera states:

> Nowadays the basic structural principle of texts written for the theatre increasingly often turns out to be their immanent theatricality, which is, however, no longer understood as a reflection upon theatre as a domain of artistic activity or as an extensive metaphor of human life, but rather as a means of inducing the audience to watch themselves as subjects which perceive, acquire knowledge and partly create the objects of their cognition.[12]

In German-language theatre, major examples of this kind of writing would be texts by Heiner Müller (*Hamletmaschine*) and by Austrian playwright Elfriede Jelinek. British and American authors whose texts could be described as postdramatic include, for example, Sarah Kane (especially *4:48 Psychosis* and *Crave*), Martin Crimp (e.g., *Attempts on Her Life, Face to the Wall, Fewer Emergencies*), and Suzan Lori-Parks (e.g., *The America Play, Imperceptible Mutabilities in the Third Kingdom*). All these writers produce what could be called 'open' or 'writerly' texts[13] for performance, in the sense that they require the spectators to become active co-writers of the (performance) text. The spectators are no longer just filling in the predictable gaps in a dramatic narrative but are asked to become active witnesses who reflect on their own meaning-making and who are also willing to tolerate gaps and suspend the assignment of meaning.

In the Epilogue to this book, Lehmann considers the politics of postdramatic theatre, arguing that it is not the direct political content or thematics which makes this theatre political but the 'implicit content of its mode of representation'. The turn to performance is thus precisely not a turn to performativity in the sense of Austin's speech act theory.[14] While performance can address, show, destabilize and interrupt the 'performativity' of nationalism, racism, sexism or ageism, it does so not through a direct efficacy or real doing, not primarily by producing political meaning, but through something Lehmann calls 'afformance art'. With this term Lehmann locates the political in perception itself, in art as a poetic *interruption* of the law and therefore of politics.

Post-1960s institutional context, memory, history and palimpsest

Together with the turn to performance in practice and theory, the development of a laboratory-based theatre studies is an important context for the development of postdramatic theatre. In Germany, Hans-Thies Lehmann himself, together with Andrzej Wirth, was instrumental in establishing a more practice-based theatre studies education by developing the Institut für Angewandte Theaterwissenschaft (Applied or Practiced Theatre Studies) at the University of Giessen between 1982 and 1988. This historical development away from Drama or Theatre Studies (*Theaterwissenschaft*) as a branch of Literature or the purely historical study of theatre and towards Theatre Studies as an independent academic discipline and integrated practical and theoretical training ground for practitioners of theatre, dance and performance, occurred a good ten to twenty years earlier in Britain and in the USA.[15] Just as many of Germany's new directors, authors and companies (e.g. René Pollesch, She She Pop, Showcase Beat Le Mot, Rimini-Protocol) have come out of the University of Giessen and younger programmes (e.g. at the University of Hildesheim), many of the contemporary experimental companies working in Britain and the USA today are comprised of graduates from the relatively young academic disciplines of Drama, Theatre Studies and Performance Studies. While the international Centre for Performance Research in Wales has just celebrated its thirtieth anniversary, companies like Forced Entertainment, whose members originally graduated from Exeter University's Drama department (founded as a course in 1968 and as a separate section in 1976), have just celebrated their twentieth anniversary.

What does this institutional history mean for the theatre these companies make? I would argue that, despite the playful innocence exuded by many of the performances, most of the practitioners of contemporary experimental theatre are actually well versed in the historical avant-garde, the neo- and post-avant-garde and so-called modern drama. This includes the intimate knowledge of playwriting that was already to a large extent postdramatic, such as the work of Samuel Beckett or Peter Handke, references to which can often be traced in the work of Forced Entertainment, for instance. Hence, while this can by no means serve as the only context or 'explanation' for the work (many practitioners also came from the visual arts), it is significant that this work is often 'postdramatic' even on the level of biographical trajectories.

Secondly, this institutional context means that there are by now artistic networks, collaborations and occasional intertextual references to each other's work. The work of these companies, especially The Wooster Group, Forced Entertainment and Goat Island, by now has a firm place in Theatre Studies curricula and has generated its own history. Younger companies have grown up having been taught about the work of these pioneering experimental companies or increasingly having been taught *by* them or worked with them. The Wooster

Group under the direction of Elizabeth LeCompte, for example, has always very actively encouraged other artists through internships, associations, its annual Visiting Artists Series and more recently the Emerging Artist Series at the Performing Garage. It has profoundly influenced the work of other New York companies such as Elevator Repair Service, the New York City Players (director Richard Maxwell), The Builders Association (director Marianne Weems) and Cannon Company (director Richard Kimmel).[16] Younger companies are often registering and at times deliberately referencing the impact of pioneering companies in their own theatre making. An extreme case is Stan's Café's 1999 curious 'revival' of *The Carrier Frequency*, a show by Impact Theatre Cooperative (1978–85), as part of Birmingham's Towards the Millennium 80s Festival. As the director, James Yarker, recalls, while the 1980s were not so long ago for most of the arts organizations present at the planning meeting, for Stan's Café (as graduates from Lancaster University): 'this was our history'. So they volunteered to restage *The Carrier Frequency*, explaining that this show 'was regularly cited as a seminal piece of physical theatre but that, as it was made in 1984 when we were fifteen and deeply un-cool, none of us had seen it'.[17] Stan's Café 'invited a number of guest artists to help revive the show. Working from a documentation video, using the original soundtrack and text, a version of *The Carrier Frequency* was staged fifteen years after its premiere.'[18] The choice for this revival, it seems, was strangely appropriate, as the apocalyptic show made in 1984 (!) – 'set in a post-nuclear world, where brutalised steel and concrete structures rise from a giant pool of water' and 'depict[ing] six figures lost in an absurd and exhausting ritual, trying to revive a departed civilisation' – would have resonated with new millennial angst in 1999. Similarly, the ghost of *The Carrier Frequency* could also be seen to have haunted *Ark* (1999–2000) by Imitating the Dog, another company which emerged from Lancaster University. *Ark* saw a 'group of lost survivors try[ing] to come to terms with the expiring world around them, aided by their short-wave radio which sporadically spews out pockets of information – foreign voices, songs, memories, reference points.'[19]

Such palimpsestuous intertextuality and intratextuality are a significant quality of much postdramatic theatre. The quality of a palimpsest, of going over or writing over the same terrain, in one respect is often simply the product of the devising and rehearsal process, of companies using and reusing the materials left on stage or found in the rehearsal room or recycling material from previous shows in new contexts. As Robin Arthur recalled in the performance *A Decade of Forced Entertainment*:

> There was something about the way things got used and re-used, the way things moved in and out of the work. So much of the work had this complex interior history, where a single line of text in one show would become a title or even a whole character several years later.[20]

It is not just the company's interior history, however, that accounts for the palimpsestuous quality of its work. It also has to do with the way much of the work tries to 'map' British history, personal micro-histories and public macro-histories and their hopelessly overlapping 'site-specific' inscriptions:[21]

> Claire: They drew a map of the country and marked on it the events of the last 10 years – the sites of political and industrial conflict, the ecological disasters, the showbiz marriages and celebrity divorces. On the same map they marked the events of their own lives – the performances they'd given, the towns and cities where they'd stayed, the sites of injuries and fallings in or out of love.
>
> They drew a map of the country and marked on it the events of the previous 300, then 400, then 500 years. They kept on going until the beginnings of geological time. Until the map was scribbled over a thousand times – utterly black.[22]

Self-reflective performance lectures such as this (*A Decade of Forced Entertainment*) or Tim Etchell's writings and presentations about 'Performance Writing' are by no means exercises in self-indulgence. They stem from a pedagogical desire to:

> open the door to a broad, adventurous description of what writing for performance might mean – beyond ideas of playwrighting which is still, sadly, the measure too often employed in the UK, despite a rich history of writers in theatre spaces who are doing something quite different. The piece talks about physical action and set construction as forms of writing, it talks about writing words to be seen and read on-stage rather than spoken, it talks about lists, about improvisation, about reading, about whispering and about collage as a form – in each case implying a critical dialogue with more traditional notions of theatre or performance writing.[23]

Like Etchells, many practitioners of contemporary experimental and post-dramatic theatre are now themselves teaching the new performance aesthetics, scenographies and writing techniques in Theatre Studies at university level – with all the problems and challenges that juggling practice, theoretical reflection and pedagogical practice bring with it.[24] Increasingly, many are also developing work within the academic framework of what in Britain has come to be recognized as 'practice as research'. While practice as research is perhaps threatening to take some of the playfulness and spontaneity out of the work, it is a way of articulating the enquiries that drive it and is promising to generate a closer integration of theory and practice. Like this book, it also ought to contribute to giving postdramatic explorations their long-overdue cultural and intellectual legitimacy.

Theatre and world in the age of media: are we post-postdrama?

Lehmann's study identifies the 'caesura of the media society' as one of the most crucial contexts for postdramatic theatre. This is immediately apparent, for example, in The Wooster Group's high-tech, intermedia aesthetics, which makes use of video, film, electronic sound effects, microphones and computer programs to disrupt, fragment and infract the dramatic text and the bodies of 'characters'. Thus, in the 2001 production *To You, the Birdie! (Phèdre)*, loosely based on Racine's *Phèdre*, the representation of bodies is sometimes split between live upper halves and pre-recorded lower halves on a screen, Phèdre's (Kate Valk's) soliloquies are often spoken into a microphone by the actor Scott Shepard, creating an electronic 'voice mask' that 'ghosts' the actress,[25] and the figures' movements are overlaid with cartoon-like amplified sound effects. The overall effect can be read as a 'posthuman . . . reconstituted alternative presence of a media driven age', as Jennifer Parker-Starbuck has argued.[26]

The impact of media on performance manifests itself not only in the use of high-tech 'multimedia' onstage, however, but sometimes also in its very opposite: theatre on a bare stage with minimalist, pared down aesthetics, which neverthe-less can only be understood by being related to life in a 'mediatized' society. Whether or not media technology is actually being used on stage, as Etchells says, 'technology will move in and speak through you, like it or not. Best not to ignore.'[27] Hence, Forced Entertainment say that they make theatre that is under-standable by anybody 'who was brought up in a house where the TV was always on'. Similarly, the Bristol based UK/German company Uninvited Guests say they 'produce performance for a media-saturated culture'.[28] Their piece *Offline*, for example, sourced text by 'wandering the web as electronic *flâneurs*' in various sordid chatrooms but presented this found text 'off-line in a distinctly low-tech environment', a carpeted stage with a few microphones and analogue sound equipment. The performers 're-embodied' the virtual voices: texts written to be read in the anonymous environment of the internet were suddenly presented live in face-to-face communication.[29]

Given that the new theatre in this way is much more immediately informed by cultural practices other than traditional drama (from visual art and live art, to movies, TV channel hopping, pop music and the internet), the question may be asked why it would still be necessary or even appropriate to relate new theatre and performance work to drama at all. While the work of The Wooster Group or The Builders Association *has* often included an engagement with classic dramatic texts (e.g. with *Three Sisters* in The Wooster Group's *Brace Up!* or with various Faust dramatizations in The Builders Association's *Imperial Motel (Faust)* and *Jump Cut (Faust)*), this is not true of much of the new theatre that Lehmann invites us to consider. What can be the point of talking about this kind of work in relation to drama? Some provisional answers can be offered here: for one, we are dealing with deep structures that still inform the expectations of the majority of the audi-ence when they come to the theatre or talk about it in everyday language. Drama and theatre, as Lehmann argues, are treated as inseparable if not synonymous in the popular imagination and come with expectations of suspenseful and exciting stories. A spectator attending *Offline* (and not having read the programme, let's say) may therefore instinctively search for cohesive characters and try to piece together a coherent plot from what the performers say – needless to say that all such expectations will be frustrated as the 'identities' the performers take on morph from one speech to the next, crossing lines of gender and sexual orientation to boot. Contemporary experimental companies have continually come up against such expectations that equate theatre with drama, be it in audience reactions or funding applications. Tim Etchells describes the refusal of financial support from the Drama Department of the Arts Council of England for Forced Entertainment's *Speak Bitterness*:

> Swathed in concerns about aesthetics, 'poor-quality' productions, 'low production values', 'lack of development' and off-the-record questions about our status as drama or 'something else', the refusal meant more than a lost project – in economics it was a body blow and in critical terms it was a recognition (and an inscription) of a culture gap that had been widening for years.[30]

In many ways, Lehmann's study is setting out to articulate and, to an extent, help to bridge this culture gap where it still exists.

Secondly, and connected to the first answer, the performances themselves – whether consciously or unconsciously – often allude to these expectations of familiar dramatic structures and theatrical conventions and deliberately confound them. Approaching these performances from the theoretical perspective of postdramatic theatre can therefore often produce surprising insights and allow us to articulate their larger philosophical implications. For example, in Forced Entertainment's *Dirty Work* (1998) two performers on a small stage with tatty red theatre curtains calmly take turns describing an 'impossible' performance with scenes ranging from small everyday occurrences to scenes from Shakespeare, from great battles from world history and nuclear explosions to a 'speck of dust'. Listening to the performers at the time, I understood how it invited us to create in our minds a 'theatre' that could not possibly be 'represented' or enacted in any normal live theatre (but was at the same time often *overrepresented* as spectacle in the media). Thinking about it with hindsight and Lehmann's discussion of Aristotle's *Poetics* in mind, I now see how the performance, though structured into four acts, defied the Aristotelian demand for the right 'magnitude' of tragedy. It tells of a theatre that cannot be taken in 'at once', that is not easily 'surveyable', and thus a theatre that does not make the world 'manageable' for us – fundamentally because the world we live in, globalized and multiply mediatized as it is, *is* less 'surveyable' and manageable than ever. Forced Entertainment say of their work that they are 'searching for a theatre that can really talk about what it's like to live through these times'.[31] Despite their non-dramatic aesthetic, the forms of theatre the company have developed in fulfilment of this 'mission statement' – from long-durational performances (such as *And on the Thousandth Night, Speak Bitterness, Quizzola* and *Who Can Sing a Song to Unfrighten Me?*) to more meta-theatrical works (such as *First Night, Dirty Work,* and *Bloody Mess*) can be curiously reminiscent of Shakespeare's theatre, as Lehmann observed in a more recent essay:

> The impression of an open world without borders . . . is nearly always present in Shakespeare's theatre. Empires of thought and matter – wide and inexhaustible, endless in their various aspects, from those encompassing the world to the most banal – are travelled by this theatre with the breath of *Welt-Zeit* (worldtime), back and forth, between fairy tales and reality, dream and triviality, the cosmos and the inn, between Lear and Falstaff, the sublime and the inebriated, tragic and comic. . . . It is just that kind of feeling one has when watching Forced Entertainment, for here too, the theatre is reaching effortlessly across the most varied areas imaginable, amalgamating wit, black humor, fear, and melancholy.[32]

Such postdramatic theatre has thus not given up on relating to the world but crucially no longer *represents* the world as a surveyable whole: 'Here, "world" does not mean the walled-off (by a fourth wall) fictional totality, but a world open to its audience, an essentially possible world, pregnant with potentiality.'[33]

Another example of such open theatre which turns the audience into an active participant is Chicago-based Goat Island's new work *When will the September roses bloom? Last night was only a comedy* (2005). Quite a while into the performance of this piece, a performer interrupts to apologize to the audience – in a stuttering, faltering manner – that the company is lacking a beginning. Somewhere in the middle, another performer explains that 'there is a hole in this performance' – after which all performers disappear behind a cardboard disc, only to reappear as disembodied heads in a film projected onto the disc. Somewhere near the end, the company explain that they do not yet have an ending ('check our website' the performer says). Then they state that miraculously they have found the missing beginning: a 'pep talk' addressed to dancers at the beginning of a long rehearsal process is spoken into a microphone by another performer, who reads the text (borrowed from the musical *42nd Street*) several times, each time omitting more words. Moreover, the second version of the performance on the following night swaps some parts around. Goat Island's rehearsal process had begun with the question 'How do you repair?' and in its movement work, structure and spoken text draws on repair manuals, the poetry of Paul Celan, Jean Amery's description of his torture in prison, Simone Weil's *Gravity and Grace* and Lilian Gish's silent film *The Wind*, to name but a few.[34] Like some of the fragile materials used – one-legged stools, cardboard tables and crutches in pieces – the structure of the performance text itself self-consciously announces that it, too, could be seen as in need of repair. It does not add up to an Aristotelian dramatic fictional *whole* but instead is full of *holes*. The onus is on the spectator/witness to help 'repair' – perhaps by piecing together information seen over the two nights – or to help bear the trauma of living in a damaged world.

In a very different way, Station House Opera's latest performance *Mare's Nest* defied the Aristotelian demand for a fictional 'whole' through an ingenious and complex stage setup of two back-to-back video screens, each with a platform and stairs leading up to it and a door through it. The performance consisted of a mix of filmed and live action, so that four people – strangely reminiscent of characters from a Hitchcock film – and 'their life size video doubles inhabit a real and imaginary, half-physical and half-virtual space, often occupying both at once'.[35] In addition, the virtual room created on screen was populated by fantasy figures (naked men in fancy masks and headgear) that had been filmed near the actual theatre location, thus further confusing the real and the imaginary. The spectators were free to position themselves wherever they wished around this setup and to take in whatever they could or chose to take in. Thus, in a very real sense, everyone created their own narrative through the performance but no one was ever able to totalize it.

The above performance example and its use of film vignettes, as well as the use of film and television references in the work of The Wooster Group, The Builders Association, Plane Performance (especially *SET*), Imitating the Dog (*Five Miles and Falling, Hotel Methuselah*) and many others, also point to yet another answer to our initial question about the relevance of relating this kind of work to the dramatic tradition. As Philip Auslander has argued, when film and then television first emerged they 'remediated' theatre, modelling themselves on theatre and on dramatic structures. While early film 'remediated theatre by adopting the narrative structures and visual strategies of nineteenth-century melodrama', television in addition 'could remediate theatre at the ontological level through its claim to immediacy'.[36] Important dramatic structures and expectations are thus still sedimented in film and television. When contemporary experimental live performance now uses or references media, it is partially 'remediating' film and television but not in order insidiously to 'replicate' them to maintain its legitimacy (as Auslander argues mostly with respect to rock concerts and Broadway theatre production[37]) but in order to probe their status and impact on us in a self-conscious manner – including their history of remediating theatre.

Postmodern and postdramatic theory

Despite the fact that Lehmann opts for the term 'postdramatic' instead of 'postmodern' to describe the new theatre, his theory of postdramatic theatre is of course resonating with many aspects of postmodernist and poststructuralist thinking. Notably Lyotard's analysis of the postmodern condition as an 'incredulity towards grand narratives'[38] has a bearing on it, since the connection between the historical dominance of drama and a teleological philosophy of history runs deep. As Lehmann explains in his section on 'Drama and dialectic' the structure of classical drama with its conflicts and resolutions has been the model for a desired, imagined or promised development of history. The experiences of World War II, the Holocaust and Hiroshima, however, have fundamentally shaken the belief in this historical model, which explains why postwar practitioners such as Samuel Beckett, Tadeusz Kantor and Heiner Müller eschew the dramatic form in the wake of these events.

The application of postmodern and especially poststructuralist discourses to contemporary theatre and performance has certainly generated a wealth of insightful studies and is an ongoing endeavour of which this study is ultimately a part. Yet apart from a problematic inflationary and often superficial use of the term 'postmodern theatre' or worse 'postmodern *drama*', and apart from the difficulties surrounding any categorical definition of what the 'postmodern' actually is[39] (depending also on whether it is approached through Lyotard, Baudrillard or Jameson to name but some of the major thinkers), scholars and practitioners have sometimes expressed unease about the fact that these discourses originated outside of theatre and performance. Thus Johannes Birringer states:

> What postmodern theories of textuality and visual representation (and the spectating subject examined by film theory) lack is a more concrete historical understanding of the complex and conflicted relations of text and language to performance and space in the theatre. Even more importantly they lack a concrete theatrical knowledge of the reconceptions and revisions of various approaches to the acting in, and staging of, textual and contextual (scenographic, choreographic and musical) work carried out by several generations of avant-garde artists in this century.[40]

More recent studies, including Birringer's own, have since partially rectified this situation. Nick Kaye's rigorous theorization of the relationship between postmodernism and performance has argued against the model of a 'postmodern style' (derived from a discourse on postmodern architecture) and – turning the tables – has instead proposed that 'performance may be thought of as a primary postmodern mode'.[41] Lehmann's study could be seen to act as a further corrective and as providing the 'missing link' by tracing a trajectory from *within* theatre aesthetics. For, as Wessendorf puts it succinctly:

> Even though the concept of postdramatic theatre is in many ways analogous to the notion of postmodern theatre, it is not based on the application of a general cultural concept to the specific domain of theatre, but derives and unfolds from within a long-established discourse on theatre aesthetics itself, as a deconstruction of one of its major premises.[42]

To practitioners, the term 'postdramatic theatre' may in the end be just another 'describing word', as Forced Entertainment's Claire Marshall says in interview about the term postmodernism: 'You don't set out to make a postmodernist [or postdramatic] piece of work.'[43] Nevertheless, for practitioners, students, scholars and fans of contemporary theatre, the analyses provided in this book should contribute an invaluable theoretical vocabulary for reflecting on this work and for articulating its aesthetics and politics.

Note on the translation and acknowledgement

Translation is a curious activity of moving from one 'way of meaning' (Benjamin's *Art des Meinens*) to another – with inevitable gains and losses. The translation itself tends to become 'invisible', not unlike the performance dimension in a Naturalist play. I have occasionally retained the German terms in brackets but have overall opted for readability and accessibility for the Anglophone reader. Every effort has been made to track down existing English translations (or originals) for quotations in the text. The reader should note that the book has been somewhat abridged from the original – especially the chapter 'Aspects' has been shortened – but this does not affect the overall argument.

I would like to express my thanks to Kate Newey, Clare Grant and Tim Moss for feedback on draft chapters and the introduction, to the virtual community of fellow translators in the LEO dictionary forum, to our readers Erika Fischer-Lichte and Heike Roms for their enthusiastic and constructive comments on the project, to Minh Ha Duong for her careful reading and intelligent editing of the whole manuscript, to Frances Brown for meticulous copy-editing, to Jonathan Munby for his loving support behind the scenes, and finally to Hans-Thies Lehmann for his generosity and encouragement in a productive and inspiring collaboration.

Prologue

The stakes

With the end of the 'Gutenberg galaxy' and the advent of new technologies the written text and the book are being called into question. The mode of perception is shifting: a simultaneous and multi-perspectival form of perceiving is replacing the linear-successive. A more superficial yet simultaneously more comprehensive perception is taking the place of the centred, deeper one whose primary model was the reading of literary texts. Slow reading as much as theatre, which is laborious and cumbersome, is in danger of losing its status compared to the more profitable circulation of moving images. Literature and theatre, which are aesthetically mutually dependent on each other in a productive relation of repulsion and attraction, are both being demoted to the status of minority practices. Theatre is no longer a mass medium. To deny this becomes increasingly ridiculous, to reflect on it increasingly urgent. In the face of the pressure created by the attraction of the united forces of speed and surface, theatrical discourse emancipates itself from literary discourse but at the same time draws nearer to it in terms of its general function within culture. For both theatre and literature are textures which are especially dependent on the release of active energies of imagination, energies that are becoming weaker in a civilization of the primarily passive consumption of images and data. Neither theatre nor literature is essentially characterized by reproduction but rather organized as a complex system of signifiers.

At the same time, the cultural 'sector' increasingly falls prey to the laws of marketability and profitability, and here an additional disadvantage becomes apparent: theatre does not produce a tangible object which may enter into circulation as a marketable commodity, such as a video, a film, a disc, or even a book. The new technologies and media are becoming increasingly 'immaterial' – 'Les Immatériaux' was the title of an exhibition organized in 1985 by Jean-François Lyotard. Theatre, by contrast, is especially distinguished by the 'materiality of communication'. Unlike other forms of artistic practice it is marked by the especially heavy weight of its resources and materials. Compared to the poet's pen and paper, or the painter's oils and canvas, it requires a lot: the continuous activity of living people; the maintenance of theatre spaces; organizations, administrations and crafts; in addition to the material demands of all the arts themselves that are united in the theatre. Nevertheless, this seemingly antiquated institution still finds a surprisingly stable cultural place in society next to technically advanced media (which are increasingly often incorporated into theatrical performance).

Theatre is the site not only of 'heavy' *bodies* but also of a *real gathering*, a place where a unique intersection of aesthetically organized and everyday real life takes place. In contrast to other arts, which produce an object and/or are communicated through media, here the aesthetic act itself (the performing) as well as the act of reception (the theatre going) take place as a real doing in the here and now. Theatre means the collectively spent and used up lifetime in the collectively breathed air of that space in which the performing *and* the spectating take place. The emission and reception of signs and signals take place simultaneously. The theatre performance turns the behaviour onstage and in the auditorium into a *joint text*, a 'text' even if there is no spoken dialogue on stage or between actors and audience. Therefore, the adequate description of theatre is bound to the reading of this total text. Just as much as the gazes of all participants can virtually meet, the *theatre situation* forms a whole made up of evident and hidden communicative processes. This study concerns itself with the question of how scenic practice since the 1970s has made use of this basic given of theatre, has specifically reflected on it and directly turned it into the content and theme of its presentation. For the theatre shares with the other arts of (post)modernity the tendency for self-reflexivity and self-thematization. Just as, according to Roland Barthes, in modernism every text poses the problem of its own possibility (can its language attain the real?), radical staging practice problematizes its status of illusory reality. At the mention of 'self-reflexivity' and 'auto-thematic structure' one may at first think of the dimension of the text, since it is language *par excellence* that opens up the free play of a self-reflexive use of signs. Yet in theatre the text is subject to the same laws and dislocations as the visual, audible, gestic and architectonic theatrical signs.

Its profoundly changed mode of theatrical sign usage suggests that it makes sense to describe a significant sector of the new theatre as 'postdramatic'. At the same time, the new theatre *text* (which for its part continually reflects its constitution as a linguistic construct) is to a large extent a 'no longer dramatic' theatre text. By alluding to the literary genre of the drama, the title 'Postdramatic Theatre' signals the continuing association and exchange between theatre and text. Nevertheless, the discourse of *theatre* is at the centre of this book and the text therefore is considered only as one element, one layer, or as a 'material' of the scenic creation, not as its master. In no way does this involve an a priori value judgment. Important texts are still being written, and in the course of this study the often dismissively used term 'text theatre' will turn out to mean a genuine and authentic variant of postdramatic theatre, rather than referring to something that has supposedly been overcome. However, in view of the wholly unsatisfactory theoretical analysis of the newly produced *scenic* discourses (in comparison with the analysis of *drama*), it seems appropriate to consider even the dimension of the text from the perspective of theatrical reality.

The 'principles of narration and figuration' and the order of a 'fable' (story) are disappearing in the contemporary 'no longer dramatic theatre text' (Poschmann).[1] An 'autonomization of language'[2] develops. Retaining the dramatic dimension to different degrees, Werner Schwab, Elfriede Jelinek, Rainald Goetz, Sarah Kane and René Pollesch, for example, have all produced texts in which language appears not as the speech of characters – if there still are definable characters at all – but as an autonomous theatricality. With her 'theatre as an oralic institution', Ginka Steinwachs tries to create the scenic reality as a heightened poetic-sensual reality of language. A concept that may illuminate what is happening here is Elfriede Jelinek's idea of juxtaposed 'language surfaces' (*Sprachflächen*) in place of dialogue. As Poschmann explains,[3] this form is directed against the 'depth' of speaking figures, which would suggest a mimetic illusion. In this respect, the metaphor of 'language surfaces' corresponds to the turning point of painting in modernity when, instead of the illusion of three-dimensional space, what is being 'staged' is the picture's plane-ness, its two-dimensional reality, and the reality of colour as an autonomous quality. The interpretation that this autonomization of language bears witness to a lack of interest in the human being,[4] however, is not a foregone conclusion. Is it not rather a matter of a changed perspective on human subjectivity? What finds articulation here is less intentionality – a characteristic of the subject – than its failure, less conscious will than desire, less the 'I' than the 'subject of the unconscious'. So rather than bemoan the lack of an already defined image of *the* human being in postdramatically organized texts, it is necessary to explore the new possibilities of thinking and representing the individual human subject sketched in these texts.

Intentions

This study does not aim to be a comprehensive inventory. Rather it attempts to develop an aesthetic logic of the new theatre. That this has hardly been undertaken yet is – among other reasons – due to the fact that theoreticians whose thinking could correspond to the tendencies of radical theatre rarely encounter this theatre and engage with it. Philosophers, while contemplating the 'theatre' as a concept and idea with conspicuous frequency and even turning 'scene' and 'theatre' into key concepts of theoretical discourse, rarely write concretely about specific theatre forms or practitioners. Jacques Derrida's readings of Artaud, Gilles Deleuze's comments on Carmelo Bene or Louis Althusser's classic text on Bertolazzi and Brecht are the more notable exceptions confirming the rule.[5] The affirmation of a theatre-*aesthetic* perspective may, however, necessitate the remark that aesthetic investigations always involve *ethical*, moral, political and legal questions in the widest sense. Art, and even more so theatre which is embedded in society in multiple ways – from the social character of the production and the public financing to the communal form of reception – exists in the field of *real socio-symbolic practice*. While the common reduction of the aesthetic to social positions and statements remains empty, inversely all aesthetic interrogation is blind if it does not recognize the reflection of social norms of perception and behaviour in the artistic practice of theatre.

The description of all those forms of theatre that are here considered as post-dramatic is intended to be useful. What is at issue is, on the one hand, the attempt to place the theatrical development of the twentieth century into a perspective inspired by the developments of the new and newest theatre – developments which are obviously still hard to categorize – and, on the other hand, to serve the *conceptual* analysis and *verbalization of the experience* of this often 'difficult' contemporary theatre and thus to promote its 'visibility' and discussion. For it cannot be denied: the new forms of theatre have certainly marked the work of some of the most significant directors and companies of our time. They have found a significant, mostly younger audience who have flocked and continue to flock to venues like the Mickery Theater (Amsterdam), Kaaitheater (Brussels), Kampnagel (Hamburg), Mousonturm und TAT in Frankfurt, Hebbel-Theater (Berlin), Szene Salzburg, the Edinburgh Festival, the Barbican's BITE series, Riverside Studios, BAC and the ICA in London, Arnolfini (Bristol), Chapter Arts Centre (Cardiff), Nuffield Theatre (Lancaster), Tramway (Glasgow), PS122 (New York), Walker Arts Centre (Minneapolis), Wexner Centre for the Arts (Ohio State University), MCA (Chicago), PICA (Portland), On the Boards (Seattle), Highways Performance Space (Los Angeles) and Performance Space (Sydney) to name but a few. They have received an enthusiastic reception among a number of critics and some of their aesthetic principles have managed to 'infiltrate' the established theatre (albeit mostly in a watered down form). Yet the majority of spectators, who – to put it crudely – expect from the theatre the illustration of classic texts, may well accept the 'modern' set but subscribe to a comprehensible fable (story), coherent meaning, cultural self-affirmation and touching theatre feelings. With this audience the postdramatic theatre forms of a Robert Wilson, Jan Fabre, Einar Schleef or Jan Lauwers – to name but a few of the more 'accepted' theatre practitioners of the 1980s and 1990s – have met with little understanding. But even spectators who are convinced of the artistic integrity and the quality of such theatre often lack the conceptual tools to articulate their perception. This is demonstrated by the predominance of purely negative criteria. The new theatre, one hears and reads, is not this and not that and not the other, but there is a lack of categories and words to define or even describe what it is in any positive terms. This study aims to go some way towards correcting this situation and at the same time encourage ways of working in the theatre that expand our preconceptions of what theatre is or is meant to be.

Furthermore, this essay aims to facilitate an orientation in the variegated field of the new theatre. Much of it is only briefly sketched and would already serve its purpose if it inspired more detailed analyses. A comprehensive 'overview' of the new theatre in all its variants is obviously impossible anyway, and not only because of its limitless diversity. This is indeed a study dedicated to 'contemporary theatre'[6] but only in so far as it attempts to define theoretically how we recognize what makes it truly contemporary. Only a fragment of the theatre of the last thirty years is being considered here. The goal was not to find a conceptual framework that accommodates everything. The task in each case was to decide whether an aesthetic attests to true 'contemporaneity' or whether it merely perpetuates old models with technical accomplishment. Classical idealistic aesthetics had the concept of the 'idea' at its disposal: the design of a conceptual whole which allows the details to concretize (to grow together) as they unfold simultaneously in 'reality' and in 'concept'. Every historical phase of a particular art could thus be regarded by Hegel as a concrete and specific unfolding of the idea of art, every work of art as a special concretization of the objective spirit of an epoch or 'artistic form'. The idea of an 'epoch' or a historical state of the world gave idealism its unifying key, which made it possible to place art historically and systematically. If the confidence in such constructions – for example in that of 'the' theatre, of which the theatre of a particular epoch is a specific unfolding – has disappeared, then the pluralism of phenomena forces us to recognize the unforeseeability and suddenness of the *invention*, its indeducible moment or event.

At the same time, the heterogeneous diversity of forms unhinges all those methodological certainties that have previously made it possible to assert large-scale causal developments in the arts. It is essential to accept the coexistence of divergent theatre forms and concepts in which no paradigm is dominant. A conceivable consequence would be to leave it at a purely additive description, which would at least seemingly do justice to all the variants of the new theatre. But we cannot be satisfied with restricting ourselves to an atomizing historico-empirical listing of everything that exists. This would only be the transferral of a historicist contentedness – according to which everything is worth attending to simply because it once existed – to the present. As theatre studies scholars, we must not approach our own present with the gaze of the archivist. Therefore we must find a way out of this dilemma, or at least an attitude to it. The academic industry only seemingly solves the difficulties arising from the disappearance of overarching historical and aesthetic ordering models: mostly through the splintering into pedantic specializations. These in themselves, however, can be nothing more than increasingly laboriously packaged pieces of data collection, no longer of interest or support even to theorists in neighbouring fields. Another answer consists in theatre studies placing its bets on the much called upon interdisciplinarity. The impulses resulting from this orientation are certainly very important. Yet it has to be stated that especially under the banner of an interdisciplinary approach scholars often evade the very cause and *raison d'être* for the theorizing – namely the aesthetic experience itself in its unprotected and unsecured experimental character. The latter is often sidestepped as a disturbing element in favour of large (and, in the name of interdisciplinarity, increasingly larger-scale) strategies of categorization.

Not wanting to succumb to the metamorphosis of thought into the equally meaningless exercises of either archiving or categorizing, I propose a double path. On the one hand, following Peter Szondi, I want to read the realized artistic constructions and forms of practice as answers to artistic questions, as manifest reactions to the representational problems faced by theatre. In this sense, the term 'post*dramatic*' – as opposed to the 'epochal' category of the 'postmodern' – means a concrete problem of theatre aesthetics: thus Heiner Müller could state that he found it increasingly difficult even to articulate himself in a dramatic form any longer. On the other hand, I will claim here a certain (controlled) trust in a personal – or, to quote Adorno, 'idiosyncratic' – reaction. Where theatre caused me 'shock' through enthusiasm, insight, fascination, inclination or curious (not paralysing) incomprehension, the field marked by my experiences was carefully surveyed. However, only the course of the explication itself will justify the leading selection criteria.

Trade secrets of dramatic theatre

For centuries a paradigm has dominated European theatre that clearly distinguishes it from non-European theatre traditions. For example, Indian Kathakali or Japanese Noh theatre are structured completely differently and consist essentially of dance, chorus and music, highly stylized ceremonial procedures, narrative and lyric texts, while theatre in Europe amounted to the representation, the 'making present' (*Vergegenwärtigung*) of speeches and deeds on stage through mimetic dramatic play. Bertolt Brecht chose the term 'dramatic theatre' to designate the tradition that his epic 'theatre of the scientific age' intended to put an end to. In a more comprehensive sense (and also including the majority of Brecht's own work), however, this term can be used to designate the core of European theatre tradition in modern times. Inherent in it is a certain conglomeration of motifs – partially conscious and partially taken for granted as self-evident – that is frequently still unquestioningly regarded as constitutive for 'the' theatre. Theatre is tacitly thought of as the *theatre of dramas*. Among its consciously theorized elements are the categories of 'imitation' and 'action'/'plot', as much as the virtually automatic intimate connection of the two. As an associated, rather unconscious motif of this classical theatre conception we can point out the attempt to form (or strengthen) a social bond through theatre, a community uniting the audience and the stage emotionally and mentally. 'Catharsis' is the displaced theoretical name for this – by no means primarily aesthetic – function of theatre: the bringing about of affective recognition and solidarity by means of the drama and the affects represented and transmitted to the audience within its frame. These traits cannot be separated from the paradigm of 'dramatic theatre', whose significance therefore reaches far beyond the validity of a simple genre classification.

Dramatic theatre is subordinated to the primacy of the text. In the theatre of modern times, the staging largely consisted of the declamation and illustration of written drama. Even where music and dance were added or where they predominated, the 'text', in the sense of at least the imagination of a comprehensible narrative and/or mental *totality*, was determining. Despite an ever increasing characterization of dramatis personae through the non-verbal repertoire of gesture, movement and psychologically expressive mime, the human figure even in the eighteenth and nineteenth centuries was still centrally defined through speech. The text, in turn, functioned primarily as role script. The use of choruses, narrators, interludes, plays-within-a-play, prologues and epilogues, asides, and a thousandfold more subtle openings of the dramatic cosmos – including in the end even the Brechtian repertoire of epic ways of playing – could all be incorporated and added to the drama without destroying the specific experience of dramatic theatre. Whether or not lyrical forms of language were effective within the dramatic texture, and to what degree epic dramaturgies were applied, made no difference in principle: the drama was able to incorporate all of these without losing its dramatic character.

Although it remains debatable to what degree and in what way the audiences of former centuries were taken in by the 'illusions' offered by stage tricks, artful lighting, musical background, costumes and set, it can be stated that dramatic theatre was the formation of illusion. It wanted to construct a *fictive cosmos* and let all the stage represent – be – a world (this inversion is the aesthetic implication of the Shakespearean 'All the world's a stage . . .') abstracted but intended for the imagination and empathy of the spectator to follow and complete the *illusion*. For such an illusion neither completeness nor even continuity of the representation is necessary. What is necessary, however, is the principle that what we perceive in the theatre can be referred to a 'world', i.e. to a totality. Wholeness, illusion and world representation are inherent in the model 'drama'; conversely, through its very form, dramatic theatre proclaims wholeness as the *model* of the real. Dramatic theatre ends when these elements are no longer the regulating principle but merely one possible variant of theatrical art.

Caesura of the media society

One commonly held view is that the experimental forms of contemporary theatre since the 1960s all have models in the period of the historical avant-gardes. This study proceeds from the conviction, however, that the undoubtedly deep caesura caused by the historical avant-gardes around 1900, despite their revolutionary innovations, largely maintained the essence of the 'dramatic theatre'. The newly emerging theatre forms continued to serve the – now modernized – representation of textual worlds; they plainly sought to save the text and its truth from disfigurement through a theatre practice that had become conventional; only within limits did they question the traditional model of theatrical representation and communication. Certainly Meyerhold's means of staging 'alienated' the staged plays in an extreme manner but they were still presented in a cohesive totality. Certainly the theatre revolutionaries broke with almost all conventions but even in their turn towards abstract and alienating means of staging they mostly still adhered to the mimesis of action on stage. By comparison, the spread and then omnipresence of the *media* in everyday life since the 1970s has brought with it a new multiform kind of theatrical discourse that is here going to be described as *postdramatic theatre*. It will not be disputed that the important art and theatre revolution that occurred around the turn of the twentieth century historically paved the way – on the contrary, we will devote a whole section to the antecedents, first beginnings and anticipations of postdramatic theatre that were developed at this time. For all the similarities in expressive forms, however, one has to consider that the same means can radically change their meaning in different contexts. The formal languages developed since the historical avant-gardes have become an arsenal of expressive gestures, which in postdramatic theatre serve as theatre's response to changed social communication under the conditions of generalized information technologies.

One of the salutary effects of this study is that the demarcation of a new theatre continent with other criteria, values and processes has created the necessity to reveal a number of 'un-thought' implications of that which even nowadays shapes the common understanding of theatre. Apart from this critique of a series of – on closer inspection rather questionable – self-evident notions in the theory of theatre, it is necessary to postulate postdramatic theatre energetically as a concept contradictory to these seemingly self-evident concepts. Developed as a way of defining the contemporary, it can retroactively allow the 'non-dramatic' aspects of the theatre of the past to stand out more clearly. The newly developed aesthetic forms allow both the older forms of theatre *and* the theoretical concepts used to analyse them to appear in a changed light. To be sure: one always has to be cautious with the assertion of caesuras in the history of an art form, above all when they are of a very recent date. There may be a danger in overestimating the depth of the rupture postulated here: the destruction of the foundations of dramatic theatre – which after all have been valid for hundreds of years – and the radical transformation of scenic practice in the ambiguous light of media culture. But the obverse danger (especially in academia) of perceiving the new always as only a variant of the well known seems to threaten with yet more disastrous misjudgments and blindness.

Names

The following list offers a kind of *panorama* of the field of study that opens up under the name of postdramatic theatre. It is concerned with phenomena of a most heterogeneous kind, with world famous theatre practitioners, as much as with companies hardly known beyond a small circle. Every reader will discover a more or less long list of names familiar to them. Not all of the practitioners have created a whole 'oeuvre' that can be considered postdramatic in its entirety – if we can use the term 'oeuvre' for directors, theatre companies, theatre productions and actions. Not all of them are extensively discussed in this book. Accordingly, the following belong among this, in every way incomplete, 'namedropping' for a postdramatic theatre: Robert Wilson, Jan Fabre, Jan Lauwers, Heiner Goebbels, Einar Schleef, Jürgen Manthey, Achim Freyer, Klaus Michael Grüber, Peter Brook, Anatoli Vassiliev, Robert Lepage, Elizabeth LeCompte, Pina Bausch, Reinhild Hoffmann, William Forsythe, Meredith Monk, Anne Teresa de Keersmaeker,

Meg Stuart, En Knap, Jürgen Kruse, Christof Nel, Leander Haussmann, Frank Castorf, Uwe Mengel, Hans-Jürgen Syberberg, Tadeusz Kantor, Eimuntas Nekrosius, Richard Foreman, Richard Schechner, John Jesurun, Theodoros Terzopoulos, Giorgio Barberio Corsetti, Emil Hrvatin, Silviu Purcarete, Tomaz Pandur, Jerzy Grotowski, Eugenio Barba, Saburo Teshigawara, Tadashi Suzuki. Countless action theatres, performance artists, happenings and theatre styles inspired by happenings also belong here: Bobby Baker, Hermann Nitsch, Otto Mühl, The Wooster Group, Survival Research Laboratories, Squat Theatre, The Builders Association, Magazzini, Falso Movimento, Theatergroep Hollandia, Theatergroep Victoria, Matschappej Discordia, Theater Angelus Novus, Hotel Pro Forma, Serapionstheater, Sydney Front, Bak-Truppen, Remote Control Productions, Tg STAN, Suver Nuver, La Fura del Baus, Goat Island, DV8 Physical Theatre, Forced Entertainment, Station House Opera, Vincent Dance Theatre, Desperate Optimists, Reckless Sleepers, Théâtre de Complicité, Teatro Due, Societas Raffaello Sanzio, Théâtre du Radeau, Akko-Theater, Gob Squad. Numerous theatre companies, small, medium and large projects and productions, which are associated with one or more of the 'theatre languages' indicated by the named names. Younger theatre practitioners like Stefan Pucher, Helena Waldmann, René Pollesch, Michael Simon. Authors whose work is at least partially related to the postdramatic paradigm: in the German-speaking countries above all Heiner Müller, Rainald Goetz, the Vienna School, Bazon Brock, Peter Handke, Elfriede Jelinek . . .

Paradigm

The plethora of phenomena in the theatre landscape of the last few decades that have challenged the traditional forms of drama and 'its' theatre with aesthetic consistency and inventiveness suggests that it is justified to speak of a new *paradigm of postdramatic theatre*. Paradigm is an auxiliary term used here to indicate the shared negative boundary demarcating the internally highly diverse variants of the postdramatic theatre from the dramatic. These works of theatre also become paradigmatic because they are widely recognized – albeit not always welcomed – as an authentic testimony of the times, and as such develop their own yardstick. The term paradigm is not intended to promote the illusion that art, like science, could conform to the developmental logic of paradigms and paradigm shifts. When discussing postdramatic stylistic moments one could easily point out those that the new theatre shares with the traditional dramatic theatre. In the emergence of a new paradigm, the 'future' structures and stylistic traits almost unavoidably appear mixed in with the conventional. An analysis that resigned itself to a mere inventory of the motley costumed styles and varieties would miss the actual underlying productive processes. Without the development of categories for stylistic traits, which in each case are only impurely realized, these traits would not even stand out. For instance, narrative fragmentation, heterogeneity of style, hypernaturalist, grotesque and neo-expressionist elements, which are all typical of postdramatic theatre, can also be found in productions which nevertheless belong to the model of dramatic theatre. In the end, it is only the constellation of elements that decides whether a stylistic moment is to be read in the context of a dramatic or a postdramatic aesthetics. One thing is certain: today a Gotthold Ephraim Lessing, who could develop 'the' dramaturgy of a post-dramatic theatre, is unthinkable. The theatre of sense and synthesis has largely disappeared – and with it the possibility of synthesizing interpretation. Rec-ommendations, let alone prescriptions, are no longer possible, merely partial perspectives and stuttering answers that remain 'works in progress'. The task of theory is to articulate, conceptualize and find terms for that which has come into being, not to postulate it as the norm.

Postmodern and postdramatic

For the theatre of the time span we are concerned with here – roughly the 1970s to the 1990s – the term *postmodern theatre* has become established. This can be sorted in many ways: the theatre of deconstruction, multimedia theatre, restora-tively traditionalist theatre, theatre of gestures and movement. The difficulty of comprehending such a wide field in terms of 'epoch' is evident in many studies that try to characterize the 'postmodern theatre' since 1970 through a long and impressive list of features. Some of the key words that have come up in the inter-national postmodernism discussion are: ambiguity; celebrating art as fiction; celebrating theatre as process; discontinuity; heterogeneity; non-textuality; plural-ism; multiple codes; subversion; all sites; perversion; performer as theme and protagonist; deformation; text as basic material only; deconstruction; considering text to be authoritarian and archaic; performance as a third term between drama and theatre; anti-mimetic; resisting interpretation. Postmodern theatre, we hear, is without discourse but instead dominated by mediation, gestuality, rhythm, tone. Moreover: nihilistic and grotesque forms, empty space, silence. Such key-words, as much as they often hit upon something real about the new theatre, can neither be cogent individually (much of it – ambiguity, resisting interpretation, multiple codes – is obviously also true for previous forms of theatre), nor can they collectively offer more than catchphrases which necessarily have to remain very general (deformation) or name very heterogeneous traits (perversion, subver-sion). Much of it also provokes opposition: of course there is 'discourse' in postmodern theatre, for instance. Like any other artistic practice, it is not exempt from the modern development that analysis, 'theory', reflection and self-reflection invade art to a previously unknown degree. Postdramatic theatre knows not only the 'empty' space but also the overcrowded space. It can indeed be 'nihilis-tic' and 'grotesque' – but so is *King Lear*. Process, heterogeneity or pluralism in turn are true for all theatre – the classical, modern and 'postmodern'. When Peter Sellars staged *Ajax* in 1986 and *The Persians* in 1993, his productions, like his original stagings of Mozart operas, were called 'postmodern' merely because he rigorously and irreverently brought classical material into the contemporary, everyday world.

Choice of term

The term and subject of 'postdramatic theatre' that I introduced into the debate some years ago have been picked up by other theoreticians, so for this reason, too, it made sense to stay with this coinage. The present study takes up questions that could only be hinted at in my earlier opposition of the 'predramatic' discourse of Attic tragedy and 'postdramatic' contemporary theatre.[7] In passing, and related to but diverging from the emphasis attempted here, Richard Schechner has applied the word 'postdramatic' to happenings; he once spoke of the 'postdramatic theatre of happenings'.[8] Similarly *en passant* and with a view to Beckett, Genet and Ionesco, he also, somewhat paradoxically, talked about the 'postdramatic drama',[9] in which no longer the 'story' but what Schechner calls the 'game' becomes the 'generative matrix' – albeit within the frame of what, according to our use of terms, is a 'dramatic' structure of stage fiction and situation. With respect to newer theatre texts, scholars have talked about 'no longer dramatic theatre texts', as already mentioned, but what is still missing is an attempt to survey the new *theatre* and the diversity of its theatrical means in more detail in the light of postdramatic aesthetics.

One could cite other reasons in favour of the term 'postdramatic' – notwithstanding the understandable scepticism towards coinages with the prefix 'post'. (Heiner Müller once said he knew only one postmodern poet: August Stramm – a modern poet who worked at the post office.) This scepticism, however, seems to be more justified towards the concept of postmodernism, which claims to achieve the definition of a whole epoch. Many traits of theatre practice that are called postmodern – from the seeming to the real randomness of means and quoted forms, to the unabashed use and combination of heterogeneous styles, from a 'theatre of images' to mixed media, multimedia and performance – by no means demonstrate a renunciation of modernity on principle. Yet they do show a renunciation of the traditions of dramatic form. The same is true for numerous texts by authors ranging from Heiner Müller to Elfriede Jelinek that have been labelled as 'postmodern'. When the progression of a story with its internal logic no longer forms the centre, when composition is no longer experienced as an organizing quality but as an artificially imposed 'manufacture', as a mere sham of a logic of action that only serves clichés (something Adorno abhorred about the products of the 'culture industry'), then theatre is confronted with the question of possibilities beyond drama, not necessarily beyond modernity. Heiner Müller said in a conversation with Horst Laube in the mid-1970s:

> Brecht thought epic theatre was impossible; it would only become possible if the perversion of turning a luxury into a profession were to cease – the constitution of theatre out of the division of stage and auditorium. Only if this is abolished, at least in tendency, does it become possible to make theatre with a minimum of dramaturgy, almost without dramaturgy. And that's what it's about now: to produce a theatre without effort. I realize

when I go to the theatre that it is increasingly boring to me to follow one plot for an evening. That is actually no longer interesting to me. If one plot starts in the first image, and then an entirely different one is continued in the second one, and then a third and a fourth starts, then it's entertaining and pleasurable, but it's no longer the perfect play.[10]

In the same context, Müller bemoans that the method of collage is not yet sufficiently utilized in theatre. While the large theatres, under the pressures of conventional norms of the entertainment industry, tend not to dare to deviate from the unproblematic consumption of fables, the newer theatre aesthetics practise a consistent renunciation of the one plot and the perfection of drama – without this implying a renunciation of modernity *per se*.

Tradition and the postdramatic talent

The adjective 'postdramatic' denotes a theatre that feels bound to operate beyond drama, at a time 'after' the authority of the dramatic paradigm in theatre. What it does not mean is an abstract negation and mere looking away from the tradition of drama. 'After' drama means that it lives on as a structure – however weakened and exhausted – of the 'normal' theatre: as an expectation of large parts of its audience, as a foundation for many of its means of representation, as a quasi automatically working norm of its drama-turgy. Müller calls his postdramatic text *Description of a Picture*,[11] a 'landscape beyond death' and 'explosion of a memory in a withered dramatic structure'. This describes postdramatic theatre: the limbs or branches of a dramatic organism, even if they are withered material, are still present and form the space of a memory that is 'bursting open' in a double sense. Even in the term 'postmodern', wherever it is used in more than a token sense, the prefix 'post' indicates that a culture or artistic practice has stepped out of the previously unquestioned horizon of modernity but still exists with some kind of reference to it. This may be a relation of negation, declaration of war, liberation, or perhaps only a deviation and playful exploration of what is possible beyond this horizon. Similarly, one can speak of a 'post-Brechtian theatre', which is precisely not a theatre that has nothing to do with Brecht but a theatre which knows that it is affected by the demands and questions for theatre that are sedimented in Brecht's work but can no longer accept Brecht's answers.

Postdramatic theatre thus includes the presence or resumption or continued working of older aesthetics, including those that took leave of the dramatic idea in earlier times, be it on the level of text or theatre. Art in general cannot develop without reference to earlier forms. It is only a question of the level, consciousness, explicitness and special manner of reference. Nevertheless, one has to distinguish between the recourse to earlier forms within new forms and the (false) appearance of the continued validity and necessity of the traditional 'norms'. The claim that postmodern theatre needed classical norms in order to establish its own identity by way of a polemical distancing from it[12] could be based on a confusion between the perspective from outside and the internal aesthetic logic. For, it is often rather the critical talk *about* the new theatre that seeks such recourse. What is actually hard to shake off is the classical *terminology* that turns the power of tradition into aesthetic norms. It is true that new theatre practice often establishes itself in the public consciousness through polemical differentiation from customary practice and thus creates the appearance that it owes its identity to the classical norms. Provocation alone, however, does not make a form; even provocative, negating art has to create something new under its own steam. Through this alone, and not through the negation of classical norms, can it obtain its own identity.

Drama

Drama and theatre

'Epicization' – Peter Szondi, Roland Barthes

Modern theatre, as Peter Szondi observed, already substantially negated the outmoded model of drama in important aspects. This then posed the question: And what is taking its place? Szondi's classical response was to theorize the new forms of texts that had emerged from what he described as the 'crisis of drama' as variants of an 'epicization', thus turning the epic theatre into a kind of universal key for understanding the recent developments. This answer can no longer suffice. Faced with the new tendencies of dramatic writing since 1880, which he reflects upon in terms of a form–content dialectic, Szondi's sweeping *Theory of the Modern Drama* contrasts the model of the ideal 'pure drama' with *one* particular counter-tendency. Almost without explanation, based only on his recourse to the classical opposition of epic and dramatic representation in Goethe and Schiller, Szondi says right at the beginning:

> Since modern theatrical works develop out of and away from the Drama itself, this development must be considered with the help of a contrasting concept: 'Epic' will serve here. It designates a common structural characteristic of the epos, the story, the novel, and other genres – namely, the presence of that which has been referred to as the 'subject of the epic form' or the 'epic *I*'.[1]

This contrast has narrowed the perspective for many dimensions of *theatrical* developments since the 1960s. One exacerbating factor for the nearly uncontested acceptance of this conception of the epic as *the* successor to the dramatic has been the overpowering authority of Brecht. For a long time this meant his work was the central reference point in considering newer theatre aesthetics – a circumstance which, despite all its productive outcomes, has led to outright blocks in perception and an overly hasty agreement about what matters in 'modern' theatre.

The case of Roland Barthes is a revealing one. He concerned himself intensely with the theatre between 1953 and 1960, acting in a student company himself (Darius in *The Persians*), and together with Bernard Dort founding the important journal *Théâtre populaire*. His theoretical writings are deeply informed by the model of theatre: time and again, Barthes refers to topoi of the theatre such as 'scene', 'staging', 'mimesis', etc. His articles about Brecht – written after the Berliner Ensemble's epoch-making tour to Paris in 1954 – are still worth reading today. Barthes was so shaken by this experience that he subsequently declared his reluctance to write about any other kind of theatre from then on. After his 'illumination' through Brecht's theatre, he no longer had a fancy for less accomplished theatre. Barthes had grown up in the 1920s with the theatre of the so-called 'Cartel' (Jouvet, Pitoëff, Baty, Dullin), in whose work he saw, retrospectively, a passionate clarity ('une sorte de clarté passionnée'). Even then, this seemed more important to him than the emotionality of theatre. Such concentration on rationality, on the Brechtian distance between the showing and the shown, the represented and the mode of representation, *signifiant* and *signifié*, brought about a semiological productivity but also a peculiar blindness. Barthes could not 'see' the whole line of new theatre that led from Artaud and Grotowski to The Living Theatre and Robert Wilson, despite the fact that his semiotic reflections, for example about the image, the *sens obtus* (obtuse sense), the voice, etc., are of great value for the description of precisely this new theatre. Brecht became a (perceptual) block for Barthes. One could say, Brechtian aesthetics represented for him – all too comprehensively and all too absolutely – *the* one and only model of a theatre of inner distance. This all-too-bright light eclipsed the possibility that there might be entirely different strategies for overcoming the naïveté of an illusory reality, psychological empathy and non-political thinking. After Brecht we saw the emergence of absurdist theatre, the theatre of scenography, the *Sprechstück*, visual dramaturgy, the theatre of situation, concrete theatre and other forms that are the subject of this book. Their analysis can no longer make do with the vocabulary of the 'epic'.

The estrangement of theatre and drama

Starting in the *Theory of the Modern Drama* itself and more so in his subsequent studies on lyrical drama, Szondi himself expanded his diagnosis and amended his one-sided interpretation of the metamorphosis of drama as epicization. Yet a whole host of prejudices still block comprehension of the very transformation process of which phenomena like the epicizing tendency and the lyrical theatre are themselves only moments: namely the transformation that has *mutually estranged theatre and drama and has distanced them ever further from each other*. The dissolution processes of drama on the textual level that Szondi described correspond with the development towards a theatre which is no longer even based on 'drama' – be it (to use the categorizations of dramatic theory) open or closed, pyramidal or circular, epic or lyrical, focused more on character or more on plot. Theatre without drama does exist. What is at stake in the new theatre development are the questions in which way and with what consequences the

idea of theatre as a representation of a *fictive* cosmos in general has been rup-
tured and even relinquished altogether, a cosmos whose closure was guaranteed
through drama and its corresponding theatre aesthetic. Certainly, even throughout the modern era, the modern theatre for its devotees was an event in which
the dramatic text played only one part – and often not the most important – of
the experiences sought. Yet despite all the individual entertaining effects of the
staging, the textual elements of plot, character (or at least dramatis personae)
and a moving story predominantly told in dialogue remained the structuring
components. They were associated with the keyword 'drama' and informed not
only its theory but also the expectations of theatre. This explains why many
spectators among the traditional theatre audience experience difficulties with
postdramatic theatre, which presents itself as a meeting point of the arts and
thus develops – and demands – an ability to perceive which breaks away from
the dramatic paradigm (and from literature as such). It is not surprising that
fans of other arts (visual arts, dance, music) are often more at home with this
kind of theatre than theatregoers who subscribe to literary narrative.

'Dramatic discourse'

Mainly for terminological reasons, I do not speak of 'dramatic discourse', as
used by Andrzej Wirth, although I am frequently in agreement with Wirth's
clear-sighted observations.[2] He put the emphasis on theatre turning into an
instrument, as it were, through which the 'author' (director) addresses 'his'/'her'
discourse directly to the audience. The salient point of Wirth's description is that
this model of 'address' becomes the basic structure of drama and replaces the
conversational dialogue. It is no longer the stage but the theatre as a whole
which functions as the 'speaking space' (*Sprechraum*). This indeed captures a
crucial change and a structure concerning, for example, the theatre of Robert
Wilson, Richard Foreman and other exponents of American avant-garde
theatre. Key influences for this development, according to Wirth, are Brecht's
epicization (his model of the 'street scene' contains no dialogue), the incoherence
of dialogue in the Theatre of the Absurd and the mythic and ritual dimensions
of Artaud's vision for the theatre. For Wirth, the disintegration of dialogue in
texts by Heiner Müller, the 'polyphonic discourse' in Peter Handke's *Kaspar* and
the direct audience address (*Offending the Audience*) constitute 'a new model of epic
theatre'. He conceives of the trajectory Brecht – Artaud – Theatre of the
Absurd – Foreman – Wilson as an 'emergence of a quasi intercontinental idiom
of contemporary drama', as 'dramatic discourse' leading to a redefinition of the
actor, who is used by the director as a 'button in the communication machine of
theatre':

> The emerging 'model character' of the theatre is radically epic. And in this
> theatre without dialogue the figures only seem to be speaking. It would be
> more accurate to say that they are being spoken by the author of the script
> or that the audience lends them its inner voice.[3]

These were important impulses *avant la lettre* for an understanding of the theatre of the 1980s and 1990s, and they have maintained much of their pertinence. At the same time, one cannot stop here, especially since Wirth outlined his ideas only briefly and in the form of theses. To begin with, the discourse model, with its duality of point of view and vanishing point, omnipotent director here and solipsistic viewer there, preserves the classical ordering model of perspective that was characteristic of drama. The 'polylogue' (Kristeva) of the new theatre, however, often breaks away from such an order centred on *one* logos. A *disposition of spaces of meaning and sound-spaces* develops which is open to multiple uses and which can no longer simply be ascribed to a single organizer or organon – be it an individual or a collective. Rather, it is often a matter of the authentic presence of individual performers, who appear not as mere carriers of an intention external to them – whether this derives from the text or the director. They act out their own corporeal logic within a given framework: hidden impulses, energy dynamics and mechanics of body and motorics. Thus, it is problematic to see them as agents of a discourse of a director who remains external to them. (A special case are the speakers in texts by Heiner Müller, who in the absence of an autonomous characterization have to be understood as 'vehicles of a discourse'.) It is true more of the classical director that he lets the players speak 'his' discourse, or rather that of the author, whom he takes under his care, and thus communicates with the audience. Artaud's critique of the traditional bourgeois theatre focused precisely on this: that the actor in it is only an agent of the director who, in turn, only 'repeats' the word prescribed to him by the author (the author himself being already bound to a representation, and thus repetition, of the world). This theatre of a logic of the double is precisely what Artaud wanted to exclude. In this, in any case, postdramatic theatre follows him: it wants the stage to be a beginning and a point of departure, not a site of transcription/copying. Only if we understood *dis-currere* literally as a 'running apart' could we speak of a 'discourse' of the creator with respect to the new theatre. Rather, it seems it is exactly the *omission* of an originary source/agency of discourse combined with the pluralization of sending agencies/sources on stage that lead to new modes of perception. The model of an 'address', therefore, requires further specification to apply to the new forms of theatre. Terminologically it is also misleading to adhere to the concept of drama by talking about the '*dramatic* discourse' in opposition to dialogue. Instead, we have to comprehend a much more radical distancing of theatre from the dramatic-dialogic conception as such. Only in a very limited sense can postdramatic theatre, therefore, be qualified as 'radically epic'.

Theatre after Brecht

Andrzej Wirth writes:

> Brecht called himself the Einstein of the new dramatic form. This self-assessment is no exaggeration if one understands the epoch-making theory

of epic theatre as an extremely effective and operative invention. This theory has given an impulse for the dissolution of the traditional stage dialogue into the form of the discourse or solilogue. Brecht's theory implicitly indicates that in the theatre a statement is articulated through the equal participation of verbal and kinetic elements (Gestus) and is not simply of a literary nature.[4]

Yet, do the impulses cited here really come from Brecht's theatre or not in equal measure from its contestation? Is Gestus, understood so generally, not at the heart of playing in *all* theatre? And can we – without thoroughly rereading his texts – separate out the 'operative' inventions by Brecht from the conventions of the *theatre of stories (Fabel-Theater)* which he still took for granted but which the new theatre breaks away from? With these questions, the theory of a post-dramatic theatre can connect with Wirth's lucid reflections on the Brechtian heritage within the new theatre.

What Brecht achieved can no longer be understood one-sidedly as a revolutionary counter-design to tradition. In the light of the newest developments, it becomes increasingly apparent that, in a sense, the theory of epic theatre constituted a *renewal and completion of classical dramaturgy*. Brecht's theory contained a highly traditionalist thesis: the *fable (story)* remained the *sine qua non* for him. Yet from the point of view of the fable, the decisive elements of the new theatre of the 1960s to the 1990s cannot be understood – nor even the textual forms of that theatre literature (Beckett, Handke, Strauss, Müller, Kane, etc.). Post-dramatic theatre is a *post-Brechtian theatre*. It situates itself in a space opened up by the Brechtian inquiries into the presence and consciousness of the process of representation within the represented and the inquiry into a new 'art of spectating' (Brecht's *Zuschaukunst*). At the same time, it leaves behind the political style, the tendency towards dogmatization, and the emphasis on the rational we find in Brechtian theatre; it exists in a time *after* the authoritative validity of Brecht's theatre concept. The complexity of these relations is marked by the fact that Heiner Müller considered Robert Wilson Brecht's legitimate heir: 'On this stage, Kleist's marionette theatre has a space to play, and Brecht's epic dramaturgy a place to dance.'[5]

Suspended suspense

Theatre and drama seem so closely related and quasi identical to many (even to many theatre studies scholars), a tightly embracing couple, so to speak, that despite all radical transformations of theatre, *the concept of drama has survived as the latent normative idea of theatre*. When everyday speech normally identifies drama and theatre (spectators will say after a theatre visit that they liked the 'play' when they possibly mean the performance and, in any event, do not clearly distinguish between the two), then it is basically not so far off from a large part of theatre criticism. For here, too, the choice of words and an implicit or even explicit equation of theatre with staged drama perpetuate the no longer accurate

assumption of a virtual identity of both and hence imperceptibly turn it into a
norm. To take this stance, however, marginalizes crucial realities of theatre –
and not just of contemporary theatre. Ancient tragedy, Racine's dramas and
Robert Wilson's visual dramaturgy are all forms of theatre. Yet, assuming the
modern understanding of drama, one can say that the former is 'predramatic',[6]
that Racine's plays are undoubtedly dramatic theatre, and that Wilson's 'operas'
have to be called 'postdramatic'. When it is obviously no longer simply a matter
of broken dramatic illusion or epicizing distance; when obviously neither plots,
nor plastically shaped dramatis personae are needed; when neither dramatic-
dialectical collision of values nor even identifiable figures are necessary to
produce 'theatre' (and all of this is sufficiently demonstrated by the new theatre),
then the concept of drama – however differentiated, all-embracing and watered
down it may become – retains so little substance that it loses its cognitive value.
It no longer serves the purpose of theoretical concepts to sharpen perception but
instead obstructs the cognition of theatre, as well as the theatre text.

Among the external reasons why one nevertheless has to continue to read
the new theatre with reference to and in differentiation from the category of
'drama' is the tendency of daily press reviews to operate with value judgments
that are determined by the polarity of 'dramatic' and 'boring'. The need for
action, entertainment, diversion and suspense employs the aesthetic rules of the
traditional concept of drama, though mostly unconsciously so, in order to
measure theatre that quite obviously refuses such demands according to these
standards. Peter Handke's *Across the Villages: A Dramatic Poem* opened at the
Salzburger Felsenreitschule in 1982. While critics here complained that no
Dionysian–tragic conflict appeared in it ('a play more for quiet reading'), Urs
Jenny praised the subsequent Hamburg production by Niels-Peter Rudolph for
having revealed a 'suspenseful drama' in the 'poem'. The quality of the
Hamburg production – the only one I know – consisted, however, in its differentiated rhythm designed to carry the grand form intended by Handke. In any
event, the author was certainly not concerned with writing a 'suspenseful
drama'. It is telling that even in an academic analysis of this case, the criterion
itself remains unchallenged and valid as a matter of course.[7] With the criterion
'suspense' the classical understanding of drama, or more precisely a certain
ingredient of it, lives on. Exposition, ascending action, peripeteia and catastrophe: as old-fashioned as it may sound, these are what people expect of an
entertaining story in film and theatre.

The fact that classical aesthetics – and not only that of theatre – of course
had the notion of dramatic tension ought not be confused with the ideal of
'suspense' in the age of the mass media entertainment, which, despite all technologies of simulation, is deeply N aturalistic. Here it is about nothing else
but the 'content', there about the logic of tension and release, suspense in the
sense of musical, architectonic, generally compositional tension. With respect to
the new theatre, however, the conceptual complex drama/suspense leads to
judgments that are nothing but prejudices. If texts and staged processes are
perceived according to the model of suspenseful dramatic *action*, the *theatrical*

conditions of perception, namely the aesthetic qualities of theatre *as* theatre, fade into the background: the eventful present, the particular semiotics of bodies, the gestures and movements of the performers, the compositional and formal structure of language as a soundscape, the qualities of the visual beyond representation, the musical and rhythmic process with its own time, etc. These elements (the form), however, are precisely the point in many contemporary theatre works – by no means just the extreme ones – and are not employed as merely subservient means for the illustration of an action laden with suspense.

'What a drama!'

Colloquial language, too, creates expectations that tend to govern the reception. 'That was a drama', people say, referring to a situation or event of daily life that was extraordinary or full of excitement. *Excitation* and *event* are two connotations of this word. 'The dramatic abduction ended without bloodshed', the news-reader says. He means to say that for a long time the outcome of the events was uncertain, creating a 'dramatic' suspense with regard to the further develop-ment and the *end*. This is what the epithet 'dramatic' means when added to an occurrence, action or mode of acting. When a mother comments on the suffer-ing of her child who was not allowed to go to the cinema, 'What a drama that was!', the word distances the incident, it resonates with irony about the paltry cause. Yet we still find an actual similarity to drama here: *suffering*, at least dis-appointment, as much as the – presumably quite expressive – *manifestation of feelings* as a reaction to the refusal. Two points are remarkable about this every-day usage. On the one hand, it concentrates on the *serious* side of the dramatic play whose model forms the background. People say, something is 'dramatic' and mean a situation is serious. We do not speak of comic entanglements in real life as dramas (possibly, due to the fact that since the eighteenth century the French '*drame*' and drama have been in common usage for serious bourgeois tragedy). On the other hand, it is interesting to note that the everyday usage of the word lacks almost all reference to the basic pattern of drama, which Hegel denotes with the term 'dramatic collision', and which in some form or another is at the heart of almost every theory of drama. According to this Hegelian notion, drama is a conflict of ethical attitudes, in which the dramatic person is completely identifying with an objectively founded 'pathos', i.e. seeking to assert the validity and acceptance of his/her position passionately and at the expense of the whole self. This model of dramatic antagonism hardly makes itself felt in everyday language use. People also call a long search for a lost pet, in which no oppositions, enemy positions, etc. occur, a 'drama'. Apparently, the words 'drama' and 'dramatic' in everyday language are associated more with an atmosphere, a sense of heightened excitation, anxiety and uncertainty than with a certain structure of events.

'Formalist theatre' and imitation

In front of paintings by Jackson Pollock, Barnett Newman or Cy Twombly every viewer understands at once that one can hardly speak of an imitation of a pre-existent reality here. Certainly, there have been adventurous theoretical attempts – for example in the eighteenth century – to salvage the principle of imitation even for music, for example by understanding it as the mimesis of affects. And Marxist theoreticians sought to rescue the principle of art as a reflection or 'mirror' of reality for non-representational painting. Affects or mental states are not visual or auditory, however, and thus the reference of aesthetic creations to them is more complex – a kind of 'allusion'. Since the beginning of modernism, the painted work has often rejected representation and obviously has to be comprehended as positing a new reality in its own right: as a gesture and innervation made manifest; as a statement affirming its own reality; as a *trace* no less concrete and real than a bloodstain or a freshly painted wall. In these cases, aesthetic experience demands – and makes possible – reflected visual pleasure, conscious experiencing of purely (or predominantly) visual perception as such, independent of any recognition of represented realities. In the domain of visual arts, this shift in attitude has long been considered a foregone conclusion. In the face of stage 'action' and the presence of human performers, however, the insight into the reality and legitimacy of the abstract is obviously more difficult. In theatre, the reference to 'real' human behaviour seems to be too direct. This is why here 'abstract action' is considered to be only an 'extreme'[8] – and thus ultimately negligible for the definition of theatre. Yet, at the latest the theatre of the 1980s has obliged us to see, to put it in Michael Kirby's terms, that 'abstract action', a 'formalist theatre' where the real process of 'performance' replaces 'mimetic acting' – that theatre with lyrical texts, in which virtually no plot is represented – can by no means still be described as an 'extreme' but is an essential dimension of the reality of the new theatre.[9] It is born out of a different intention than wanting to be repetition and double – however differentiated, condensed and artistically formed – of another reality. This shifting of media boundaries displaces plot-oriented drama from the aesthetic centre of theatre – though of course by no means from its institutional centre where the traditional drama is still firmly rooted.

Mimesis of action

Aristotle's poetics couples imitation and action in the famous formula that tragedy is an imitation of human action, 'mimesis praxeos'. The word drama derives from the Greek δρᾶν = to do. If one thinks of theatre as drama and as imitation, then action presents itself automatically as the actual object and kernel of this imitation. And before the emergence of film indeed no artistic practice other than theatre could so plausibly monopolize this dimension: the mimetic imitation of human action represented by real actors. With a certain necessity the fixation on action seems to entail thinking the aesthetic form of theatre as a variable dependent on another reality – life, human behaviour, reality, etc. This reality always precedes the double of theatre as the original. Fixated onto the cognitive programme 'Action/Imitation', the gaze misses the texture of written drama as much as that which offers itself to the senses as pre-sentational action, in order to assure itself only of the represented, the (assumed) 'content', the signification, and finally the meaning, the sense.

While for good reason no poetics of drama has ever abandoned the concept of action as the object of mimesis, the reality of the new theatre begins precisely with the fading away of this trinity of drama, imitation and action. It is a trinity in which theatre is regularly sacrificed to drama, drama to the dramatized, and finally the dramatized – the real in its continual withdrawal – to its concept. Without freeing ourselves from this model, we will never be able to realize to what extent all that we recognize and feel in life is thoroughly shaped and struc-tured by art: shaped and structured by ways of seeing, feeling, thinking, 'ways of meaning' (Benjamin's 'Art des Meinens') articulated only in and by art – so much so that we would have to admit that the real of our experiential worlds is to a large extent created by art in the first place. One only has to remember that aesthetic articulations in general (transversely to the conceptual grids) invent perceptive images and differentiated worlds of affects or feelings that did not exist in this way before or outside of their artistic representation in text, sound, image or scene. Whatever so-called 'defiant', 'rebellious', 'triumphant' and other affective gestures a listener finds shaped and united in a Beethoven symphony, these did not even exist outside of this specific and unique 'inven-tion' of a sound organization. Human sentiment imitates art, as much as, the other way round, art imitates life. Victor Turner made the important distinction between 'social drama', which takes place in social reality, and what he called 'aesthetic' drama, primarily in order to show how the latter 'reflects' hidden structures of the former. He emphasized, however, that conversely the aesthetic articulations of social conflicts in turn offer models for their perception and are partially responsible for the modes of ritualization in real social life. He argued that aesthetically formed drama produces images, structured forms of develop-ment and ideological patterns that give order to the social, its organization and perception.[10]

'Energetic theatre'

Jean-François Lyotard cites a nice example from Bellmer, in which representa-tion becomes a problem: 'I have a toothache, I clench my fist, my nails dig into the palm of my hand. Two investments of the libido. Shall we say that the action of the palm represents the passion of the tooth? Is there no possibility to reverse one and the other, a hierarchy of one position over the other, power of one over the other?'[11] Lyotard speaks of a changed idea of theatre that we have to assume in order to be able to conceive of a theatre beyond drama. He calls it 'energetic theatre'.[12] This would be a theatre not of meaning but of 'forces, intensities, present affects'.[13] If one does not even realize the 'energetic', for example, in Einar Schleef's chanting and moving choruses stomping towards the audience, searching instead exclusively for signs and 'representation', one will imprison the scenic in the model of mimesis, plot, and thus 'drama'. These choruses relate to that reality not as representation, however, but rather like the clenching of the fist to the toothache in Bellmer. Of course, Lyotard could already find images and concepts in Artaud's works which show that, in theatre, gestures, figurations and arrangements are possible that refer to an 'elsewhere' in a different way than iconic, indexical or symbolic 'signs'. They allude or point towards it and at the same time offer themselves as an effect of a flux, an innervation or a rage. Energetic theatre would be theatre beyond representation – meaning, of course, not simply without representation, but not governed by its logic. For postdramatic theatre one would have to postulate a kind of making of signs that Artaud names at the end of 'The Theatre and Culture' (in *The Theatre and Its Double*) with his call for 'being like victims burnt at the stake, signaling through the flames'.[14] One does not have to take on the tragic overtones of this image in order to gain an idea decisive for the new theatre: namely, that of a signalling shooting up and crystallizing from reactive vocal, physical and visceral gestures. This idea is more compatible with Adorno's idea of mimesis – which he understands as a presymbolic, affective 'becoming-like-something', in the sense of Roger Caillois' 'mimétisme' – rather than with mimesis in the narrow sense of imitation.[15]

Artaud's 'signaling through the flames', as well as Adorno's mimesis, includes shock and pain as constitutive for theatre. Neither does Lyotard's image of an energetic theatre of intensities suppress this element. Artaud and Adorno also insist, however, that the spasm (*Zuckung*) organizes itself into a *sign* or – as Adorno says – that mimesis is realized through a process of aesthetic rationality and 'construction'. It gains its logic, as much as its sound material, through a musical organization. It would not represent a logic (for example of a plot) given prior to the theatrical signs. A statement by Adorno on this topic seems strangely reminiscent of Lyotard's example:

> Art is no more a replica of an object than it is an object of cognition. Otherwise it would debase itself by becoming a mere duplicate of something. (Husserl, incidentally, leveled a cogent critique against duplication in the area of discursive knowledge.) Actually, what happens is that art makes a gesture-like grab for reality, only to draw back violently (*zurückzucken*) as it touches that reality.[16]

It will become apparent in the following explorations that the term 'postdramatic theatre' is intimately related to that of 'energetic theatre'. Yet it is preferable to the latter in order not to lose sight of the ongoing dispute with the tradition of theatre and the discourse about theatre and of the manifold intermixtures of the theatrical 'gesture' with the practices and procedures of representation.

Drama and dialectic

Drama, history, meaning

In classical aesthetics, the dialectic of the form of drama and its philosophical implications were of central concern. Therefore, a consideration of what is being left behind when drama is being left behind is best started here. Drama and tragedy were considered the highest form or one of the highest forms of the appearance of Spirit. Drama took on a distinguished role in the canon of the arts because of the dialectical essence of the genre (dialogue, conflict, solution; a high degree of abstraction essential for the dramatic form; exposition of the subject in its state of conflict). As *the* art form of process, it is, even to date, identified with the dialectical movement of alienation and sublation. Thus, Szondi attributes dialectic to the genre of drama and to tragedy.[17] Marxist theoreticians have sometimes claimed drama to be the embodiment of the dialectic of history. Historians have time and again taken recourse to the metaphors of drama, tragedy and comedy to describe the sense and inner unity of historical processes. This tendency has been furthered by the objective element of theatricality in history itself. Thus, above all the French Revolution with its grand entrances, speeches, gestures and exits has time and again been conceived of as a drama with conflict, solution, heroic roles and spectators. To view history as drama, however, almost inevitably introduces teleology, pointing towards a finally meaningful perspective – reconciliation in idealist aesthetics, historical progress in Marxist historiography. *Drama promises dialectic.*[18] Some scholars were so carried away by this aesthetic meaningfulness of history that they went so far as to say that history itself had an objective dramatic beauty.[19] Conversely, authors like Samuel Beckett and Heiner Müller avoided the dramatic form not least of all because of its implied teleology of history.

The tight entanglement of drama and dialectic and, more generally, of *drama and abstraction* has often been noted. Abstraction is inherent to drama. Conscious of this, Goethe and Schiller consequently put at the forefront of their contemplations about the difference between drama and epic the question of the right choice of subject (appropriate to the form of drama). Which subject is suitable for letting the coherence of the interpreted Being shine out, without excessive embellishments of factual information clouding the view onto the abstract structures of fate, the 'tragic collision', the dialectic in dramatic conflict and the reconciliation? The gesture of the epic writer precisely emphasizes the accessory detail (which in drama appears as a laborious waste of time) in order to evoke a sense of plenitude and credibility. By contrast, drama is based on a feat of abstraction that sketches a model world in which the plenitude not of reality in general but of human behaviour in the state of an experiment becomes evident. Long before Brecht's invention of a 'theatre of the scientific age', the dramatic form *qua* abstraction tended towards the conceptual, towards pointed and contracted condensation. This is also the basis for the often-observed similarity of novella and drama.

Aristotle: the ideal of surveyability (synopton)

Aristotle's *Poetics* conceptualizes beauty and the order of tragedy according to an analogy with logic. Thus the rule that tragedy has to be a 'whole' with beginning, middle and end, coupled with the demand that the 'magnitude' (the temporal expansion) should be just enough for the movement to a 'peripeteia' (a sudden reversal in the plot), and from there to a conclusive catastrophe, is conceptualized according to the example of logic. For the *Poetics* drama is a structure that gives a logical (namely dramatic) order to the confusing chaos and plenitude of Being. This inner order, supported by the famous unities, hermetically seals off the meaningful form, which the artefact tragedy represents, from outside reality and, at the same time, constitutes it internally as an unbroken, complete unity and wholeness. The 'whole' of the plot, a theoretical fiction, founds the logos of a totality, in which beauty is intrinsically conceived of as mastery of the temporal progress. Drama means a flow of time, controlled and surveyable. Just as peripeteia can be shown to be actually a logical category, anagnorisis, another profound idea of the *Poetics*, namely the extraordinary emotional effect of recognition, is a motif related to *cognition*. But in a special way: for the shock of anagnorisis ('You are my brother Orestes!', 'I myself am the son and murderer of Laios!') in tragedy renders manifest the concurrence of insight and helpless loss of meaning. The painful light of recognition casts light on the whole and, at the same time, poses it as an unsolvable riddle: according to which rules has the now brightly lit constellation come about? Thus, the moment of recognition is ironically the caesura, the *interruption* of recognition. This remains implicit in the *Poetics*, for Aristotle is concerned with the philosophical in tragedy. He regards mimesis as a kind of 'mathesis', a learning that becomes more pleasurable through the enjoyment of recognizing the object of mimesis – a pleasure only needed by the masses, not actually by the philosopher:

> [U]nderstanding is extremely pleasant, not just for philosophers but for others too in the same way, despite their limited capacity for it. This is the reason why people take delight in seeing images; what happens is that as they view them they come to understand and work out what each thing is (e.g. 'This is so-and-so').[20]

Tragedy appears as a para-logical order. The criterion of 'surveyability', too, serves as an intellectual processing unclouded by confusion. Beauty, the *Poetics* argues, cannot be thought without a certain magnitude (expansion):

> For this reason no organism could be beautiful if it is excessively small (since observation becomes confused as it comes close to having no perceptible duration in time) or excessively large (since the observation is then not simultaneous, and the observers find that the sense of unity and wholeness is lost from their observation, e.g. if there were an animal a thousand miles

long). So just as in the case of physical objects and living organisms, they should possess a certain magnitude, and this should be such that it can readily be taken in at one view [*eusynopton*], so in the case of plots: they should have a certain length, and this should be such that it can readily be held in memory.[21]

The drama is a model. The perceptible has to yield to the laws of comprehension and memory retention. The priority of drawing (logos) over colour (senses), which later becomes important in the theory of painting, is already called upon for comparison here, with the ordering structure of the fable-logos towering above all: 'If someone were to apply exquisitely beautiful colours at random he would gives less pleasure than if he had outlined an image in black and white.'[22] That tragedy, according to Aristotle, due to its logical-dramatic structure could even do entirely without a real staging, that it would not even need the theatre to develop its full effect, is only the logical conclusion and extreme consequence of this 'logification'. Theatre itself, the visible staging ('opsis') is already for Aristotle the realm of the incidental, the merely sensuous – and, notably, ephemeral and transitory – effects, later increasingly also the site of 'illusion', deception and imposture. By contrast, dramatic logos since Aristotle has been attributed with the advance of logic behind deceptive illusion. Its dramaturgy reveals the 'laws' behind the appearances. Not without reason Aristotle considers tragedy more 'philosophical' than historiography: it demonstrates an otherwise hidden logic according to conceptual 'necessity' and equally analytically graspable 'probability'. As the belief in the possibility of such '*modelability*' – strictly separated and separable from everyday reality – disappeared, the reality or 'worldliness' of the theatrical process itself came to the fore. The *border* between world and model that had promoted a sense of security dissolved. With that, an essential basis of dramatic theatre broke down that was axiomatic for occidental aesthetics, namely the totality of the logos.

The complicity of drama and logic, and then drama and dialectic, dominates the European 'Aristotelian' tradition – which turns out to be highly alive even in Brecht's 'non-Aristotelian drama'. The beautiful is conceptualized according to the model of the logical, as its variant. A climax of this tradition is Hegel's aesthetics. Under the general formula of the beautiful ideal as a 'sensuous appearance of the idea', it unfolds a complex theory of actualization of the Spirit in the respective artistic material, all the way up to poetic language. At the same time, it can be shown through Hegel's aesthetics why the idea of drama could have been so powerful: it could never have developed such a far-reaching efficacy if it had not been designed deeper and richer in contradictions than its abridgement to the dramaturgical result, i.e. the schema of the dramatic genre, would suggest. I shall, therefore, sketch the complex line of Hegel's speculative theory of drama in some of its aspects by drawing on reflections by Christoph Menke.[23]

Hegel 1: the exclusion of the real

Drama as an essentially dialectical genre is at the same time the exquisite place of the tragic. Theatre after drama, we might thus suspect, would be a theatre without the tragic. This conjecture is fed by Hegel's placing of tragedy in pre-modernity. Just as art, according to Hegel, comes to an end when the Spirit is at home with itself in the realm of complete conceptual abstraction and no longer in need of sensuous materialization, there is also a 'past of the tragic',[24] which Hegel in turn ties to 'dramatic poetry'. In art, the highest form and the most beautiful form are not the same. The ideal joining of the sensuous and the spiritual reached its height in classical sculpture of the gods, of which Hegel can say (not without pathos but with strict dialectical logic): 'Nothing can be or become more beautiful.'[25] The reason given by Hegel as to why Greek classical sculpture nevertheless remains inadequate and forces a further progress of art and Spirit is its lack of subjective internalization and animation (which can then be found in the 'Romantic art form', exemplarily in the image of the Virgin Mary). Hence the well-known remark about ancient sculptures that they were tinged with an air of mourning. For in post-antiquity, the height of *beauty*, the perfect merger of the sensuous and the spiritual, has to be overcome through the progress of *Spirit* in favour of a progressive intellectual abstraction. This leads to ever higher but no longer more beautiful creations, until in the 'absolute Spirit' a state of being is reached that has, in the last instance, to be thought of as beyond any shape or form.

While in classical sculpture, i.e. in visual art, the absolute of beauty has been reached, Hegel regards Sophocles' *Antigone* by contrast as the 'most satifying work of art'[26] of both the new and the ancient world – yet only in a certain respect: namely as the ideal representation of the division and reconciliation of the objective form and the subjective form of ethical spirit. Classical tragedy, as a creation of ethical conflict, goes beyond 'mere' perfect beauty, even within the realm of the 'classical art form'! It is *more than beautiful*, already on the way to pure concept and subjectivity. Menke therefore proposes to bring together Hegel's representation of the 'dissolution' of the 'classical art form' with the theorem of the end of art in modernity in such a way that actually only the conception of this 'dissolution' makes sense of that theorem. 'Drama for Hegel is on its way to a "no longer beautiful" art, even in its Greek form. In drama begins the end of art, *within* art'.[27] Thus, according to a sort of 'unofficial logic' of Hegel's teleological discourse – at least since the *Phenomenology of Spirit* – we arrive at a kind of 'marginal position' of drama, in so far as, within the area of the beautiful, it renders beauty itself questionable in its capacity for reconciliation. If Hegel understands artistic beauty as a many-layered reconciliation of opposites, especially of beauty and the ethical order, then one can indeed maintain that within the term 'drama' Hegel emphasizes those traits of the aesthetic that let reconciliation fail. Drama is not simply the (unproblematic) appearance but, at the same time, the manifest crisis of beautiful ethity (*Sittlichkeit*).

In the philosophy of drama we find, at the height of its classical formulation,

a remarkable 'two-faced-ness':[28] on the one hand, the affirmation of the successful reconciliation of beauty and ethicity (*Sittlichkeit*) – 'the sense's pleasure and the
soul's content' (Schiller) – but on the other hand, the conflictuous manifestation
of their division. Let us take a closer look at this rupture within tragedy. Compared with the epic, Hegel considers tragedy a 'higher language'. In the form of
the epic, the abstract divergence of Moira (Fate/Necessity) and impersonal
singer makes the hero appear in such a way that 'in his strength and beauty [he]
feels his life is broken and sorrowfully awaits an early death'.[29] The contingency
of the epic plenitude of action knows no dialectical necessity yet. Hence, the
voice of the epic narrator, which remains external to the hero, has to be
replaced with the actual dramatic structure of fate and – in the same move –
with the self-articulation of the human being (through the scenic embodiment).
Menke shows that, if Hegel's argument is read carefully, in tragedy the strangeness of tragic fate (already inherent in the epic) as a 'subjectless power, without
wisdom, indeterminate in itself', a 'cold necessity', indicates not only a power
that shatters beauty but also that the dramatic reconciliation itself already
carries the poisonous kernel of its failure within it. Namely in this way: in
Hegel's understanding, the experience of 'fate' forms the kernel of the drama.
This, however, is an 'ethical' experience: something eludes the control of ethical
volition, throwing a 'contingency' into the dramatic play – and thereby into the
play of the Spirit. This is fatal for the ethical concept. This contingency or 'plurality', appearing in the divine as much as among humans, destroys any
possibility of ultimate reconciliation. What marks the dramatic is a rupture that
it tries to mend scantily in order to maintain the 'truth' of reconciliation through
a stylization that empties the drama of material reality. Drama, as a beautiful
art, 'casts everything aside which in appearance does not conform to the true
concept and only through this *purification* brings about the ideal'.[30]

It is this 'catharsis' of the dramatic form that, together with the semblance of
reconciliation, also produces the beginnings of the destruction of this semblance.
For what motivates the internally necessary *exclusion of the real*, which at the same
time endangers the claim to comprehensive mediation, is nothing less than the
principle of drama itself. It is that dialectical abstraction that makes drama possible as a form in the first place, yet, in the same move, removes it from the
realm of aesthetic reconciliation, a reconciliation that occurs by means of the
permeation of *sensuous* subject-matter. In the shape of an insolubly contradictory
experience of the ethical problem and abjected materiality, there already
slumber in the depths of dramatic theatre those tensions that open up its crisis,
dissolution and finally the possibility of a non-dramatic paradigm. If there is
anything the classical ideal lacks, it is the possibility of accepting that which is
impure and alien to sense/meaning. Pointedly and convincingly, Menke concludes that, with the help of Hegel, modernity can already be thought of as a
world 'beyond beautiful morality's deficiency . . . of having to exclude all deficiency'. Beyond an aesthetic of mediation with its central aesthetic paradigm of
drama, a modernity (or postmodernity) becomes thinkable – for theatre, too –
which 'does not exclude multiplicity and difference but instead tolerates them'.[31]

From postclassical times to the present, theatre has gone through a series of transformations that assert the right of the disparate, partial, absurd and ugly against the postulates of unity, wholeness, reconciliation and sense. In content and form, theatre has increasingly incorporated all that which – filled with disgust – one did not want to 'take on' before. Rethinking the internal ambiguity (*Doppelbödigkeit*)[32] of the classical tradition itself makes it clear, however, that this 'other' of classical theatre was already present in its own most thoroughgoing philosophical interrogation, namely as a hidden possibility of rupture within the frame of the work of reconciliation strained to its maximum. Thus, *post*dramatic theatre, again and most definitely, does *not* mean a theatre that exists 'beyond' drama, without any relation to it. It should rather be understood as the unfolding and blossoming of a potential of disintegration, dismantling and deconstruction within drama itself. This virtuality was present, though barely decipherable, in the aesthetics of dramatic theatre; it was contemplated in its philosophy, but only, as it were, as a current under the sparkling surface of the 'official' dialectical procedure.

Hegel 2: the performance

For Hegel it was essential and not (as with Aristotle) merely accidental to drama that the 'persons' were embodied by real people with their own voices, physicality and gestures. For him there is a unique 'performative self-reflection of drama' which, as Menke can demonstrate, points in the same direction as the latent rift in fine arts owing to the 'deficiency of its reconciliation work'.[33] By achieving the realization no longer with the one voice of a narrator or singer but through a necessary *plurality* of voices, the particular, 'individual' subjects receive such an autonomous justification in themselves that it becomes impossible to relativize their respective individual right in favour of a dialectical synthesis. Moreover, the actors, whom Hegel regards as 'statues' made to move and brought into relation with one another, realize a displacement that is scandalous for Hegel's objective idealism: in so far as in the drama it is only empirical human beings who help the spiritual ideal, the artistic beauty (the dramatic heroes), to become reality, they develop an 'ironic performance consciousness'. What results is, in other words, the (for Hegel) unthinkable phenomenon that the particular and preconceptual – the mere individual real player – stand above the moral content. The latter, the Spirit, here depends on the mere particular representational achievement of the player instead of imposing its law on the particular. Menke comments, 'instead of being "merely a tool" disappearing in its role, the actor experiences a reversal of the dependence between beauty or rather the ethical order and subjectivity . . . The basic experience of the actor is the production of the ethically valid through individuals.'[34]

The active performance character of drama (read: the theatre) thus opens up a tension between the made and the making, which in performance comes to light in such a way that the 'actual human beings' (the actors) 'design' the 'personae', the masks of the heroes, and portray them 'not in the form of a narrative, but in the actual speech of the actors themselves'.[35] For this reason, there can also occur an 'unmasking' of this, in Hegel's view, 'reversed' relationship between subjectivity and objective ethical content: namely, when in the comical parabasis the actors step out of character and play with the mask. With great acuteness, Hegel sees the peculiarity of the experience of *theatre*, that it presents the unity of spiritual reality and material execution as a 'hypocrisy':[36] 'the hero who appears before the onlookers splits up into his mask and the actor, into the person in the play and actual self'.[37] This is merely very obtrusively noticeable in the comical parabasis where the 'self' at one moment acts in the mask and at the next appears 'in his own nakedness and ordinariness'.[38] The theatrical play in general presents something fundamentally unthinkable for the philosophy of the Spirit: the in and of itself essence-less subjective self of the player who produces signs artificially, this merely individual accidental I, experiences itself as the founder and donor of the essential, of the ethical content, as the creator of the dramatis personae, i.e. figures who already unite the beautiful and the ethical: 'The pretensions of universal essentiality are uncovered in the self . . . The self, appearing here in its significance as something actual, plays with the mask it once put on in order to act its part.'[39]

In this reality of the theatre Hegel has to see a 'general dissolution of the shapes of the essentiality as a whole in their individuality'.[40] Consequently, this tendency of dissolution must logically, in terms of the history of Spirit, lead to the emergence of abstraction and the dialectical consciousness of 'rational thinking', namely from tragic and comic drama to Greek philosophy. Drama is necessarily positioned at the margins of art, at the borderline that separates the ideal of art, the 'sensuous appearance of the idea', and the somewhat shapeless philosophical abstraction. It makes sense that Menke connects this inner tension, the incompleteness of drama, with the Romantic transcendentalization of poetry. And it makes sense that he understands Hegel's theory of drama as a metaphor for a notion of art that already contains those motifs of argumentation within it that turn the 'official' concept of the ideal as sensuous appearance of the idea into an unattainable phantasm. Thus, the 'end of art' appears less as a historical and (art-)philosophical thesis than as an end of the 'classical' idea of art, an end of art within art, that has always already begun. From the perspective of the newer development of art and theatre forms, which seek to depart from the Gestalt as totality, mimesis and model, Hegel's presentation of the ancient development strikes us as a model for the dissolution of the dramatic concept of theatre.

Prehistories

Towards a prehistory of postdramatic theatre

Theatre and text

Theatre and drama have existed, and still exist, in a relationship of tension-ridden contradictions. To emphasize this state of affairs and consider the whole extent of its implications are the first prerequisite for an adequate understanding of the new and newest theatre. The cognition of postdramatic theatre starts with ascertaining to what extent its existence depends on the mutual emancipation and division between drama and theatre. A genre history of drama in and of itself is therefore only of limited interest to theatre studies. Yet, since the theatre in Europe has practically and theoretically been dominated by drama, it is advisable to use the term 'postdramatic' in order to relate the newer developments to the past of dramatic theatre, that is, not so much to the changes of theatre *texts* as to the transformation of theatrical modes of expression. In post-dramatic forms of *theatre*, staged text (*if* text is staged) is merely a component with equal rights in a gestic, musical, visual, etc., total composition. The rift between the discourse of the text and that of the theatre can open up all the way to an openly exhibited discrepancy or even unrelatedness. The historical drifting apart of text and theatre demands an unprejudiced redefinition of their relationship. It proceeds from the reflection that theatre existed first: arising from ritual, taking up the form of mimesis through dance, and developing into a full-fledged behaviour and practice before the advent of writing. While 'primitive theatre' and 'primitive drama' (*Ur*-theatre and *Ur*-drama) are merely the object of reconstructive attempts, it seems to be an anthropological certainty that early ritual forms of theatre represented affectively highly charged processes (hunting, fertility) with the help of masks, costumes and props, in such a way that dance, music and role-play were combined.[1] Even if this physically semiotic, motor practice already represented a kind of 'text' before the advent of writing, the difference with respect to the formation of modern literary theatre is still apparent. The written text, literature, took on the rarely contested leading role of the cultural hierarchy. Thus, even the connection of text with a musicalized form of speech, dance-like gesture and splendid optical and archi-tectonic décor that was still present in baroque representational theatre could vanish in bourgeois literary theatre: the text *as an offer of meaning* reigned; all other theatrical means had to serve it and were rather suspiciously controlled by the authority of Reason.

There have been attempts to make allowances for the newly raised awareness of the autonomy of non-literary elements of theatre by defining 'drama' very widely. Thus, Georg Fuchs wrote in *The Revolution of Theatre*: 'Drama in its simplest form is rhythmic movement of the body through space'. Here 'drama' means scenic action, and thus, to all intents and purposes, theatre. Fuchs also considered everything that may occur in variety theatre, 'dance, acrobatics, juggling, tightrope walking, conjuring, wrestling and boxing, dressage of and performing with animals, musical, masquerade, and whatever else' as simple forms of drama.[2] (In theatre utopias of the first half of the twentieth century one occasionally comes across discourses identifying theatre as *cultic* action with 'drama' and demarcating this symbolic, cultic action from that of the *mimus*' imitation of reality.) However, such a terminological identification of drama with all levels of theatricality cancels out the productive historical and typological differentiations between the different ways in which theatre and dramatic literature have met and separated from each other in modernity. It therefore makes sense to define 'drama' more narrowly and to agree that in approaches such as Fuchs' the dimensions of the agonal and theatrical are indistinguishably merged with drama – aspects that are rightfully distinguished in the minds of theatre practitioners, readers and theoreticians. The same also applies to certain remarks by Heiner Müller that the basic element of theatre *and* of drama was that of *transformation*, death being the last transformation and theatre always having to do with symbolic death: 'The essential thing about theatre is transformation. Dying. And the fear of this last transformation is general, one can rely on it, one can depend on it.'[3]

Discussing the appearance of reconciliation in Goethe's *Elective Affinities*, Walter Benjamin writes:

> The mystery is, on the dramatic level, that moment in which it juts out of the domain of language proper to it into a higher one unattainable for it. Therefore, this moment can never be expressed in words but is expressible solely in representation: it is the 'dramatic' in the strictest sense.[4]

In this sense, the 'dramatic' is without connection to anything that is understood by it in theatre studies debates. Benjamin's wording relates what he describes as the 'dramatic' to the silent agon of the physical competitions rooted in cult. What is at stake is the (Christian) surpassing of the agon through Grace, Redemption or 'Language' beyond, or in any case at the limit of, human language. No doubt there is a relative justification in identifying theatre and drama, and this is evident where Benjamin's conception of the dramatic emphasizes its greatest proximity to pantomime and muteness, which are, so to speak, only framed by language. Yet, precisely for this reason it will be useful to regard the Benjaminean 'dramatic' as belonging to *theatre*: as ritual and ceremony, 'poetry' of the stage, and extra-linguistic or at least borderline linguistic semiosis. This notion of the 'dramatic' points to theatre as an unfathomable experience of metamorphosis, in which there is no arresting of the utopian, anxiety-ridden whirl of transformations that the theatre manifests; in which there is only the feast and no fixing that could protect from the vertigo and dizziness of theatre. Rather, what is at issue here is the reality (albeit one always remaining in the twilight) of an overcoming of death through its staging. As Primavesi emphasizes, 'in holding on to the silent *physis*, the "dramatic" can guarantee redemption from the myth of guilt and of beauty only where the body – as in theatre – remains withdrawn from comprehension'.[5]

The twentieth century

Towards the end of the nineteenth century, dramatic theatre had reached the end of a long blooming as a fully perfected discursive formation. Shakespeare, Racine, Schiller, Lenz, Büchner, Hebbel, Ibsen and Strindberg could thus be experienced as variants of one and the same discursive form – despite all their differences. Within this frame, the internally highly divergent types and individual appearances, too, presented themselves as variations of a discursive formation, for which the amalgamation of drama and theatre is essential. The development of that discursive formation towards the postdramatic will now be briefly traced. The 'take off' towards a formation of postdramatic discourse in theatre can be described as a series of stages of *self-reflection, decomposition* and *separation* of the elements of dramatic theatre. The path leads from the grand theatre at the end of the nineteenth century, via a multitude of modern theatre forms during the historical avant-garde and then the neo-avant-garde of the 1950s and 1960s, to the postdramatic theatre forms at the end of the twentieth and the beginning of the twenty-first centuries.

First stage: 'pure' and 'impure' drama

The initial situation is a still intact predominance of drama, whose essential moments are clearly developed in the idea(l) and partially in the practice of the 'pure drama'. 'Drama' is not just an aesthetic model but carries with it essential epistemological and social implications: the objective importance of the hero, of the individual; the possibility of representing human reality through language, namely through the form of stage dialogue; and the relevance of individual human behaviour in society. Parallel to and before 'pure drama' (in medieval times, in Shakespeare, in baroque theatre), considerable deviations from the model already existed. They can roughly be described as 'epic' elements of drama, and for our purposes one could designate the abundance of these forms as 'impure drama'. For these forms, too, the essential form semantics of drama can be demonstrated at each point: the embodiment of characters or allegorical figures through actors; the representation of a conflict in 'dramatic collision'; a high degree of abstraction of world representation in comparison to the novel and the epic; the representation of political, moral and religious issues of social life through the dramatization of their collision; a progressive action even in the case of extensive de-dramatization; the representation of a world even in the case of minimal real action.

Second stage: crisis of drama, theatre goes its own way(s)

Under the premise of a theatre that is not yet changed in revolutionary ways, the crisis of drama occurs from about 1880 onwards. What is being shaken during this crisis and subsequently declines is a series of previously unquestioned constituents of drama: the textual form of a dialogue charged with suspense and pregnant with decisions; the subject whose reality can essentially be expressed in interpersonal speech; the action that unfolds primarily in an absolute present. Szondi differentiates the well-known 'solutions' or 'rescue attempts' the authors arrive at under the impression of a rapidly changing world and a changing image of the human subject: *I* Dramaturgy (*Ich-Dramatik*), static drama (*drame statique*), conversation play, lyrical drama, Existentialism and constraint, etc.[6] In parallel and in analogy to the crisis of drama as a theatre-related text form, there emerges a first scepticism towards the sheer compatibility of drama and theatre. Thus, Pirandello was convinced of the incompatibility of theatre and drama.[7] Edward Gordon Craig explicated in the 'First Dialogue' of the *Art of Theatre* that one should not stage Shakespeare's great plays at all! This would even be dangerous because the acted Hamlet would kill some of the infinite wealth of the imaginary Hamlet. (Later Craig actually undertook a production of the play and declared the attempt had proved his thesis that the play was unstageable.) Theatre is here recognized as something that has its own different roots, preconditions and premises, which are even hostile to dramatic literature. The text should recede from the theatre, Craig concludes, precisely because of its poetic dimensions and qualities.

New forms of texts develop that contain narration and references to reality only in distorted and rudimentary shape: Gertrude Stein's 'Landscape Play', Antonin Artaud's texts for his 'Theatre of Cruelty', Witkievicz's theatre of 'pure form'. These 'deconstructed' kinds of *texts* anticipate literary elements of post-dramatic *theatre* aesthetics. Gertrude Stein's texts will only find their congenial theatre aesthetics with Robert Wilson. Artaud's theatre remained a vision, like-wise that of Witkievicz, which points ahead to the Theatre of the Absurd. The French director Antoine Vitez, someone who stages classical texts with sparse and functional theatrical means, knew what he was talking about when he said that since the end of the nineteenth century all great works written for the theatre were marked by a 'total indifference' towards the problems their texture posed for scenic realization.[8] Thus, a rift, a separation, developed between theatre and text. Gertrude Stein was (and still is) considered to be 'unplayable' – which is true if her texts are measured by the expectations of dramatic theatre. Asking merely how 'successful' her texts were on stage, one would have to attest her unequivocal failure as a theatre author. Yet in the forms of her texts, too, a dynamic force declares itself, which eventually dissolves the tradition of dramatic theatre.

The autonomization of theatre is not the result of the self-importance of (post)modern directors craving recognition, as which it is often dismissed. The emergence of a director's theatre was, rather, potentially established in the aesthetic dialectics of dramatic theatre itself, which in its development as a 'form of presentation' increasingly discovered the means and devices that are inherent to it even without regard to the text. At the same time, one has to realize the productive side in some twentieth-century and contemporary authors' lack of consideration for the possibilities of the theatre: they write in such a way that the theatre for their texts largely still remains to be invented. The challenge to discover new potencies of the art of theatre has become an essential dimension of writing for the theatre. Brecht's demand that authors should not 'supply' the theatre with their texts but instead change it has been realized far beyond his imagination. Heiner Müller could even declare that a theatre text was only good if it was unstageable for the theatre as it is.

Autonomization, retheatricalization

In parallel to the crisis of drama and in the course of the general art revolution around 1900, a crisis of the discourse form of *theatre* itself occurs. Out of the rejection of traditional forms of theatre develops a new autonomy of theatre as an independent artistic practice. Only since this caesura has theatre abandoned orienting the choice of its means securely around the requirements of the drama to be staged. This orientation had meant not just a certain limitation but at the same time a certain security for the criteria of theatre crafts, a logic and system of rules for the use of theatrical means that serve the drama. Hence, a loss occurred along with the newly acquired freedom, which, from a productive point of view, has to be described as the *entry of theatre into the age of experimentation*. Since it became conscious of the artistic expressive potential slumbering within it, independent of the text to be realized, theatre, like other art forms, has been hurled into the difficult and risky freedom of perpetual experimentation.

While the 'theatricalization' of theatre leads to liberation from its subjection to drama, this development is accelerated by another media-historical caesura: the emergence of film. What until then had been the inherent domain of theatre, the representation of acting people in motion, is taken over by motion pictures which in this respect soon surpass theatre. While, on the one hand, theatricality is comprehended as an artistic dimension independent of the dramatic text, on the other, through the contrast with the technically produced 'image movement' (Deleuze), one simultaneously begins to realize the live process (as opposed to the reproduced or reproducible appearances) as a *differentia specifica* of the theatre. This rediscovery of the presentational potential peculiar to theatre, and only to theatre, raises the question: what is unmistakable and irreplaceable about it compared to other media? Indeed this question has since accompanied theatre, and not just because of the rivalry with other art forms. Rather, it clearly demonstrates one of the two general logics according to which new forms of artistic representation develop: the logic according to which the emergence of a new medium of form creation and world representation almost automatically entails that the media now suddenly defined as 'older' begin to inquire what is specific to them *as art forms* and what should hence be displayed consciously and emphatically after the appearance of new technologies. Under the impression of new media, the old ones become *self-reflexive*. (It happened thus with painting when photography emerged, with theatre when film emerged and with the latter when television and video emerged.) Even if this change outshines everything else only in a first phase of reaction, from then on self-reflexivity remains a permanent potential and necessity, forced by the coexistence and competition (paragon) of the arts. The other regularity within the development of the arts seems to be that dynamism grows from decomposition. When in visual arts the dimension of representation separated from the experience of colour and form (photography here and abstraction there) the individual elements, thus thrown back upon themselves, could gain acceleration and new forms could come about. From the *decomposition* of the whole of a genre into its individual elements develop new languages of form. Once the formerly 'glued together' aspects of language and body separate in theatre, character representation and audience address are each treated as autonomous realities; once the sound space separates from the playing space, new representational chances come about through the autonomization of the individual layers.

The concentration on theatricality, as opposed to the literary, photographic or filmic representation of worlds, can be described as 'retheatricalization' and marks the movements of the historical avant-garde. Erika Fischer-Lichte's studies[9] in particular have focused on this concept (first introduced as a keyword by Fuchs), emphasizing among other things its connection with the productive reception of (European and non-European) non-literary theatre traditions in the historical avant-gardes. The aim was not only the remembering of the purely aesthetic means of theatricality. It was not just a matter of a retheatricalization immanent to theatre but at the same time of an opening of the theatrical sphere to others: to cultural, political, magical, philosophical, etc. forms of practice, to gathering, feast and ritual. To be avoided, therefore, are theoretical abridgements in the direction of an aesthetization of the avant-gardes, which could be suggested by the use of the term 'retheatricalization' in the context of classical modernism. The desire of the avant-gardes to overcome the boundaries between life and art (the failure of which does not condemn them, of course) was just as much a motif of retheatricalization.

In the course of this development, we see the emergence of the 'directors' theatre' or 'theatre of direction' (*Regietheater*), as it has been called with the intention of either praise, description or defamation. The autonomization of theatre and with it the increased importance of directing are arguably irrevocable. Without wanting to disregard all justified dislike of mediocre directors in theatre, who enclose important texts into their comparatively limited horizon, it has to be emphasized that the hue and cry about directors' arbitrariness in most cases stems from a traditional understanding of text theatre (in the nineteenth-century sense) and/or the unwillingness to engage with unfamiliar theatre experiences altogether. Meanwhile, the differentiation of a theatre of directors from a theatre of the actor or the author concerns our topic only marginally: a directors' theatre (*Regietheater*) is arguably a precondition for the postdramatic disposition (even if whole collectives take on the direction), but dramatic theatre, too, is largely a directors' theatre.

With the new insistence on the intrinsic value of theatre around the turn of the century there is another context to be kept in mind: the entertainment and spectacle theatre of the late nineteenth century in particular had strengthened the more ambitious directors in their conviction that there was a conflict between the text and routinized theatre. For Craig, as much as for Chekhov and Stanislavski, Claudel and Copeau, the reclamation of complexity and truth for the theatre was a central motif of their endeavours. Even if one was quickly moving away from the traditional presentation of drama, and even if some of the advocates of autonomy and 'retheatricalization' of the theatre advanced to the demand for a banning of the text altogether, radical theatre was not moti-vated simply by contempt for the text but also by the attempt of *rescue*. The emerging 'theatre of directors' was often precisely concerned with wrenching texts away from convention and saving them from arbitrary, banal or destruc-tive ingredients of 'culinary' theatrical effects.[10] Whoever calls for rescuing text theatre from the crimes of directing nowadays should remember this historical context. The tradition of the written text is under more threat from museum-like conventions than from radical forms of dealing with it.

Third stage: 'neo-avant-garde'

For the genealogy of postdramatic theatre, the theatrical departure of the neo-avant-garde is important. In the Federal Republic of Germany, the so-called 'reconstitution phase' after World War II encouraged a questionable limitation of culture and theatre to an apolitical 'humanism'. On the one hand, no fewer than one hundred new theatres were built during the economic boom of the 1950s but, on the other hand, the scene was dominated by Gustaf Gründgen's conservatism and the attempt to forget the political past and instead return to 'culture'. The experimental attempts in Germany still seem quite timid at a time when new paths are being forged in the USA at Black Mountain College: John Cage, Merce Cunningham, Allan Kaprow and others take the stage.

During the late 1950s, the international departure begins. It marks the start not only of the avant-garde but also of pop culture which transforms all areas of private and public life. Rock music (Chuck Berry, Elvis Presley) for the first time in history produces music deliberately and exclusively targeted at young people. The triumphal procession of youth culture starts. In Germany, which in visual arts and everyday culture willingly follows American trends, an enthusiastic reception of plays by Beckett, Ionesco, Sartre and Camus starts as a reaction against the fossilized *Bildungstheater* (highbrow educational/cultural theatre). The confluence of philosophy and Theatre of the Absurd with Existentialism finds just as much of a strong echo in Germany as the belated cognizance of artistic developments such as Surrealism and Abstract Expressionism. The reception of Kafka starts and serial music and Art Informel are making themselves felt. While in the German Democratic Republic – especially after the triumphal international tour of the Berlin Ensemble – Brecht's aesthetics seems to set the tone (though in day-to-day reality it is actually treated as suspect and is opposed in the name of a so-called 'social realism'), in the Western world and especially in West Germany a new theatre of provocation and protest develops around 1965. The productions of Peter Weiss' *Marat/Sade* in Berlin and London (by Konrad Swinarski and Peter Brook respectively) become emblematic for this theatre revolt.

Culminating in the revolution of 1968, the 1960s see the development of a new spirit of experimentation in all arts. The new 'Bremen style' causes a stir: under the direction of Kurt Hübner a new political and formally protesting young theatre comes about, marked by Peter Zadek, Wilfried Minks and Peter Stein. The latter leaves for Berlin in 1969 and for decades makes the Berliner Schaubühne an internationally leading theatre. In the USA a multifariously creative avant-garde is working, with the visual arts, theatre, dance, film, photography and literature becoming a 'creative community' that turns the transgression of artistic borders into a norm and lets the conventional theatre appear as antiquated. The new art of the 'environment' (already anticipated in Kurt Schwitter's *Merzbauten*) draws close to the theatre scene through its conceptual integration of the real presence of the viewer (Rauschenberg) into the work. Christo's packaging projects interact as 'works' with the visitors flocking to them. 'Action painting' is already a painting ceremony with resonances of a theatrical situation, although after the artistic action, emphasized in its own right, the work here still exists for itself as an object linked in idea with the 'scene' of its genesis. Yves Klein directs the performers of his 'anthropometries' as art spectacles with music in front of an audience. With happenings, and all the more so with the Vienna actionists, the action takes on the traits of a ritual. In 1969, Richard Schechner stages *Dionysius 69*, in which the spectators are invited to get into physical contact with the players.

Also in the 1960s, the 'Theatre of the Absurd' is at the centre of interest. It renounces the visible meaningfulness of the dramatic action but in the midst of the decomposition of sense sticks surprisingly strictly to the classical unities of drama. What still links Ionesco, Adamov and the other variants of this theatre qualified as 'absurd' or 'poetic' to the classical tradition is the *dominance of speech*. While for Ionesco words become 'écorces sonores démunies de sens' ('sonorous shells devoid of meaning'), it is precisely through this quality that plays like *La Cantatrice chauve* (*The Bald Prima Donna*) are in the end meant to express a truth of the 'world' in a new light, the reality, as Ionesco writes, 'dans sa véritable lumière, au delà des interprétations et d'une causalité arbitraire' ('in its true light, beyond interpretations and an arbitrary causality').[11] Even the theatre of a rigorous critique of meaning understood itself as a design of *a world*, the author

as its creator. Even as a game of the absurd, theatre remained a world representation. And just like the new political theatre of provocation, the absurd theatre
remains pledged to the hierarchy that in dramatic theatre ultimately subordi-
nates the theatrical means to the text. The plexus of the dominance of the text,
the conflict of figures, and the totality of plot and world representation (however
grotesque these may be) that characterize dramatic theatre remain intact.

Reviewing the Theatre of the Absurd in Esslin's description, one might initially feel transported into the postdramatic theatre of the 1980s. There is 'no
story or plot to speak of' here; the plays 'are often without recognizable characters', but instead have 'almost mechanical puppets'; they 'often have neither a
beginning nor an end', and instead of being a mirror of reality seem to be
'reflections of dreams and nightmares' consisting of 'incoherent babblings'
instead of 'witty repartee and pointed dialogue'.[12] Is the theatre of Robert
Wilson being described here? Since one can indeed diagnose something like
an 'absence de sens' in postdramatic theatre, a comparison suggests itself with
the Theatre of the Absurd, which already carries the renunciation of sense and
meaning in its name. The atmosphere the Theatre of the Absurd feeds off
is based on a *Weltanschauung* and is politically, literarily and philosophically
founded: the experience of barbarism in the twentieth century (the Holocaust),
the real possibility of the end of history (Hiroshima), meaningless bureaucracies
and political resignation. The Existentialist retreat to the individual and the
absurd are closely related. Comic despair becomes the basic mood in Frisch,
Dürrenmatt, Hildesheimer and others. The motto 'Only comedy can still get to
us' ('Uns kommt nur noch die Komödie bei' – Dürrenmatt) expresses the loss
of the possibility of a tragic interpretation of the world as a whole. Along with
French Existentialist films, Stanley Kubrick's *Dr Strangelove or: How I Learnt to Stop
Worrying and Love the Bomb* (1964) remains the congenial cinematic translation of
this experience. However, the different *Weltanschauung* gives an entirely different
meaning to all motifs of discontinuity, collage and montage, decomposition of
narration, speechlessness and withdrawal of meaning shared by the absurd and
the postdramatic theatre. While Esslin rightly places the formal elements of the
absurd into a context of themes determined by *Weltanschauung* and emphasizes
especially the 'sense of metaphysical anguish at the absurdity of the human condition',[13] for the postdramatic theatre of the 1980s and 1990s the disintegration
of ideological certainties represents no longer a problem of metaphysical anguish
but a cultural given.

Absurdist theatre corresponds with the lyrical drama which belongs to the
genealogy (not the type) of postdramatic theatre. The title of Tardieu's second
theatre collection (*Poème à jouer*, 1960) indicates the direction. A play like
Conversation-Sinfonietta builds a musical composition out of fragments of everyday
language. In *L'ABC de notre vie* (written in 1958, premiered in 1959) one finds the
genre description 'poem for the stage' for solo voice and choir. The premiere
production used music by Anton Webern. There is also a play without any
figures in which only voices sound in an empty room (*Voix sans personne*). Compared to postdramatic theatre, the 'poetic theatre', which Esslin wanted to

distinguish from the Theatre of the Absurd,[14] is actually not so different from it. 'Poetic theatre' is a type of literary theatre in the tradition of dramatic theatre, while a gulf separates it from postdramatic theatre. In conclusion we can state that the Theatre of the Absurd, like Brecht's theatre, belongs to the dramatic theatre tradition. Some of its texts explode the frame of dramatic and narrative logic. Yet the step to postdramatic theatre is taken only when the theatrical means beyond language are positioned equally alongside the text and are systematically thinkable without it. Hence we cannot speak of a 'continuation' of absurdist or epic theatre in the new theatre[15] but must name the rupture: that epic as much as absurdist theatre, though through different means, clings to the presentation of a fictive and simulated text-cosmos as a dominant, while postdramatic theatre no longer does so.

The genre of *documentary theatre* developing in the 1960s also points some way beyond the tradition of dramatic theatre. In place of the dramatic representation of the events themselves one finds here scenes of court trials of incidents, interrogations and witness statements. One could object that court scenes and cross-examinations of witnesses are also a means of traditional theatre to create suspense. Yet while this is true for many dramatic plays, it is not pertinent here because in documentary theatre little depends on the outcome of the process of investigation or that of arriving at a verdict. What is thematically at stake here (political or moral guilt in nuclear weapons research, the Vietnam War, imperialism, and the responsibility for concentration camp atrocities) has long been historically and politically decided outside of the theatre. The documentary play in this respect confronts a similar kind of difficulty as every historical drama attempting the impossible: namely, how to represent the historically already known events as uncertain and to be decided upon only in the course of the dramatic procedure. Suspense is not located in the progress of events but is an objective, intellectual, mostly ethical one: it is not a matter of a dramatically narrated, 'discussed' world.[16] On the other hand, less consistent authors like Rolf Hochhuth could not avoid the temptation to change the documentary material back into dramatic currency, evoking sharp criticism, for example, from Adorno.

It is questionable whether the much implored political claim of documentary theatre could be upheld by adapting it formally to the dramatic norm. Peter Iden claimed in 1980 that Rolf Hochhuth's *The Deputy* had remained 'too unselfconscious towards its own dramatic form' and therefore had not really been political theatre, while, by contrast, the famous staging of *Tasso* by Peter Stein had been political.[17] It had become apparent that the treatment of classic plays in the theatre was increasingly translating the 'dramatic within the material into a drama of the collapsing of all traditional means' (though the metaphor of drama for the loss of outmoded means of representation may be considered inappropriate). The actual conflict of the dramatic subject matter had 'shifted into the way it was dealt with'.[18] This remark captures the sharp opposition to dramatic traditionalism, and the attempts at a different, new practice of theatre in Peter Stein's *Tasso*. (Of course, Stein himself consciously decided not to continue this departure or this dismantling of theatre. Rather he soon developed (with support from Dieter Sturm) a rightly praised, rather neo-classical Schaubühne aesthetics, which was at times one of the most brilliant realizations of the dramatic theatre in an age when it was questioned.) What is so forward-looking about the documentary theatre is less the desire for direct political action, and even less its conventional dramaturgy, than a trait likely to provoke rejection and criticism. While it 'dramatized' documents, it simultaneously demonstrated a distinct tendency towards oratorio-like forms, towards *rituals*, as which interrogation, report and court also present themselves. This becomes strikingly apparent in Peter Weiss' *The Investigation*, which not coincidentally arose from his reading of Dante and his plan to write a kind of *Inferno* himself. The horror of the Auschwitz death camps is presented in cantos, heightening the material of the statements into a recitative that appears liturgical.

One can say that the prominent *texts* of those years question the dramatic model of communication more clearly than the practice of directing. Thus, the genealogy of postdramatic theatre includes Peter Handke's *Sprechstücke*. The theatre here doubles itself, citing its own speech. Only through the detour of an internal erosion of theatrical signs, via a radically self-referential quality, does the indirect 'message' occur, and reference to the real take place. The problematization of 'reality' as a reality of theatrical signs becomes a metaphor for the depletion, the empty circularity of the most common figures of speech. If signs can no longer be read as a reference to a certain referent then the audience helplessly confronts the alternative of either thinking nothing in the face of this absence or instead reading the forms themselves, the language games and the players in their here and now presented 'being-as-it-is' (*Sosein* – Heidegger). In as much as it still has all the criteria of dramatic theatre as its *topic*, a text like *Offending the Audience* in a way remains bound to it as 'metadrama or metatheatre',[19] as Pfister says (with classic indecisiveness). At the same time, however, it also points to the future of theatre after drama.

The mentioned variants of neo-avant-gardist theatre each sacrifice certain parts of dramatic representation but in the end preserve the crucial unity: the close connection between the text of an action, report or process and the theatrical representation oriented towards it. This connection ruptures in the postdramatic theatre of the last decades. Intermediality, the civilization of images and scepticism towards grand theories and meta-narratives[20] dissolve the hierarchy that had previously guaranteed not just the subjection of all theatrical means to the text but also the coherence among them. It is no longer just a matter of affirming and recognizing the independent achievement of the staging as an artistic design. Instead the relationships that are constitutive for dramatic theatre are inverted, first in a subterraneous manner, then openly. The focus is no longer on the questions whether and how the theatre 'corresponds to' the text that eclipses everything else, rather the questions are whether and how the texts are suitable material for the realization of a theatrical project. The aim is no longer the wholeness of an aesthetic theatre composition of words, meaning, sound, gesture, etc., which as a holistic construct offers itself to perception.

Instead the theatre takes on a fragmentary and partial character. It renounces the long-incontestable criteria of unity and synthesis and abandons itself to the chance (and risk) of trusting individual impulses, fragments and microstructures of texts in order to become a new kind of practice. In the process it discovers a new continent of performance, a new kind of presence of the 'performers' (into which the 'actors' have mutated) and establishes a multifarious theatre land-scape beyond forms focused on drama.

A short look back at the historical avant-gardes

A discussion of the new theatre forms (roughly from around 1970 and into the first decade of the twenty-first century) has to have recourse to the historical avant-gardes because here the conventional classical dramaturgy of unity was first disrupted. Of course this cannot involve adding to the rich scholarship on this epoch or creating an inventory of the manifold influences of the historical avant-garde on postdramatic theatre. This chapter can only highlight some especially prominent positions and developments that are of special interest in the light of postdramatic theatre.

Lyrical drama, Symbolism

In his analysis of what he calls 'formalist' theatre, Michael Kirby proposes a distinction between an 'antagonistic' and a 'hermetic' model of the avant-garde. He rightly remarks that the prevalent conviction according to which avant-garde theatre started in 1896 with the theatre scandal around Alfred Jarry's *Ubu Roi* in Paris is at least one-sided. Only the 'antagonistic' line begins here (at the time, the word 'merde' mentioned at the beginning of the play could still 'épater le bourgeois'!) and leads via Futurism, Dada and Surrealism to the aesthetics of provocation of our own day. Alongside it and earlier, however, beginning in Symbolism, is what Kirby calls the 'hermetic avant-garde':

> Avant-garde theatre began – before that first performance of *Ubu Roi* – at least with the Symbolists. Symbolist aesthetics demonstrate a turning inward, away from the bourgeois world and its standards, to a more per-sonal, private, and extraordinary world. Symbolist performance was done in small theatres. It was detached, distant, and static, involving little physi-cal energy. The lighting was often dim. The actors often worked behind scrims . . . The art was self-contained, isolated, complete in itself. We can call this the 'hermetic' model of avant-garde performance.[21]

The theatre of the Symbolists marked a step on the way to postdramatic theatre because of its undramatic stasis and the tendency towards monological forms. Stéphane Mallarmé focuses on an idea of *Hamlet* according to which this play actually only has a single hero who lets all other figures recede to the rank of 'extras'. From here may be traced a line to the way in which Klaus-Michael Grüber stages *Faust* or Robert Wilson *Hamlet*: as a neo-lyrical theatre that understands the scene as a site of an 'écriture' in which all components of the theatre become letters in a poetic 'text'. Significantly, Maeterlinck remarks that 'la pièce de théâtre doit être avant tout un poème' ('the play has to be above all a poem'). Afterwards he explains that because of the annoying pressure of those 'circumstances' which for our 'conventions' count as reality the poet cheats a little bit and introduces allusions to everyday life here and there ('ça et là'). These motifs, which for the poet Maeterlinck signify no more than a necessary compromise, are usually perceived by people as the only important thing, as he complains, while for the poet – the playwright – they are superficial conces-sions[22] to the wishes of the audience who desire a representation of that which it takes for recognizable reality. The same is also true, as Maeterlinck expressly says, for what is called the 'étude des caractères'. What is renounced in these theses is the whole construction of tension, drama, story and imitation. As wit-nessed in the name *drame statique* (static drama), at the same time the classical idea of progressing, linear time is deserted in favour of a planar 'image-time', of a time-space.

Stasis, ghosts

It is well known that at this time Asian theatre becomes a source of inspiration for the theatre in Europe. Paul Claudel enthusiastically states the opposition to drama: 'Le drame, c'est quelque chose qui arrive, le No, c'est quelqu'un qui arrive' ('The drama is something that happens, the Noh is someone who arrives').[23] Only a few explanations are needed to find in this phrase the essen-tial opposition of dramatic and postdramatic theatre: appearance instead of plot action, performance instead of representation. The Noh Theatre for Claudel is a kind of one-person drama that exhibits the same structure as a dream.[24] Searching for a 'nouveau cérémonial théâtral' (Mallarmé) one finds in Japanese Noh a total theatre with a metaphysical horizon. Like the ode in Mallarmé's Symbolism, the Catholic mass, too, can advance to a model for theatre. It is obvious that the ceremonial character of Asian theatre offers encouragement for such visions. While it has almost nothing in common with the realist European 'drama', it makes space for a ritual mode of perception that allows us to trace a trajectory from Asian theatre via Maeterlinck and Mallarmé to Wilson.

In the concentration upon ritual, an experience manifests itself which can hardly be characterized other than with the old-fashioned word fate. In Maeter-linck the theme becomes explicit and central. His theatre is meant to articulate not the trivial causality of everyday experience but rather the fateful surrender of the human being to a law that remains unknowable. It would be wrong to dismiss such (certainly problematic) conceptions simply for reasons of ideologi-cal critique. Even if Wilson's so-called 'Theatre of Images' produces a peculiar aura of fatefulness because the figures seem to be at the mercy of a mysterious magic, this theatrical play cannot be identified with a declared thesis or ideology of fate. The aim of Maeterlinck's 'static' dramaturgy is to communicate an experience of being at the mercy of higher powers, an experience which in Noh Theatre comes about through the embeddedness of human life in the world of returning spirits. It is no coincidence that for Wilson, as for Maeterlinck, puppets, moving automata and marionettes are located at the heart of their idea of theatre. In the early essay 'Un théâtre d'androides' Maeterlinck writes 'Il semble aussi que tout être qui a l'apparence de la vie sans avoir la vie, fasse appel à des puissances extraordinaires . . . ce sont des morts qui semblent nous parler, par conséquent, d'augustes voix'. ('It seems also that every being that has the appearance of life without being alive makes us think of extraordinary powers . . . These are the dead who thus seem to be speaking to us with august voices').[25] The postdramatic theatre of a Tadeusz Kantor with its mysterious, animistically animated objects and apparatus, as much as the historical ghosts and apparitions in the postdramatic text of a Heiner Müller, exist in this tradition of theatrical appearances of 'fate' and ghosts, who, as Monique Borie has shown, are crucial for understanding the most recent theatre.[26]

Stage poetry

There remains, however, one important difference between the new theatre and the Symbolist idea of theatre: the latter aims at a dominance of the poetic *language* of the stage, as opposed to the then prevalent spectacle theatre. Yet it is no longer – as in dramatic theatre – the *role* script that is regarded as the essence of the theatre text but instead the *text as poetry*, which in turn is meant to correspond to the 'poetry' peculiar to the theatre. Maeterlinck too (like Craig) claims that the great plays of Shakespeare cannot be performed, that they are not 'scenic', and that staging them is dangerous.[27] With that, the dissolution of the traditional amalgamation of text and stage has become thinkable, but also the possibility of their reconnection in a new way. By regarding the theatre text as an independent poetic dimension and simultaneously considering the 'poetry' of the stage uncoupled from the text as an independent atmospheric poetry of space and light, a new theatrical disposition becomes possible. In it, the automatic unity of text and stage is superseded by their separation and subsequently in turn by their free (liberated) combination, and eventually the free combinatorics of all theatrical signs.

Viewed thus from the point of view of postdramatic theatre, the lyrical and Symbolist drama of the *fin de siècle* moves from the periphery to the centre of historical interest. In order to reach a new poetry of theatre it puts an end to the axioms of dramatic plot and story. 'Maeterlinck's demand for a "théâtre statique"', as Bayerdörfer writes,

> is the first anti-Aristotelian dramaturgy of European modernism, more radical than many that follow, for it abandons the Aristotelian key moment of the definition, the dramatic action (pragma). Maeterlinck maintains, by the way, that the most important traits of his 'static theatre'

had already been realized before Aristotle in ancient Greek tragedy, especially in Aeschylus.[28]

Certainly one could cite other, historically earlier forms that had already taken leave of the dramatic maxims. Mono- and duo-drama and melodrama at the end of the eighteenth century, for example, represent a kind of short tragedy that restricts itself to one scene or situation and which was occasionally already called 'lyrical drama'. Thus Sulzer says in his *Theorie der schönen Künste* (1775): 'The name of the lyrical drama indicates that no gradually unfolding action takes place here, with plots, intrigues and crisscrossing ventures, as in drama made for the theatre.'[29] As Szondi explains, the genre situation is, however, a different one for Mallarmé, Maeterlinck, Yeats or Hofmannsthal. Here this form becomes a 'sign for the historical impossibility of the tragedy in five acts'.[30] For Szondi, Hofmannsthal's early play *Gestern* is a 'drama en miniature', as the basic law of the dramatic genre of the 'proverbe' (a French type of play with the reversal of the hero's initial thesis) conforms to the law of the dramatic peripeteia.[31] With *Der Tod des Tizian* starts a series of his real lyrical dramas, 'whose basic blueprint is not the plot but the situation, the scene, as in Mallarmé's *Hérodiade*, as in de Régnier's *La Gardienne* and as in Maeterlinck's two works *L'Intruse* and *Les Aveugles*, which appeared in 1890'. The 'static, single-track, plot-less nature of the lyrical drama' manifests a 'reaction to drama or the difficulty of the drama of Maeterlinck's time'[32] which is going to lead to the forms of modern drama and to a changed theatre practice. Szondi's commentary[33] on the Symbolist staging practice, for example in Henri de Regnier's lyrical drama *La Gardienne* is illuminating. The poem was read by actors in the orchestra pit invisible to the audience, while on stage the action took place as a pantomime behind a gauze veil. On the one hand, this was a bold and groundbreaking idea, 'to pull apart movement and language' and 'through this dissociation of scenic action and word' take leave of the traditional 'conception of dramatis personae as self-contained, plastic figures'. On the other hand, this decomposition of the dramatic model could only come into its own when the illusion of represented reality was consistently abandoned, which only happened in the later postdramatic forms of theatre. Szondi may get to the crux when he attributes the flop of this new staging style at the time to the 'contradiction between the anti-illusionism of the split into silent play and voice, on the one hand, and the illusionist means, on the other, whereby the play and the voices were meant to gain an aura of the mysterious'.[34] Looking back from the age of 'high tech theatre', however, one harbours the suspicion that the merely episodic existence of lyrical drama could also be due to the fact that practitioners did not yet have the technical means for giving the stage poetry such a density that poetic word and stage reality would not hopelessly fall apart.

Acts, actions

Another question to consider is what kind of relationship postdramatic theatre shows with those avant-garde movements that wrote onto their banners the destruction of any coherence, the privileging of nonsense and action in the here and now (Dada), thus giving up theatre as a 'work' and meaningful concept in favour of an aggressive impulse, an event that implicated the audience in its actions (Futurism), or sacrificed the narrative causal nexus in favour of other representational rhythms, especially of dream logic (Surrealism). This is, in Kirby's sense, the 'antagonistic line' of the avant-garde. Dada, Futurism and Surrealism demand an intellectual, mental/nervous and also physical attack on the spectator. The fundamental *shift from work to event* was momentous for theatre aesthetics. It is true that the act of viewing, the reactions and latent or acute 'responses' of the spectators, had always been an essential factor of theatrical reality. Now, however, they become an active *component* of the event, so that, for this reason alone, the idea of a coherent formation of a theatre 'work' necessarily becomes obsolete: theatre that includes the actions and utterances of the visitor as a constitutive element can practically and theoretically no longer be self-contained. The theatre event thus makes explicit the nature of process that is peculiar to it, including its inherent unpredictability. Analogously to the differentiation between the 'closure' of the book (the 'clôture' as theorized by Derrida) and the open processuality of the text, the theatre work, closed in itself – albeit extended over time – is superseded by the exposed act and process of an aggressive, enigmatically esoteric or communal theatrical communication. In this turn to a performative *act*, in place of a well-made *message*, one can see an updating of the early Romantic speculations about art, which sought a 'sympoetry' of reader and author. This conception is incompatible with the idea of an aesthetic totality of the theatre 'work'. If we wanted to cite the ancient image for the symbol – a shard of pottery is broken in two and later the edge of the fracture on the one half identifies its bearer as 'authentic' when it joins the other edge – the theatre likewise manifests itself only as the one half and awaits the presence and gesture of the unknown spectators who realize the edge of the fracture through their intuition, their way of understanding, and their imagination.

Speed, numbers

Modern theatre was crucially influenced by popular forms of entertainment, of which especially the *number format* is noticeable. It has its place in cabaret and variety theatre, revue, nightclub, circus, grotesque film or the shadow plays emerging in Paris around 1880. In particular new film technology with the accompanying cinema culture turns the number format, episode form and kaleidoscope into a principle. At first visited only by the lower classes, variety goes upmarket, becomes 'presentable' and a favourite amusement for the upper classes as well (e.g. the Berliner Wintergarten). The enthusiasm for dancing and the pleasure in the perfection of the revues spreads to the avant-garde, new body images become a theme. Cabaret and variety thrive on the principle of parabasis, the player's stepping out of character and addressing the audience directly. Cabaret is based on the possibility of allusions to everyday reality shared by players and audience and hence contains a performance moment that is inseparably connected to urban life: to a city culture in which jokes and information are immediately understood. All this contributed to the erosion of the ivory tower of art and, at the same time, inspired the desire for a theatre that could be a similarly topical, participatory event in the here and now for all involved. Owing to its sensuality, entertainment value and lack of consideration towards 'good taste', that Oskar Panizza predicted in 1896, the variety theatre would soon be preferred to theatre.[35]

The principle of the destruction of coherence is connected to the transformation of everyday experience, which seems to make a calm theatre impossible. In 1900, Otto Julius Bierbaum notes: 'The city dweller of today has . . . variety nerves; he is rarely capable of following great dramatic connections, of tuning his emotional life for three hours of theatre to one tone; he wants diversity – variety.'[36] This clearly shows that the formal principle of a succession of numbers is directly related to the temporal structure of the staging. An urban perception that has become more impatient demands acceleration, which can also be found in the theatre. The tempo of vaudeville with its techniques of quick punch lines, brevity and wit cannot remain without effect on the 'higher' forms of theatre. Music gains greater importance as an interlude and intermezzo, 'songs' now offering what *Lieder* used to offer in the *Volksstück*; one-act plays gain ground in dramatic writing. The destruction of theatre time into ever more tiny pieces is thus influenced by the new fast pace. Later, postdramatic theatre will carry this demolition of the continuum into the staging of classical drama, as well. While, on the one hand, dramatic rhythm dissolves into stasis and later into 'durational aesthetics', on the other, theatre accelerates the rhythm to such an extent that drama falls apart, too. In many productions of the 1980s and 1990s the dismemberment of actions and time into individual numbers is very pronounced. The dialectic connection of the two time distortions – duration and acceleration – becomes apparent as soon as one focuses on the development of the peculiar time aesthetics of postdramatic theatre.[37]

Landscape Play

Along with Craig, Brecht, Artaud and Meyerhold, two further ancestors of the contemporary theatre are Gertrude Stein and Stanislaw Ignacy Witkiewicz. It has been noted that Gertrude Stein's texts exhibit a relation to Cubism. Witkiewicz came to theatre from painting. This fact is revealing: the prehistory of postdramatic theatre includes conceptions that think of theatre, stage and text rather like a landscape (Stein) or as a construction that deforms reality (Witkiewicz). Both conceptions remained theoretical, at least for the theatre. Stein's texts were hardly produced and became more effective as a productive provocation, while Witkiewicz formulated a theory that his own plays only partially corresponded to. Both conceptions are at war with the dynamic time aspect of the art of theatre. Their innovative potential becomes apparent only in retrospect, after the static moment emerges as a possibility for theatre within a media society. When Gertrude Stein speaks of her idea of the 'Landscape Play', it appears as a reaction to her basic experience that theatre always made her terribly 'nervous' because it referred to a *different* time (future or past) and demanded a constant effort on the side of the viewer contemplating it. Instead of following it with 'nervous' – we may as well translate this as 'dramatic' – tension, one ought to contemplate what was happening on stage as one would otherwise contemplate a park or a landscape. Thornton Wilder remarked: 'A myth is not a story read from left to right, from beginning to end, but a thing held full in-view the whole time. Perhaps this is what Gertrude Stein meant by saying that the play henceforth is a landscape.'[38]

In Stein's texts the – relatively sparing – explanations of her theatre concept are repeatedly linked to images of actual landscapes. If it is often tempting to describe the stagings of the new theatre as landscapes, this is rather due to traits anticipated by Stein: a *defocalization* and equal status for all parts, a renunciation of teleological time, and the dominance of an 'atmosphere' above dramatic and narrative forms of progression. It is less the pastoral than the conception of theatre as a *scenic poem as a whole* that becomes characteristic. Elinor Fuchs rightly remarks that it is above all 'the lyrical mode, essentially static and reflective, that is the key to linking Foreman back to Stein and Maeterlinck, and horizontally to Wilson and many of his contemporaries creating landscape stagings'.[39] Gertrude Stein simply transferred the artistic logic of her texts to theatre: the principle of a 'continuous present', of syntactic and verbal concatenations that mark time seemingly statically (similar to the later 'minimal music') but in reality continuously create new accents in subtle variations and loops. Stein's written text in a way already *is* the landscape. To a previously unheard of extent it emancipates the clause from the sentence, the word from the clause, the phonetic from the semantic potential and the sound from the cohesion of meaning. Just as in her texts the representation of reality recedes in favour of the play of words, in a 'Stein theatre' there will be no drama, not even a story; it will not be possible to differentiate protagonists and even roles and identifiable characters will be missing. For postdramatic theatre Stein's aesthetics is of great importance, although more subconsciously so outside America. Bonnie Marranca emphasizes her effect on the avant-garde and performance.[40] After the performance of *Ladies Voices* by The Living Theatre in 1951 (!) and the occasional performance of other pieces by Gertrude Stein by theatres and companies like the Judson Poets Theatre, La MaMa, the Performance Group and others since the 1960s, it was Richard Foreman (in Germany renowned for his *Doctor Faustus Lights the Lights*, performed in 1982 at the Freie Volksbühne, Berlin) and Robert Wilson who from the 1970s carried a use of language inspired by Stein into the theatre.

'Pure form'

Gertrude Stein's ideas share points of contact with the 'theory of pure form' by Stanislaw Ignacy Witkiewicz, also known as Witkacy. His fundamental idea is the termination of mimesis in theatre. The play is to adhere solely to the law of its internal composition. Ever since Cézanne in painting and modern French poetry in literature, the autonomization of the signifier has been observable, its play becomes the predominant aspect of aesthetic practice. Painting accentuates the perceptual demand to realize the inexpressible of the graphic quality itself as intensely as that which is expressed and represented by the image. Poetry demands a reading that follows the play of linguistic signifiers that initially may seem empty of meaning. The typeface and sound of language as such, its material reality as tone, graphics, rhythm, Mallarmé's famous 'music in the letters' ('la musique dans les lettres') are to be received simultaneously with the meaning. Latently this already heralds the development of the theatricalization of the arts: reading and viewing become more staging than interpreting. The theatre itself, however, only catches up with the developments of other arts later, with theories such as those by Stein and Witkiewicz. The latter is a precursor of Absurdist theatre but also anticipates theses by Artaud, sometimes in a surprisingly similar wording. In his text *New Forms of Painting*,[41] Witkiewicz theorizes that the theatre of 'pure form' has to be considered as an *absolute construction* of formal elements and does not represent a mimesis of reality. In this, and only in this way, is it able to represent a metaphysics. Witkiewicz's thinking is pessimistic. He is convinced that even the sense for metaphysical unity will disappear, but until then individual manifestations of this cohesion are possible, in theatre, too. The latter's task consists in communicating a sense of 'unity' of the cosmic whole through diversity. Witkiewicz sees models for this in ancient tragedy, medieval mystery plays and the theatre of the Far East. Yet, because theatre has the disadvantage of consisting of heterogeneous elements, Witkiewicz considers it one of the 'complex' arts, for which – in contrast to painting – the 'pure form' is never entirely achievable but only ever to a degree. This can never be a matter of a theatre that deals with the conflicts of 'normal' people, however, but only one that obeys the motto of 'distancing oneself from life'. Instead of the mimesis of reality, it has to be a strictly external, pure construction, which presupposes a methodical 'deformation of psychology and action' (a thesis Witkiewicz shares with Surrealism and the later Theatre of the Absurd). Such a theatre would unite a complete arbitrariness of elements with respect to real life with an utmost precision and perfection of the execution.

These thoughts, far removed from common theatre reality,[42] are especially informed by painting, from which Witkiewicz repeatedly takes his examples. This orientation towards painting gives his theory, as well as his plays, a static character.[43] Yet, his ideas have found a realization in newer forms of theatre, their alienation from theatre measured by the yardstick of dynamic dramatic theatre here turning out to be their strength. In his theory of 'pure form' we find only a single example of an imagined scenic realization. What he describes there could be an actual staging by Robert Wilson: three figures, dressed all in red, enter, bow, before whom no one knows, one declaiming a poem. A gentle old man appears with a cat on a leash. All this takes place in front of a black curtain that now opens onto a view of an Italian landscape. Later on a glass falls off a small table, all fall onto their knees and cry. The gentle old man turns into an angry murderer and kills a little girl who has entered the stage from the left. Witkiewicz ends his description, only excerpts of which are reported here, with the following remark: 'En sortant du théâtre, on doit avoir l'impression de s'éveiller de quelque sommeil bizarre, dans lequel les choses le plus ordinaires avaient le charme étrange, impénétrable, caractéristique du rêve et qui ne peut se comparer à rien d'autre.'[44] ('On leaving the theatre, one must have the impression of waking from a strange sort of sleep in which even the most ordinary things had the strange impenetrable character of a dream and which cannot be compared to anything else.')

Expressionism

Expressionism, too, develops motifs of theatre that get their breakthrough in postdramatic theatre. Its combination of cabaret and dream play and its linguistic innovations such as telegram style and broken syntax undermine the uniform perspective onto the logic of human action; the sound is intended to transport affects rather than messages. It wants to go beyond drama as interpersonal dramaturgy of conflict and beyond the motifs inherent to it. It emphasizes the forms of monologue and choir and a more lyrically than dramatically determined succession of scenes, e.g. already in Strindberg's *Ich-Dramatik* and in static drama. Expressionism seeks ways of representing the unconscious whose nightmares and images of desire are not bound to any dramatic logic. While Wedekind's *Lulu* plays show desire in a dramatic process, Oskar Kokoschka's *Murder, Hope of Women* subsequently offers a montage of individual images without a clear narrative logic. When it was staged as part of the Vienna Kunstschau in 1908, the theme of the human being as a creature of drives was shown through extreme body contortions and painted body surfaces, masks and grimaces.[45] The model of the acausal and kaleidoscopic succession of images and scenes of the dream gains power. In the episodic dramaturgy of the static drama, the archaic and the primitive become expressible as a social reality. Redemption in Barlach, pathos in Kaiser and idealism in Toller are forms of elevation and abstraction, less mimesis of real actions than symbolic-mental actions. But once *the unconscious* and the imagination are acknowledged as realities in their own right, the structure of drama – which could claim to have offered an adequate representation of what happens between human beings in the reality of *consciousness* – becomes obsolete. On the contrary, the surface logic of drama and external succession of actions prove to be an obstacle to the articulation of unconscious structures of desire. This represents the link to the emerging *expressive dance (Ausdruckstanz)*, which is an important theatrical aspect of Expressionism. The symbolic dance gestures of Mary Wigman belong to the trajectory that leads away from dance narration towards the emphasis of physical and linguistic gesture. What remains interesting about Expressionism is the convergence of two divergent tendencies: the tense will to form leading to construction (the works can be understood as highly consciously constructed effects) and the attempt to help the subjective affect to express itself.

Surrealism

Film and Expressionism concur with Surrealism in privileging an articulation based on an editing technique and collage/montage that demands and develops the speed, 'intelligence' and versatility of the associative capacity of the recipient. While the spectator of the modern theatre must develop an ever-progressing ability to connect heterogeneous elements, the gradual expansion of connections becomes increasingly less meaningful, and the ever more impatient eye is satisfied with ever more scant allusions. While the Futurist movement and Dada blossomed only for a short time, the Surrealist movement was longer lasting, probably because a pure aesthetic of speed and pure negation cannot form a canon, while the new exploration of dream, phantasm and the unconscious opened up an abundance of new subject matter. Even though Surrealism produced more literary, poetic and cinematic than theatrical manifestations, it was part of the logic of its tendency towards social and cultural revolution ('changer la vie') to seek the public, quasi-political theatre event. The transition to the theatre event is found in seed form in the format of the exhibition; the *Exposition internationale du surréalisme* was dubbed 'une œuvre d'art événement' (event art work) by André Breton. Not only had a large number of Surrealist objects been assembled here under the direction of Marcel Duchamp (well known are Bellmer's doll, Meret Oppenheimer's fur-covered teacup or Man Ray's iron with nails). The exhibition also contained inventions such as Dali's taxi, whose passengers were periodically soaked by streams of water, as well as the spacious installation of a Surrealist street, an 'environmental theatre' which incorporated the visitor.

During their time, the Surrealists produced barely any noteworthy theatre but their ideas exerted an enormous influence on the newer theatre. They aimed at a theatre of magical images and of a political gesture of revolt against the 'frame' of theatre practice. The Surrealist idea that a mutual inspiration takes place when the fantasies fed by the unconscious reach the unconscious of the recipient emphasizes a trait that is also of importance to the new 'Theatre of Situation' (the mutual inspiration of stage and audience) and the 'Environmental Theatre'. The freedom to create satire and humour is reminiscent of the 'cool fun' of playful nonsensical group practice in the new theatre. Finally, Surrealism contains the demand for a 'performance art'. Roger Vitrac's *Les Mystères de l'amour* (1923) was to activate the audience through its provocation. The author himself (played by an actor) appeared on stage. Actors were planted among the audience, the performers appearing as themselves, as well as the represented figures without a clear distinction between fiction and reality being discernible. It was a partial suspension of the distinction between the fictive cosmos of a 'drama' and the reality of the performance. There were also play and voices in the auditorium, open aggression culminating in a shot into the audience. The performance, probably the highlight of the Surrealist work in the theatre of the time, was action art, communication and aggression, dream theatre and manifestation, which in a changed form pervaded the theatre again from the 1960s onwards. Only what in Surrealism was meant to be a provocation towards an envisioned real revolution of culture and society has since largely lost this character. While Peter Brook's *Marat/Sade* and other action theatres of the 1960s may still be read from such a perspective, this is no longer true for the antiquity trilogy by Andrei Serban (1972, shown in Europe in the mid-1970s), for instance, which David Zinder claimed as neo-Surrealist.[46] Theatre abandons any attempt directly to anticipate or accelerate a revolution of social relations – not, as is carelessly imputed, due to an apolitical cynicism but because of a changed assessment of its potential efficacy.

Just as Lautréamont had already declared that poetry was produced by all, not by individuals, the Surrealist thesis said that the unconscious of every person offered the possibility for poetic creation. The task of art was thus a 'via negativa' (Grotowski), to break through the rational and conscious mental processes in order to gain access to the images of the unconscious. That the thus communicated had to remain idiosyncratic and personal (every unconscious has a discourse peculiar only to itself) leads to the further thesis that real *communication does not take place via understanding at all but through impulses for the recipient's own creativity*, impulses whose communicability is founded in the universal predispositions of the unconscious. This attitude can frequently be found among contemporary artists, Wilson being the most impressive example. His scenes are not meant to be rationally interpreted and understood but are intended to spark people's own productivity and associations in the 'magnetic field' between stage and spectators. After attending *Deaf Man Glance*, Louis Aragon composed a text that has become famous (a letter to the late *compagnon de route* in Surrealist matters, André Breton), in which he declared this spectacle to be simply the most beautiful he had ever seen, calling it the fulfilment of the hopes the Surrealists had pinned on the theatre.[47]

Panorama of postdramatic theatre

Beyond dramatic action: ceremony, voices in space, landscape

On the occasion of the Berliner Schaubühne's production of Gorki's *Summer Guests*, the adapter Botho Strauss made a note on Peter Stein's directorial decision to reorganize Gorki's dialogue material in the first and second act showing all figures on stage at the same time. Gorki himself, he wrote, had not called his piece a 'drama', 'play', 'tragedy' or 'comedy' but 'scenes'. The theatre here showed 'less a succession, a development of a story, more an involvement of inner and outer states'. This way of putting it is helpful. As is well known, it is generally painters who speak of states, the states of images in the process of creation, states in which the dynamics of image creation are crystallizing and in which the process of the painting that has become invisible to the viewer is being stored. Effectively, the category appropriate to the new theatre is not action but *states*. Theatre here deliberately negates, or at least relegates to the background, the possibility of developing a narrative – a possibility that is after all peculiar to it as a time-based art. This does not preclude a particular dynamic within the 'frame' of the state – one could call it a *scenic dynamic*, as opposed to the dramatic dynamic. The seemingly 'static' painting, too, is in reality merely the now definitive 'state' of the congealed pictorial work, in which the eye of the viewer wanting to access the picture has to become aware of and reconstruct its dynamics and process. Equally, textual theory teaches us to read the dynamic movement of becoming, the geno-text, in the congealed, now 'inert' (pheno-)text. The state is an aesthetic figuration of the theatre, showing a formation rather than a story, even though living actors play in it. It is no coincidence that many practitioners of postdramatic theatre started out in the visual arts. Postdramatic theatre is a theatre of states and of scenically dynamic formations.

By contrast, one cannot imagine a dramatic theatre that does not – in one way or another – present a dramatic action/plot. When Aristotle declares the 'mythos' – which in the *Poetics* is virtually synonymous with plot – to be the 'soul' of tragedy, he makes it clear that drama means (to all intents and purposes) an artificially constructed and composed course of action. His critic Brecht follows him in this in his 'Short Organum for the Theatre': 'And according to Aristotle – and we agree here – narrative ['Fabel' in the German original, as a translation of 'mythos'] is the soul of drama'.[1] Even in the stagnation and standstill of factual activity in Chekhov's plays, the captivated spectator follows an 'inner' action developing under the seemingly inconsequential everyday dialogue but nevertheless inevitably moving towards a minimum of external action of the story – a duel, a death, a farewell, and so on. In different ways, this core category of drama is pushed back in postdramatic theatre – in degrees ranging from an 'almost still dramatic' theatre to a form where not even the rudiments of fictive processes can be found any more. Everything indicates that the reasons why dramatic action was formerly central to theatre no longer apply: the main idea no longer being a narrative, fabulating description of the world by means of mimesis; the formulation of an intellectually important collision of objectives; the process of dramatic action as the image of the dialectics of human experience; the entertainment value of 'suspense' where one situation prepares for and leads to a new and changed situation. It goes without saying that it is not just vehement or loud acts that constitute dramatic action, as was already pointed out by Lessing. In the context of his discussion of Charles Batteux' theory of the fable he remarks that many artistic judgments 'associate too material a concept with the word action' and that 'every internal struggle of passions, every sequence of different thoughts where the one overrides the other, is an action'.[2]

Unlike diegesis, the epic-narrative mode of narration, mimesis has since antiquity signified the *embodied* representation imitating reality. The word 'mimeisthai' originally meant 'to represent through dance', not to 'imitate'. With reference to E. Utitz, Mukařovský, however, emphasizes a quality of art in the 'aesthetic function' that is different from imitation, namely 'the capacity of the *isolation* of the object touched by the aesthetic function'. It is the characteristic possibility of the aesthetic to produce a 'maximal concentration of attention onto a given object'. In the context of this argument, he gives an example directly pertinent to our analysis: the importance of the aesthetic function in any kind of *ceremony*, the aesthetically 'isolating' moment inherent to all *festivity*.[3] It is evident that there is always a dimension of the ceremonial in the practice of theatre. It is inherent to theatre as a social event – derived from its religious and cultic roots that have mostly disappeared from consciousness. Postdramatic theatre, however, liberates the formal, ostentatious moment of ceremony from its sole function of enhancing attention and valorizes it *for its own sake*, as an aesthetic quality, detached from all religious and cultic reference. Postdramatic theatre is the replacement of dramatic action with ceremony, with which dramatic-cultic action was once, in its beginnings, inseparably united.[4] What is meant by ceremony as a moment of postdramatic theatre is thus the whole spectrum of movements and processes that have no referent but are presented with heightened precision; events of peculiarly formalized communality; musical-rhythmic or visual-architectonic constructs of development; para-ritual forms, as well as the (often deeply black) ceremony of the body and of presence; the emphatically or monumentally accentuated ostentation of the presentation.

Jean Genet deliberately affirmed theatre as ceremony and consequently declared the mass to be the highest form of modern drama: 'La messe est le plus haut drame moderne.'[5] His themes – the double, the mirror, the triumph of dream and death over reality – already indicate this direction. Significantly, Genet hit upon the idea that the true site of theatre was the cemetery,[6] that theatre as such was essentially a mass for the dead. Genet, who was of special importance for Heiner Müller, agrees with the latter in the idea that theatre is a 'dialogue with the dead'. As Monique Borie states, for Genet the dialogue with the dead gives the work of art its true dimension.[7] The work of art is not directed at future generations, as is often assumed. According to Genet, Giacometti actually creates statues whose task it is to enchant the dead ('des statues qui ravissent les morts'). He says further, 'l'œuvre d'art n'est pas destiné aux générations enfants. Elle est offerte à l'innombrable peuple des morts'[8] ('the work of art is not destined for the subsequent generations. It is offered to the innumerable mass of the dead'). Heiner Müller considered the ancient theatre as an incantation of the dead. And the Japanese Noh Theatre revolves around the return of the dead with a minimum of mimesis. It thus suffices to remember these possibilities of understanding theatre quite differently in order to question the tradition of dramatic theatre in European modernity (which in turn differs from the 'predramatic' theatre of antiquity[9]). The themes of mass, ceremony, ritual had already surfaced repeatedly in early modernism. Mallarmé was already talking about a theatre of ceremony, and T. S. Eliot's confession is well known: 'the only satisfaction that I find now is in a High Mass well performed'.[10] To return to Genet: he wanted theatre to be 'la fête', a festivity, addressed to the dead. Hence he once considered it enough to hold a single performance of *Les Paravents* (*The Screens*), i.e. a singular festive ceremony. (Incidentally, Wagner's idea for the *Festspiel* originally looked like this: one should erect a theatre in the countryside, invite the audience free of charge, play, tear down the theatre and burn the score.)

In Robert Wilson's work the ceremonial aspect is obvious. Early critics, attempting to characterize their first encounter with this theatre, sometimes chose the comparison that they felt like a stranger attending the enigmatic cultic actions of a people unknown to them. In Einar Schleef's work, too, we can recognize an artistic intention towards quasi-ritual ceremonies. He not only builds on ceremonies thematized in a play in a grand, elaborate style completely out of proportion to the development of the plot (as, for example, in the *Urgötz* with a seemingly endless cortège of the court), but also stages proceedings like the symbolic feeding of the audience. It would be tempting to examine also the less obvious forms of ceremonial in postdramatic works. In the context of his reflections on the *Lehrstück*, Brecht once noted, for example, how he pictured acrobats for the – in his terminology, defamiliarizing (*verfremdende*) and epicizing – way of acting:

[they] would be people in white overalls, now three, now two, all very serious like acrobats, very serious they are and it's not clowns that are their

models, so then the proceedings could be accomplished simply like ceremonies, anger and remorse as manual tasks (*Handgriffe*), the terrible one
must not be a figure at all but rather me or another.[11]

Here one sees the connection between the tendency towards the ceremonial
and the renunciation of the classical conception of a subject that represses the
corporality (*Handgriffe*) of its seemingly only mental intentions.

In the following we shall have a look at Tadeusz Kantor, Robert Wilson and
Klaus-Michael Grüber as exemplary forms of postdramatic theatre, as 'ceremony', 'voice in space' and 'landscape'.

Kantor or the ceremony

The work of the Polish artist Tadeusz Kantor leads far away from dramatic
theatre: a rich cosmos of art forms between theatre, happening, performance,
painting, sculpture, object art and space art and, last but not least, ongoing
reflection in theoretical texts, poetic writings and manifestos. His work revolves in
obsessive form around his own childhood memories and for this reason alone
exhibits the temporal structure of memory, repetition and the confrontation with
loss and death. It seems appropriate to take a closer look at the last phase of
Kantor's theatre work, the 'theatre of death' that became famous in the 1980s,
although many of its aspects are already present or latent in his early work. As he
states in 'The Zero Theatre', Kantor wants to achieve a 'full autonomy of the
theatre, so that everything that happens on stage would become an event',[12]
stripped of any 'i r r e s p o n s i b l e illusion'.[13] There is a search here for a 'state
of non-acting'[14] and non-continuous plot structure, but instead repeatedly expres-
sionistically condensed scenes, combined with a quasi-ritualistic form of
conjuring up the past: 'This process means dismembering logical plot structures,
building up scenes, not by textual reference, but by reference to associations triggered by them.'[15]

Reminiscences of Polish history here join with the continually varied subject-
matter of religion (the Jewish rabbi, the persecution of the Jews, the Catholic
priest). Grotesquely heightened scenes of ultimate rituals constitute the leitmotif:
execution, farewell, death, burial. All figures appear as if they were already
revenants themselves. Shortly after World War II, Kantor placed the figure of
the returning Odysseus at the centre of his work: a figure symbolically returning
from the realm of the dead, who, as Kantor says, 'established a *precedent* and a
prototype for all the later characters of [his] theatre'.[16] In general, his theatre is
marked by past terror and, at the same time, by the ghostly return. It is a
theatre whose theme, as Monique Borie says, is the remains,[17] a theatre *after* the
catastrophe (like Beckett's and Heiner Müller's texts); it comes from death and
stages 'a landscape beyond death' (Müller). In this it differs from drama, which
does not show death as preceding, as the basis of experience, but instead depicts
life moving towards it. Death in Kantor's work is not dramatically staged but
ceremonially repeated. Hence, it also lacks the dramatized question about death

as a moment in which the decision about the meaning of a life occurs (as, for example, in Hofmannsthal's *Everyman*). Rather, every ceremony is actually a ceremony of the dead; it consists in the tragicomical annihilation of meaning and the showing of this annihilation – a showing which as such somehow reverses the annihilation. Thus, when the figure who obviously represents death in *Wielopole, Wielopole* or *The Dead Class* is dusting the old books, 'humiliating' and destroying them, the scene also communicates a paradoxical zest for life in its comic drive.

In Kantor's work the ceremonial form taking the place of drama is the *dance of death*. About *The Dead Class* Kantor himself stressed: 'The mystery of death, a medieval "danse macabre" takes place in a CLASS ROOM.'[18] Figures appearing in Kantor's dance of death, for example in *Wielopole, Wielopole*, are 'optical ciphers' here borrowed from the novel *The Shared Room* by Zbigniew Unilowski: 'the bigot who pushes her kneeling desk in front of her; the gambler who mechanically tosses cards onto the table rolling ahead of him; a man with a washing bowl in which he incessantly washes his feet', etc.[19] At the end of *Let the Artists Die!* (premiered in Nuremberg in 1985), soldiers are marching along to the eternal tango of war, juxtaposed with the military march 'We, the first brigade'. There is the skeleton of a horse – so that one is tempted to say with Heiner Müller, 'history rides on dead horses across the finishing line' – and ahead of it a child in a military coat far too long for it (Kantor as a little boy?). A lascivious, beautiful girl waves a black flag of anarchy over this final image, an 'angel of despair', of death or melancholia, as if correcting Delacroix with the charm of her body, as Hensel noted: the angel of liberty and of the storming of the Bastille turns into a figure of futility, melancholic eros and mourning. Kantor's scenes manifest the refusal of a dramatic representation of the all too 'dramatic' events that are the subject of his theatre – torture, prison, war and death – in favour of a pictural poetry of the stage. The 'sequences of images, often as from a slapstick movie, "dead funny" and at the same time immensely sad',[20] always move towards scenes that could occur in a grotesque drama. But the dramatic disappears in favour of *moving images* through repetitive rhythms, tableau-like arrangements and a certain de-realization of the figures, who by means of their jerky movements resemble mannequins. The theme of 'making images' incidentally also appears directly when the fat photographer in *Wielopole, Wielopole* suddenly turns her camera into a machine gun and with derisory laughter mows down a group of young soldiers posing for a photograph – at once a tragicomic emblem of murder through the fixation of images and a surrealist denunciation of war.

The visual artist Kantor, whose work in the theatre started with provocative performance actions and happenings, manifests an intention found in many postdramatic forms: to valorize the objects and materials of the scenic action in general. Wood, iron, cloth, books, garments and curious objects gain a remarkable tactile quality and intensity. How this effect is achieved cannot be easily explained. One essential factor here is Kantor's sense for what he called the 'poor object' or also the 'reality of the lowest rank':[21] chairs are well worn, walls are full of holes, tables are covered in dust or lime, old tools are rust-eaten, bleached, worn out, rotten or stained. In this state they can reveal their vulnerability and thus their 'life' with new intensity. The vulnerable human players become part of the whole structure of the stage, the damaged objects being their companions. This is also an effect enabled by the postdramatic gesture. For even when it is shown with a Naturalistic intention – where the milieu appears in its authority over people – the theatrical 'environment' in dramatic theatre functions in principle merely as a frame and background to the *human* drama and the human figure. In Kantor's theatre, however, the human actors appear under the spell of objects. The hierarchy vital for drama vanishes, a hierarchy in which everything (and every *thing*) revolves around human action, the things being mere props. We can speak of a distinct thematic of the object, which further de-dramatizes the elements of action if they still exist. Things in Kantor's lyrical-ceremonial theatre appear as reminiscent of the epic spirit of memory and its preference for things. If it was a rule of the epic mode, as opposed to the dramatic, to represent an action 'completely in the past', Kantor stresses that 'the scenes of that real action of the spectacle' should appear 'as if they were anchored in the past . . . as if the past was repeating itself, but in strangely changed forms'.[22] Through the duality of thematized memory and particular power of the reality of things a theatre develops which, as Kantor notes on the Cricot 2 Theatre, consists of 'two parallel trajectories': here 'the text purified of its superficial, storytelling structure', there the 'track of autonomous scenic action of pure theatre'.[23]

Kantor's theatre is famous for the almost life-size mannequins the actors carry around with them. For Kantor they are like the earlier, forgotten being of man, his 'I of memory' that he continues to carry around with him. But their significance goes further than this. In a kind of exchange with the living bodies and together with the objects, they change the stage into a landscape of death, in which there is a fluid transition between the human beings (often acting like puppets) and the dead puppets (appearing as if animated by children). One could almost say that the verbal dialogue of drama is replaced by a *dialogue between people and objects*. Surreal apparatuses (a mechanical cradle resembling a child's coffin; the family machine that folds out the woman's legs as though for birth; execution mechanisms) are joined up in odd ways with the extremities of the players. The repetition of trivial but poetical looking routines on and with the objects lets these actions appear as a quasi-linguistic exchange between human being and thing. Above all, in Kantor's work figures appear who act *gestically* and pantomimically and therefore, not coincidentally, seem to have escaped from grotesque slapstick movies. Drama recedes into tiny mute, scenic procedures. The hierarchy between human being and object is relativized for our perception.

Kantor clearly distances his love of mannequins from Craig's.[24] Unlike Craig, he does not polemicize against the actor (although it has to be mentioned that Craig's 'Übermarionette' by no means wants to drive the human actor from the stage but instead is meant to indicate another form of presence of the player). On the contrary: for Kantor, the imagined 'first actor' accomplished an act of 'revolutionary' and virtually holy significance. At one point someone dared to break with the ritualistic community. He was not a show-off but a heretic who by facing the community drew a dangerous barrier between himself and the 'public' that allowed him to communicate with the living from another sphere: the realm of death.[25] Through its motifs and forms Kantor's theatre corresponds in curious ways to the archaic moments of *Ur-theatre*. Monique Borie rightly points out that there is an overwhelming feeling of failure and defeat in Kantor's theatre that is reminiscent of ancient tragedy. When Kantor speaks – in a spiritual sense – of the 'consciousness of our defeat' that was at issue in theatre,[26] then this is the very motif off which Greek tragedy also fed. This correspondence, which traces a trajectory from the realm of antiquity to postdramatic theatre at the threshold of the third millennium – somehow circumventing the epoch of European dramatic theatre, so to speak – can also be observed, albeit in different manifestations, in the theatre of Grüber and Wilson.

Grüber or the reverberation of the voice in space

When speaking of a theatre 'beyond' drama, we have to include the observation that there are directors who may stage traditional dramatic texts but do so by employing theatrical means in such a way that a *de-dramatization* occurs. If in the staged text the action is relegated to the background altogether, however, it is in the logic of theatre aesthetic that the peculiar *temporality* and *spatiality of the scenic process* itself comes to the fore. It becomes more the presentation of an *atmosphere* and *state of things*. A scenic *écriture* captures the attention, compared to which the dramatic plot becomes secondary. Klaus Michael Grüber can be considered one of the exemplary 'stage authors' who have developed their own theatre idiom in this way. When in August 1989 Georg Hensel ended his long career as a critic of the *Frankfurter Allgemeine Zeitung* with a personal retrospective over fifteen years of theatre reviews,[27] he came up with the following categories to sum up the great tendencies of theatre since the mid-1970s: interpretation, reinterpretation, reconstruction and postmodernism. Rudolf Noelte for him was 'the exemplary director of interpretation'; while Claus Peymann, who in 1975 together with Achim Freyer conducted a satirical demontage of Schiller's *Robbers*, was the representative of reinterpretation. Klaus Michael Grüber appears in this panorama not only as an exponent of the 'postmodern method of directing' (with his *Empedocles. Reading Hölderlin*) but also as a representative of historical 'reconstruction', especially with his virtually unabridged version of *Hamlet* in 1982. The latter aspect falls outside of the area discussed here but it seems appropriate to mention that in parallel to Grüber's postdramatic practice, Peter Stein at the Berliner Schaubühne conceived of the theatre as the site of memory of (theatre) history, staged in an ascetic, almost chaste manner consciously opposed to the prevailing *Zeitgeist*. Thus, his productions of Chekhov quoted in detail from performances of the historic Moscow Art Theatre, and in O'Neill's

The Hairy Ape the scenic arrangements of a production by Tairov were copied. Peter Stein's staging of *Phaedra* in 1987 was part of this lineage too, a classical, historicist attitude, which over the years, however, led the Schaubühne into a certain rigidity, a perfection that often appeared 'cold' and in which the directorial craft merely seemed to celebrate itself. On the other hand, the conscious decision against any subjective ingredient demands respect and has to be acknowledged as a peculiar quality of theatrical self-reflection.

Grüber's style of de-dramaticization combines stasis and a classical economy of means. In general one can say that he removes the moment of suspense from the plays in an extreme manner. This procedure of a postdramatic *isotony*,[28] where peaks or climaxes are avoided, lets the stage appear as a tableau. The effect of this tableau increasingly intensifies by being 'charged' with the spoken word which thus unfolds primarily its mental-lyrical function of expression (Jakobson's 'emotive' dimension of language). Modern drama was a world of discussion, while the dialogue in ancient tragedy – despite the appearance of an antagonistic battle of words – is basically not a discussion: the protagonists each remain unreachable in their own world, the opponents talk at cross-purposes. The dialogue here is less conflict and altercation in the space of verbal exchange but appears rather as a 'competition of speech' (*Wettreden*), a race in words, reminiscent of the wordless wrestling in the agon. The speeches of the antagonists do not touch one another.[29] In Grüber's work, as actors working with him reported at an event organized by Georges Banu in Paris,[30] everything takes place in an atmosphere that could be entitled 'After all discussions'. There is nothing to debate any more. What is executed and spoken here has the character of a necessary, quasi-ceremonially performed, agreed upon rite.

Drama, as an exemplary form of discussion, stakes everything on tempo, dialectic, debate and solution (dénouement). But for a long time now drama has lied. Its spirit, or rather its ghost, has moved from the theatre into the cinema and increasingly into television. There the possibilities of simulating reality are much greater; there the story counts, if only because we are not meant to watch anything twice but instead consume the next product. Since the entertainment industry does not allow anything to be perceived in its contradiction, its division and doubling, anything in its strangeness, we move from the (Brechtian) V-effect to the TV-effect. There are few theatre practitioners who openly dare to *practice the difference between drama and theatre* within the framework of 'established' theatre – in Germany, apart from Grüber, one could cite Einar Schleef and some of the works by Hans Jürgen Syberberg. Their direction is (unjustly) perceived by many as simply violent, as with Schleef, or simply outmodedly classicist, as in the case of Syberberg. Despite the recognition of his exceptional genius, Grüber was no favourite of the leading critics in Germany. When his works were complex and diverted from the norm, they were considered esoteric; when they were hyperbolically true to the text, they were misunderstood as conventional (even though works like *Hamlet* or *Iphigenie in Tauris*, despite their faithfulness to the text, are highly daring readings).

While the 'dramatic collision' defines the system of drama, theatre in Grüber's work is defined as scene and situation. The spectator is there to witness the pain the actors speak of. In this way, Grüber traces a link back to that essential reality of the stage which means that here the *moment of speaking* is everything. Not the timeline of action; not the drama but the moment when the human voice is raised. A body exposes itself, suffers. The plaintive sound that it emits propagates through space and hits the spectator as a sound wave, tangentially, with disembodied force. For pity and fear, what more is needed than this? What counts in Grüber's productions is the precious moment when a body, under threat, starts to speak in the space of a scene. Incidentally, it is this constellation, not narration (which belonged to epos), that emerged in ancient theatre.[31] In Grüber's theatre, the never ending, anciently singing, Beckettian murmering voice becomes audible, a way of speaking that even in dispute resides beyond debate, speaking of the experience of infinite powerlessness, without any deceptive dynamic or pseudo-tempo. Postdramatic melancholia reconciles Aeschylus and Beckett, Kleist and Labiche in a *Trauerspiel* left to the contemplation of the spectator. In Grüber's *Iphigenie in Tauris* at the Berliner Schaubühne (1998) the heroine's report of the terror of myth (the story of the Atrides) became a quiet scenic contemplation of the unbearable. The dramatic conflict receded behind this meditation, behind the act of precise articulation. The postdramatic theme here is a *theatre of the voice*, the voice being a reverberation of past events.

The condition for the theatre of the voice is an architectural space which through its dimensions enters into a relationship with individual human speech, with the imaginary space of this voice. It is first and foremost through extremes that space becomes perceptible – for example, the oversized emptiness of the Berlin Olympia Stadium, a piece of architecture modelled on the ancient stadium and built by the Nazis to demonstrate their dominance. This Nazi building was the site of the staging of *Winterreise* (1977), the spectators, gathered into a small part of the seating area, having to connect texts from Hölderlin's *Hyperion* with sports scenes, images of cemeteries, tent camps and fastfood takeaways. For Grüber's *Faust* it was the vast church of Salpétrière. The cloister-like, cold concrete apse of the Berliner Schaubühne served as the sober space for *Hamlet*, the huge Deutschlandhalle in Berlin for Aeschylus' *Prometheus* in Handke's translation. But the space equally becomes a player in its own right as a minuscule, cramped and overflowing site. This may be an ironically babbling tiny wave that divides the stage of *Iphigenie* from the audience as an image of the wide sea; or for *Krapp's Last Tape* with Bernard Minetti a room hopelessly overfilled with plants ; or the small studio space in Berlin's Cuvrystrasse, dimly lit by small kerosene lamps in the colours of a Chagall painting, overcrowded with the bodies of travellers, a space expressing the despair in Chekhov's *On the Road* (*An der grossen Strasse*). In Grüber's work there is hardly a neutral space. By avoiding the medium space and inventing the overly large or overly small space, the axis voice/space becomes determining for this theatre. Intrigue, story or drama are hardly present; instead distance, emptiness and in-between-space are turned into autonomous protagonists. The actual dialogue takes place between sound and sound space, not between the interlocutors. The figures each speak on their own. In 1979 spectators visiting the former luxury Hotel Esplanade in Berlin found an environment of voices, projections and individual scenes connected by a reading from the 1933 novella *Rudi* by Bernhard von Brentano, a text about a proletarian child in Berlin. Grüber's action at the Weimar cemetery in the autumn of 1985 represented yet another form of scenic and spatial 'memory work': among the graves he realized Jorge Semprún's *Bleiche Mutter, zarte Schwester* (*Pale Mother, Fragile Sister*), a multi-layered text that shifts between Goethe, Buchenwald, Léon Blum, political persecution under Stalin, Brecht, Caroloa Neher and ethnic cleansing in Bosnia. Again the director left the sphere of staged drama in favour of the creation of a theatre situation (for which the unusual site was arranged by the painter and set designer Eduardo Arroyo).[32]

Wilson or the landscape

According to Richard Schechner,[33] the plot of a drama can easily be summed up by compiling a list of the changes that occur to the dramatis personae between the beginning and the end of the dramatic process. Transformations can be produced through magical procedures, disguises or masques, they can occur through new knowledge (anagnorisis) or physical processes; they can be recurring metamorphoses analogous to natural processes or belong to a temporal form that is symbolic and cyclical. At the heart of acting is perhaps not so much the transmission of meanings but the archaic *pleasure/fear (Angstlust) of play*, of metamorphosis as such. Children enjoy dressing up. The pleasure in dissimulating oneself under the mask is paired with another, no less uncanny pleasure: how the world changes under one's gaze looking out of the mask, how it suddenly becomes strange when seen from 'elsewhere'. Whoever looks through the eyes of a mask changes his gaze into that of an animal, a camera, a being unknown to itself and the world. Theatre is transformation at all levels, *metamorphosis*, and it is worth taking to heart the insight of theatre anthropology that under the conventional scheme of *action* there is the more general structure of *transformation*. This explains why abandoning the model of 'mimesis of action' by no means leads to the end of theatre. Conversely, an attention to the processes of metamorphosis leads to another mode of theatrical perception in which seeing as recognition is continually outdone by a play of surprises that can never be arrested by an order of perception. 'The crab walk of repetitive vision is perforated by a *different kind of seeing* that lurks in the recognizing way of seeing and continuously throws it off its habitual course.'[34]

Over the last thirty years hardly any theatre practitioner has changed the theatre and the scope of its means and at the same time influenced the possibilities of reimagining theatre as much as Robert Wilson. Certainly, he has not been spared the common fate whereby in his later works the theatrical means that had once, in their freshness, revealed an epochal theatre dream lose much of their magic, as they become predictable and are employed, at times, in a merely craftsman-like, slightly mannerist fashion. But this does not detract from the fact that it was Wilson who in many ways invented the most far-reaching 'response' to the question of theatre in the age of media and who simultaneously radically broadened the scope for changed conceptions of what theatre can be. In the meantime the subterranean as well as the obvious influence of his aesthetic has filtered through everywhere, and one can say that theatre at the turn of the century owes him more than any other individual theatre practitioner.

Wilson's theatre is a theatre of metamorphoses. He leads the viewer into the dreamland of transitions, ambiguities, and correspondences: a column of smoke may be the image of a continent; trees turn first into Corinthian columns, then columns turn into factory smoke-stacks. Triangles mutate into sails, then tents or mountains. Anything can change its size, as in Lewis Carroll's *Alice in Wonderland*, of which Wilson's theatre is often reminiscent. His motto could be: *from action to metamorphosis*. Like the Deleuzian machine, metamorphosis connects heterogeneous realities, a thousand plateaux and energy flows. In particular, the actors' movement in slow motion always produces an absolutely peculiar experience in Wilson's aesthetic, an experience that undermines the idea of action. We are talking here of the impression that the human actors on stage do not act of their own volition and agency. When Büchner wrote that humans are like puppets moved on invisible wires by invisible forces and Artaud spoke of 'automate personnel', then these motifs correspond with the impression that in Wilson's theatre there are mysterious forces at work who seem to be moving the figures magically without any visible motivation, objectives or connections. These figures remain solitarily spun into a cosmos, into a web of lines of forces and – quite concretely through the lighting design – 'prescribed' paths. The figures (or figurines) inhabit a magical phantasm that imitates the ancient heroes' enigmatic path of fate drawn by oracles. As in Grüber's muteness, as in Kantor's eternal tango rounds, thus also in Wilson's lines of light: the dramatic theatre, tied to human autonomy as a question and a problem, falls apart into a *postdramatic energetics*, in the sense in which Lyotard speaks of an 'energetic' instead of a representational theatre. It prescribes enigmatic patterns of movement, processes and stories of light, but hardly any action/plot.

Although one needs to distinguish between painterly and theatrical forms and to take their respective laws and rules into account, the peculiar *transformation from stage space into landscape* – Wilson calls his auditive environments 'audio landscapes' – recalls an inverse process in the nineteenth century when painting approximated a theatrical event. I am talking here of the panorama and the diorama, the gigantic transparent pictures by Daguerre, in which different kinds of lighting seemed to move sceneries, architectural structures and landscapes. For example, the interior of a church would at first seem empty but through a change in lighting one would suddenly notice visitors in it; music would be heard and finally there would be darkness again.[35] Such occurrences are reminiscent of the metamorphosis in Wilson. One can see in them an anticipation of cinema, the satisfaction of scopophilia in a manner that was felt to be sensational at the time. For our context it is important to confirm that the *theatrical* need is obviously not fixated on action alone. The artificially illuminated landscape, the 'action' of daybreak and the change of lighting equally belong to it.

In the context of Karl Friedrich Schinkel's effective transparent paintings the term 'theatre without literary text' has been used by Birgit Verwiebe.[36] And Stephan Oettermann comments that it was precisely the arresting of time in this fascinating simulation of reality in panoramas that evoked the desire for move-ment and narration (which would later be satisfied by cinema).[37] This comment can also be read in the sense that this was a point of departure for a theatrical experience dominated by the *effects of diorama (image) and parallel language.*

In Wilson's work we find a *de-hierarchization* of theatrical means connected to the absence of dramatic action in his theatre. Mostly there are neither psycho-logically elaborated, nor even individuated figures within a coherent scenic context (as in Kantor's work), but instead figures who seem to be incomprehen-sible emblems. The ostentatious mode of their appearance poses the question as to their meaning without this interrogation finding an answer. The actors 'sharing' the stage often do not even enter into the context of an interaction of any kind. And the space of this theatre, too, is discontinuous: light and colours, disparate signs and objects create a stage that no longer signifies a homoge-neous space: frequently Wilson's space is divided 'into stripes' parallel to the apron of the stage, so that actions taking place in different depths of the stage can either be synthesized by the spectator or be read as 'parallelograms', so to speak. It is thus already left to the constructing imagination of the viewer whether s/he considers the different figures on stages as existing within a shared context at all, or only as synchronically presented. It is obvious that the inter-pretability of the whole texture for this reason is close to zero. Through the montage of juxtaposed or imbricated virtual spaces, which – this is the crucial point – remain independent from one another so that no synthesis is offered, a poetic sphere of *connotations* comes into being.

What is missing here is a dramatic orientation through the lines of a story, which in painting corresponds to the ordering of the visible through perspective. The point about perspective is that it makes totality possible precisely because the position of the viewer, the point of view, is excluded from the visible world of the picture, so that the constitutive act of representation is missing in the repre-sented. This corresponds to the form of dramatic narration – even where it integrates an epic narrator. In Wilson's work it is superseded by a kind of uni-versal history that appears as a multicultural, ethnological, archaeological *kaleidoscope.* Without restraint his theatre tableaux mix times, cultures and spaces. In *The Forest* (1988) nineteenth-century industrial history is mirrored in Babylon-ian myth; at the end of *Ka Mountain and Guardenia Terrace: A Story about a Family and Some People Changing* (1972) a scale model of the New York skyline goes up in flames, behind it appear the outline of a pagoda, a great white ape as a statue whose face is burning, the three wise men from the East, an apocalyptic fire and a dinosaur: history and prehistory not in the sense of a historical-dialectic under-standing but as a dance of images. Numerous images in Wilson's work directly or indirectly conjure up old myth in an overwhelming plethora of newer histor-ical, religious, literary motifs and figures. For Wilson they all belong to the imaginary cosmos and are all in the widest sense mythological: Freud, Einstein,

Edison and Stalin; Queen Victoria and Lohengrin; Parsifal, Salome, Faust, the brothers from the Gilgamesh epic, Tankred Dorst's version of Parsifal in Hamburg, the Saint Sebastian in Bobigny, King Lear in Frankfurt am Main . . . An incomplete list of mythical, quasi- and pseudo-mythical elements of his theatre may at the same time give an indication of the playful delight he takes in quoting from the human store of images, a playfulness that is not going to allow any limits imposed on it by centripetal logic. Appearing on stage are: Noah's ark, the book of Jonas, Leviathan, ancient and modern Indian texts, a Viking ship, African cult objects, Atlantis, the white whale, Stonehenge, Mycenae, the Pyramids, the man with the Egyptian crocodile mask, enigmatic beings like Mother Earth, Bird Woman and the white bird of death, Saint Joan, Don Quixote, Tarzan, Captain Nemo, Goethe's Erl-king, Hopi Indians, Florence Nightingale, Mata Hari, Madame Curie, etc.

Wilson's theatre is *neo-mythical*, but with the myths as images, carrying action only as virtual fantasies. Prometheus and Heracles, Phaedra and Medea, the Sphinx and the dragon as the protagonists of the artistic imagination continue to live on through the centuries as narratives with a profound allegorical meaning. But at the same time they exist as mere images, familiar also to those without an 'education'. As unconsciously operating figures of cultural discourse everyone 'knows' (knowingly or unknowingly) Heracles and the Hydra, Medea and her children, the rebellious Prometheus, and the enemy brothers Polyneices and Eteocles. The same is true for postantiquity mythical figures such as Don Juan, Faust or Parsifal. In an epoch when 'normally' arranged narration hardly attains the density of the mythical any more, Wilson's theatre is trying to approach the prerational logic of a mythical world of images. If one should hesitate to accept a serious connection between Wilson's artistry and ancient myth, however, this doubt would certainly be justified: mythical imagery here takes the place of action, satisfying a 'postmodern' pleasure in the quotation of imaginary worlds whose time has passed. (On the other hand, a look back into theatre history teaches that in former epochs myth and entertainment did not have to exclude one another, either.) Wilson is part of a long tradition, from the baroque theatre of effects, the 'machines' of the seventeenth century, Jacobean masques, Victorian spectacle theatre down to the variety show and circus in modern times, all of which have always irreverently and effectively incorporated the depth of myth as much as the attraction of mythical clichés into their repertoire.

In Wilson's work the phenomenon has priority over the narrative, the effect of the image precedence over the individual actor, and contemplation over interpretation. Therefore, his theatre creates a time of the gaze. This theatre is without tragic sentiment or pity, but it does speak of the experience of time, it does testify to *mourning* (*Trauer*). In addition, Wilson's painting with light reinforces the idea of a unity of natural processes and human occurrences. It is also for this reason that whatever the players do, say and manifest in their movements loses the character of intentional actions. Their undertakings seem to be occurring as in a dream and thus 'lose the name of action', as Hamlet says. They change into an occurrence. Human beings turn into *gestic sculptures*.

The association with three-dimensional painting lets things appear as *nature morte* and players as mobile whole-figure portraits. Wilson explicitly compared his theatre to natural processes. The idea of a scenic landscape therefore also takes on the meaning attached to it in Heiner Müller's phrase of the 'landscape waiting for the gradual disappearance of man'. It is about the insertion of human actions into the context of *natural history*. As in myth, life appears as a moment of the cosmos. The human being is not separated from landscape, animal and stone. A rock may fall in slow motion, animals and plants are just as much agents of the events as the human figures. If in this way the concept of action dissolves in favour of occurrences, of continual metamorphosis, the space of action appears as a landscape continually changed by different states of light, appearing and disappearing objects and figures.

At Heiner Müller's funeral, Wilson introduced his contribution – a reading of a passage from Gertrude Stein's *The Making of Americans* in lieu of a personal text – by remarking that after reading this book he had known that he could make theatre. Indeed the elective affinity between Wilson's theatre and Gertrude Stein's texts, her notion of 'Landscape Play', is immediately evident. In both there is minimal progression, the 'continuous present', no identifiable identities, a peculiar rhythm that wins out over all semantics and in which anything fixable passes into variations and shadings. Elinor Fuchs comments in Another Version of the Pastoral':

> I experimentally suggest that a performance genre has emerged that encourages and relies on the faculty of landscape surveyal. Its structures are arranged not in lines of conflict and resolution but on the multivalent spatial relationships, 'the trees to the hills to the fields . . . any piece of it to any sky' as Stein said, 'any detail to any other detail'.[38]

Even if the coupling of new pastoral and theatre is perhaps only due to a specifically American perspective (the experience of the grandiose landscapes of the USA), it makes sense if Fuchs states about the postdramatic theatre of the Texan Robert Wilson: 'He creates within advanced culture a fragile memory bank of imagery from nature. In this way, and in a variety of others, postmodern theatre artists hint at the possibility of a post-anthropocentric stage.'[39] *Post-anthropocentric theatre* would be a suitable name for an important (though not the only) form that postdramatic theatre can take. Under this heading one could assemble the theatre of objects entirely without human actors, theatre of technology and machinery (e.g. in the mechanized presentations by Survival Research Laboratories), and theatre that integrates the human form mostly as an element in landscape-like spatial structures. They are aesthetic figurations that point utopically towards an alternative to the anthropocentric ideal of the subjection of nature. When human bodies join with objects, animals and energy lines into a single reality (as also seems to be the case in circus – thus the depth of the pleasure it causes), theatre makes it possible to imagine a reality other than that of man dominating nature.

Postdramatic theatrical signs

Retreat of synthesis

The following overview of the stylistic traits of postdramatic theatre or, to be more precise, of the ways it uses theatrical signifiers, proposes criteria and categories of description with whose help – not in the sense of a 'checklist' but as a companion for the viewing experience – a better understanding of postdramatic theatre can be gained. The term 'theatrical signs' in this context is meant to include all dimensions of signification, not merely signs that carry determinable information, i.e. signifiers which denote (or unmistakably connote) an identifiable signified, but virtually all elements of the theatre. For even a striking physicality, a certain style of gesture or a stage arrangement, simply by dint of the fact that they are present(ed) with a certain emphasis, are received as 'signs' in the sense of a manifestation or gesticulation obviously demanding attention, 'making sense' through the heightening frame of the performance without being 'fixable' conceptually. Certainly the tradition of aesthetics has also understood such density without a fixed conceptual identity as an indication of the beautiful. Thus, Kant says of the 'aesthetic idea' that it was a 'representation of the Imagination, which induces much thought, yet without the possibility of any definite thought whatever, i.e. *concept*, being adequate to it, and which language, consequently, can never . . . render completely intelligible',[40] and which opens out for the mind 'a prospect into a field of kindred representations stretching beyond its ken'.[41] This is not the place to discuss the extent to which the theory of sign usage in modern times has moved away from this way of thinking by dissolving the 'aesthetic idea's' reference to concepts of reason, which is implied by Kant. Suffice to say that one has to grant theatre signs the possibility that they can work precisely through the *retreat* of signification. While theatre semiotics nevertheless extricates the nucleus of meaning and even in the greatest ambiguity secures the remnants of signifying possibilities (without which the free play of potentialities would indeed lose its attraction), it is important simultaneously to develop forms of analysis and discourse for that which, crudely put, remains non-sense in the signifiers. In this spirit, our tentative analysis starts with the insights of theatre semiotics but at the same time tries to go beyond them by focusing on the figurations of self-cancellation of meaning.

Synthesis is cancelled. It is explicitly combated. Theatre articulates through the mode of its semiosis an implicit *thesis* concerning perception. It may appear surprising to ascribe to artistic discourse the ability to have a thesis like a theoretical discourse. Apart from exceptional cases, as for example in a successful thesis play, art certainly knows theses and theorems only *implicitly* (and these consequently always remain ambiguous). Yet this is precisely why it is one of the tasks of hermeneutics to read in the preferred forms and configurations of an aesthetic practice the hypotheses expressed in them, i.e. to take into account and practice a semantics of form. Enclosed within postdramatic theatre is obviously the demand for an open and fragmenting perception in place of a unifying and closed perception. On the one hand, the abundance of simultaneous signs in this way presents itself like a doubling of reality: it seemingly mimics the chaos of real everyday experience. But part and parcel of this quasi 'Naturalistic' stance is the thesis that an authentic manner in which theatre could testify to life *cannot* come about through imposing an artistic macrostructure that constructs coherence (as is the case in drama). It could be demonstrated that in this transformation lurks a hidden *penchant for solipsism.* The establishment and relative durability of the 'great' forms can be understood by considering that they offered the possibility of *articulating collective experiences.* Commonality is the essence of aesthetic genres. It is, however, precisely this commonality that recognizes itself via the collectively experienced form that is now put into doubt. If the new theatre wants to reach beyond a non-committal and entirely private engagement, it has to seek other ways to find transindividual points of contact. It finds them in the theatrical real- ization of freedom – freedom from subjection to hierarchies, freedom from the demand for coherency. In her essay *The Burden of the Times,*[42] Marianne van Kerk- hoven, who has gained a reputation as a dramaturg of new theatre in Belgium, relates the new theatre languages to chaos theory, which assumes that reality con- sists of unstable systems rather than closed circuits; the arts respond to this with ambiguity, polyvalence and simultaneity, the theatre with a dramaturgy that fixes partial structures rather than whole patterns. Synthesis is sacrificed in order to gain, in its place, the density of intensive moments. If the partial structures never- theless develop into something like a whole, this is no longer organized according to prescribed models of dramatic coherence or comprehensive symbolic refer- ences and does not realize synthesis. This tendency applies to all arts. Theatre, the art of the event *par excellence,* becomes the paradigm of the aesthetic. It no longer remains the relatively narrow institutional branch that it was but becomes the name for a multi- or intermedially deconstructive artistic practice of the momentary event. Yet it was technology and the separation and division of the senses in media that first called attention to the artistic potential of the decompo- sition of perception, to what Deleuze called the 'lines of flight' of the 'molecular' particles compared to the 'molar' structure as a whole.

Dream images

Considered from the point of view of reception, the retreat of synthesis is a matter of the freedom to react arbitrarily, or rather involuntarily and idiosyn- cratically. The 'community' that arises is not one of similar people, i.e. a community of spectators who have been made similar through commonly shared motifs (the human being in general), but instead a common contact of different singularities who do not melt their respective perspectives into a whole but at most share or communicate affinities in small groups. In this sense, the perturbing strategy of the withdrawal of synthesis means the offer of a commu- nity of heterogeneous and particular imaginations. Some critics may see in this only a socially dangerous or at least artistically questionable tendency towards an arbitrary and solipsistic reception, but perhaps this suspension of laws of sense formation heralds a more liberal sphere of sharing and communicating that inherits the utopias of modernism. Mallarmé once remarked that he wished for newspapers in which the inhabitants of Paris would report their dreams to each other (instead of daily events). Indeed the stage discourses often come to resemble the structure of dreams and seem to tell of the dream world of their creators. An essential quality of the dream is the non-hierarchy of images, movements and words. 'Dream thoughts' form a texture that resembles collage, montage and fragment rather than a logically structured course of events. The dream constitutes the model *par excellence* of a non-hierarchical theatre aesthetic – an inheritance of Surrealism. Artaud had already envisioned it, speaking of *hieroglyphs* in order to stress the status of theatrical signs between letter and image, between the respectively different modes of signifying and affecting. Freud, too, uses the comparison with hieroglyphs in order to characterize the kinds of signs that the dream offers for analysis. Just as the dream demands a different concept of the sign, the new theatre demands a 'sublated' semiotics and an 'abandoned' interpretation.

Synaesthesia

It can hardly be overlooked that there are stylistic traits in the new theatre that have been seen as attributes of the *tradition of mannerism*: an aversion to organic closure, a tendency towards the extreme, distortion, unsettling uncertainty and paradox. The aesthetic of metamorphosis, as it is realized in Wilson's work in an exemplary manner, can also be read as an indication of a mannerist use of signs. In addition there is the mannerist principle of equivalency: instead of contiguity, as it presents itself in dramatic narration (A is connected to B, B in turn to C, so that they form a line or sequence), one finds disparate heterogeneity, in which any one detail seems to be able to take the place of any other. As in surrealist writing games this circumstance continually leads to the intensified perception of the individual phenomenon and simultaneously to the discovery of surprising *correspondances*. Not coincidentally this term stems from poetry, and it aptly describes the new perception of theatre beyond drama as 'scenic poetry'. The human sensory apparatus does not easily tolerate disconnectedness. When deprived of connections, it seeks out its own, becomes 'active', its imagination going 'wild' – and what then 'occurs to it' are similarities, correlations and correspondences, however far-fetched these may be. The *search for traces* of connection is accompanied by a helpless focusing of perception on the things offered (maybe they will at some moment reveal their secret). As in the preclassical episteme, which according to Foucault seeks and finds everywhere a 'world of similarities',[43] the spectator of the new theatre searches – pleasurably, wearily or desperately – for the Baudelairean *correspondances* in the 'temple' of theatre. The *synaesthesia* immanent to scenic action, a main topic of modernism since Wagner (and since Baudelaire's enthusiasm for Wagner), is no longer an only *implicit* (1) *constituent* (2) of theatre presented for contemplation as a *work* of *mise en scène* (3), but instead becomes an *explicitly marked* (1) *proposition* (2) for a *process of communication* (3). It would be tempting to discuss here the different models offered by phenomenology and perception theory to understand the process of global perception (synaesthesia) which, without being homogeneous, communicates across the senses. But it has to suffice here to have marked the shifting accents sketched above. Perception always already functions *dialogically*, in such a way that the senses *respond* to the offers and demands of the environment, but at the same time also show a disposition first to construct the manifold into a texture of perception, i.e. to constitute a unity. If this is so, then aesthetic forms of practice offer the chance to intensify this synthesizing, corporeal activity of sensory experience precisely by means of a purposeful impediment: they call attention to it as a quest, disappointment, retreat and rediscovery.

Performance text

The following distinction between different levels of theatrical staging has become established: the *linguistic text*, the *text of the staging and mise en scène*, and the '*performance text*'. The linguistic material and the texture of the staging interact with the theatrical situation, understood comprehensively by the concept 'performance text'. Even if the term 'text' here is somewhat imprecise, it does express that each time there occurs a connection and interweaving of (at least potentially) signifying elements. Through the development of Performance Studies it has been highlighted that the *whole situation of the performance* is constitutive for theatre and for the meaning and status of every element within it. The mode of relationship of the performance to the spectators, the temporal and spatial situation, and the place and function of the theatrical process within the social field, all of which constitute the 'performance text', will 'overdetermine' the other two levels. While it is justified to dissect the density of the performance methodologically into levels of signification, it has to be remembered that a texture is not composed like a wall out of bricks but like a fabric out of threads. Consequently the significance of all individual elements ultimately depends on the way the whole is viewed, rather than constituting this overall effect as a sum of the individual parts. Hence, for postdramatic theatre it holds true that the written and/or verbal text transferred onto theatre, as well as the 'text' of the staging understood in the widest sense (including the performers, their 'paralinguistic' additions, reductions or deformations of the linguistic material; costumes, lighting, space, peculiar temporality, etc.) are all cast into a new light through a *changed conception of the performance text*. Even if the structural transformation of the theatrical situation, of the role of the spectator in it, and of the mode of its communicative processes is not equally pronounced everywhere, this statement still holds true: that postdramatic theatre is *not simply a new kind of text of staging* – and even less a new type of theatre text, but rather a type of sign usage in the theatre that turns both of these levels of theatre upside down through the structurally changed quality of the performance text: it becomes more presence than representation, more shared than communicated experience, more process than product, more manifestation than signification, more energetic impulse than information.

The observed peculiarities, proposed categories and types of sign usage in postdramatic theatre will be illustrated in the following with individual cases. The status of these examples is allegorical: even when they can be classed into the respective type, category or procedure in many or all traits, in principle they only demonstrate a trait more obviously which could also be extracted in other works of theatre where it may be more hidden. The 'style' or rather the palette of stylistic traits of postdramatic theatre demonstrates the following characteristic traits: parataxis, simultaneity, play with the density of signs, musicalization, visual dramaturgy, physicality, irruption of the real, situation/event. (In this phenomenology of postdramatic signs I will only marginally discuss language, voice and text which will be dealt with later.)

1 Parataxis / non-hierarchy

The de-hierarchization of theatrical means is a universal principle of postdramatic theatre. This non-hierarchical structure blatantly contradicts tradition, which has preferred a hypotactical way of connection that governs the super- and subordination of elements, in order to avoid confusion and to produce harmony and comprehensibility. In the *parataxis* of postdramatic theatre the elements are not linked in unambiguous ways. Thus Heiner Goebbels remarked in conversation:

> My collaboration with Magdalena Jetelová or with strong set designers like Michael Simon or Erich Wonder is not primarily because it has to be visual arts at all costs. I am interested in a theatre that does not incessantly multiply signs . . . I am interested in inventing a theatre where all the means that make up theatre do not just illustrate and duplicate each other but instead all maintain their own forces but act together, and where one does not just rely on the conventional hierarchy of means. That means, for example, where a light can be so strong that you suddenly only watch the light and forget the text, where a costume speaks its own language or where there is a distance between speaker and text and a tension between music and text. I experience theatre as exciting whenever you can sense distances on stage that I as a spectator can then cross . . . I therefore try to invent a stage reality that also has something to do with the buildings, with the architecture or construction of the stage and its particular laws, and which also finds resistance in these . . . I am interested, for example, in the fact that a space formulates a movement and has a time.[44]

In a similar way we can repeatedly note a non-hierarchical use of signs that aims at a synaesthetic perception and contradicts the established hierarchy, at the top of which we find language, diction and gesture and in which visual qualities such as the experience of an architectonic space – if they come into play at all – figure as subordinated aspects.

A comparison with painting may clarify the artistic consequences of de-hierarchization. In Breughel's paintings the positions of the represented figures (peasants, skaters, brawlers, etc.) appear strangely frozen and as if arrested (because of a certain plumpness they lack the suggestion of movement characteristically fixed in the tableau). This immobilization is closely related to the narrative character of the paintings. They are noticeably de-dramatized: every detail seems to be accorded the same weight, the accentuation typical for dramatic representation and the centring with its separation of major and minor matter, centre and periphery, does not take place in these 'swarming pictures'. Often the seemingly important narrative is deliberately shifted into the margins (*The Fall of Icarus*). This chronicle aesthetic understandably fascinated Brecht, who related Breughel's painting to his conception of the epic. Epicization – the negation of drama in the image – is, however, only one aspect of that aesthetic which unites the immobilization and freezing of poses with the consistent juxtaposition of signs. What happens here within the medium of painting can also be found in manifold ways in postdramatic theatrical practice: different genres are combined in a performance (dance, narrative theatre, performance, etc.); all means are employed with equal weighting; play, object and language point simultaneously in different directions of meaning and thus encourage a contemplation that is at once relaxed and rapid. The consequence is a changed attitude on the part of the spectator. In psychoanalytical hermeneutics the term 'evenly hovering attention' (*gleichschwebende Aufmerksamkeit*) is used. Freud chose this term to characterize the way in which the analyst listens to the analysand. Here everything depends on not understanding immediately. Rather one's perception has to remain open for connections, correspondences and clues at completely unexpected moments, perhaps casting what was said earlier in a completely new light. Thus, meaning remains in principle postponed. Minor and insignificant details are registered exactly because in their immediate non-significance they may turn out to be significant for the discourse of the analysand. In a similar way the spectator of postdramatic theatre is not prompted to process the perceived instantaneously but to postpone the production of meaning (semiosis) and to store the sensory impressions with 'evenly hovering attention'.

2 Simultaneity

Associated with the procedure of parataxis is the simultaneity of signs. While dramatic theatre proceeds in such a way that of all the signals communicated at any one moment of the performance only a particular one is usually emphasized and placed at the centre, the paratactical valency and ordering of postdramatic theatre lead to the experience of simultaneity. This often – and we have to add: frequently with systematic intent – overstrains the perceptive apparatus. Heiner Müller declares he wants to load so much onto the readers and spectators that they cannot possibly process everything. Frequently, language sounds are simultaneously presented on stage so that one can only partially understand them, especially when different languages are being used. Nobody is able to take in all simultaneous events in a dance performance by William Forsythe or Saburo Teshigawara. In certain performances, as for example in the performances of *Oresteia* and *Giulio Cesare* by Societas Raffaello Sanzio, the visible events on stage are surrounded and complemented by a second reality of all manner of sounds, music, voices and noise structures, so that one has to speak of the simultaneous existence of a second 'auditory stage' (Eleni Varopoulou).

Interrogating the intention and effect of simultaneity, one has to state: the *parcelling of perception* here becomes an unavoidable experience. To begin with, the comprehension finds hardly any support in overarching sequential connections of action/plot. But even the events perceived in one moment elude synthetization when they occur simultaneously and when the concentration on one particular aspect makes the clear registration of another impossible. Furthermore, the performance often leaves open whether there exists any real *connection* in what is being presented simultaneously or whether this is just an external *contemporaneity*. A systematic double-bind arises: we are meant to pay attention to the concrete particular and at the same time perceive the totality. Parataxis and simultaneity result in the failure of the classical aesthetic ideal of an 'organic' connection of the elements in an artefact. It was not least of all the idea of an analogy of the work of art and a living organic body that motivated the vehement conservative resistance against modernism's propensity for deconstruction and montage. The contrast drawn by Benjamin between an allegorical aesthetic and a symbolic aesthetic disposed towards the 'organic' ideal can also be read as a theory of theatre.[45] In this sense, the place of the *organic*, knowable whole is taken by the unavoidable and commonly 'forgotten' *fragmentary character* of perception that is explicitly rendered conscious in postdramatic theatre. The compensatory function of drama, to supplement the chaos of reality with structural order, finds itself inverted; the spectator's desire for orientation turns out to be disavowed. If the principle of the one dramatic action is abandoned, this is done in the name of the attempt to create events in which there remains a sphere of choice and decision for the spectators; they decide which of the simultaneously presented events they want to engage with but at the same time feel the frustration of realizing the exclusive and *limiting character of this freedom*. The procedure distinguishes itself from mere chaos in that it opens up chances for the recipient to process the simultaneous by means of their own selection and structuring. At the same time, it remains an aesthetic of 'meaning in retreat' since structuring is possible only with recourse to the individual substructures or microstructures of the staging and the totality is never grasped. It becomes crucial that the abandonment of totality be understood not as a deficit but instead as a liberating possibility of an ongoing (re-)writing, imagination and recombination, that refuses the 'rage of understanding' (Jochen Hörisch).

3 Play with the density of signs

In postdramatic theatre it becomes a rule to violate the conventionalized rule and the more or less established *norm of sign density*. There is either too much or too little. In relation to the time, to the space or to the importance of the matter, the viewer perceives a repletion or conversely a noticeable dilution of signs. We can recognize here an aesthetic intention to make space for a *dialectic of plethora and deprivation*, plenitude and emptiness. (It would be interesting to revisit the prehistory of empty space in theatre from this point of view – Appia's spaces of light, Copeau and his 'tréteau nu', Brecht's predilection for an empty stage, and Peter Brook's 'empty space'.) It turns out that not only can all levels of signification come to prominence in their own right but even the fact of the simple presence or absence or the unexpected density of signs as such comes to the fore. Theatre in this respect reacts to media culture. For economic, aesthetic and media specific reasons, McLuhan's world had to become a world of over-abundance. It increased the density and number of stimuli to such an extent that this plethora of images increasingly leads to a strange disappearance of the naturally, physically perceived world. While 'instrumental perception', as media theory calls it in contrast to corporeal perception, is gaining ever more impor-tance, the question of an 'appropriate' density of information, too, becomes increasingly independent from the conditions of physical, sensory perception. What remains open is the question of whether the permanent bombardment with images and signs, combined with an ever increasing rift between percep-tion and real sensual contact, will in time train the organs to register in an increasingly superficial way. If one follows Freud in assuming that impressions are inscribed as traces and 'breaches' (*Bahnungen*) in the different systems of the psychic apparatus, then it may not be an unfounded fear that the habituation of permanently repeated but ultimately unrelated, disconnected impressions will lead to increasingly shallow 'breaches' being left in the psychic apparatus, to an increasingly shallow emotional behaviour with an increasingly impermeable protection against stimulation. Consequently, the overabundant world of images could lead to the death of images, in the sense that all actual visual impressions are registered more or less only as pure information, the qualities of the truly 'iconic' aspect of the images being perceived less and less.

Lyotard's hypothesis is well known: under the 'postmodern condition', ten-dentially all knowledge that cannot take the form of information will disappear from social circulation.[46] Something similar could apply to sensory-aesthetic per-ception. Without being able to conduct the proof here, we could risk the con-tention that the viewing experience of television, compared even to the viewing experience in the cinema, leads to a reduced affectivity, a habit of processing only mental, more or less abstract information. The reduced depth and dimen-sion of the television image hardly allows for intensive visual perception. We cannot exclude the possibility that the habitual mode of such perception may reduce the capacity for libidinal 'investment' of visual, spatial and architectonic perception. In the face of our everyday bombardment with signs, postdramatic theatre works with a strategy of refusal. It practises an economy in its use of signs that can be seen as asceticism; it emphasizes a *formalism* that reduces the plethora of signs through repetition and duration; and it demonstrates a tendency to *graphism* and writing that seems to defend itself against optical opulence and redundancy. Silence, slowness, repetition and duration in which 'nothing happens' can be found not only in the minimalist early works of Wilson but also, for example, in works by Jan Fabre, Saburo Teshigawara and Michel Laub and by companies such as Théâtre du Radeau, Matschappej Discordia or Von Heyduck: little action, long pauses, minimalistic reduction, and finally a theatre of muteness and silence, which includes literary play texts such as Peter Handke's *The Hour We Knew Nothing of Each Other*. Gigantic stage spaces are provocatively left empty, acts and gestures are reduced to a minimum. On this path of ellipsis, emptiness and absence are used emphatically, comparable to certain tendencies in modern literature (Mallarmé, Celan, Ponge, Beckett) to privilege deprivation and vacuity. The play with the low density of signs aims to provoke the spectator's own imagination to become active on the basis of little raw material to work with. Absence, reduction and emptiness are not indebted to a minimalist ideology but to a basic motif of activating theatre. Deprivation as a prerequisite for new experience was explored in an especially rigorous manner by John Cage. He is often quoted as having remarked that if something is boring after two minutes, one should try it for four, if still boring, one should try eight, etc. Eventually one would discover that it is not boring at all. Similarly, Picasso is meant to have said: 'If you can paint with three colours, use two.'

4 Plethora

Exceeding the norm, just as much as undercutting it, results in what could be described less as a forming than a *deforming figuration*. Form knows *two limits*: the wasteland of unseizable extension and labyrinthine chaotic accumulation. Form is situated midway. The renunciation of conventionalized form (unity, self-identity, symmetrical structuring, formal logic, readability or surveyability (Aristotle's 'synopton'), the refusal of the normalized form of the image, is often realized by way of recourse to *extremes*. The order of images, which is tied to the 'medium' in the double meaning of the word – the organizing medium and the middle – is disturbed through the proliferation of signs. Gilles Deleuze and Felix Guattari have come up with the key term 'rhizome' for realities in which unsurveyable branching and heterogeneous connections prevent synthesis. Theatre, too, has developed a multitude of rhizomatic connections of heterogeneous elements. The division of stage time into minimal sequences, quasi-filmic 'takes', already indirectly multiplies the data for perception, because, in terms of perception psychology, a mass of unconnected elements is estimated to be larger than the same number of elements arranged in a coherent order. In dance theatre by Johann Kresnik, Wim Vandekeybus or La La La Human Steps the phenomenon of scenic overabundance is overly apparent. We could also think of the profusion in the grotesque haunted house spectacles of Reza Abdoh, or likewise of 'hypernaturalist' productions – for example, by the Belgian company Victoria – with their stage spaces completely cluttered with all sorts of objects and furniture. Certain German directors of the 1980s and 1990s have staged virtual 'battles of materials' (in the good, as well as the bad (i.e. arbitrary) sense). Following Frank Castorf's example, overabundance, chaotic arrangement and the addition of the smallest gags become a stylistic feature. An interesting variant of the plethoric aesthetic are the works of Jürgen Kruse (*Seven against Thebes, Medea, Richard II, Torquato Tasso, Knife*). Here a *theatre of props* develops. The stage is transformed into a playing field or rubbish tip littered with objects, inscriptions and signs, a field of chaotically splintered associations, whose confusing density communicates a sense of chaos, insufficiency, disorientation, sadness and *horror vacui*.

5 Musicalization

In a talk given in Frankfurt in 1998[47] about the 'musicalization of all theatrical means', Eleni Varopoulou elaborated that

> for the actor, as much as for the director, music has become an independent structure of theatre. This is not a matter of the evident role of music and of music theatre, but rather of a more profound idea of theatre *as* music. Maybe it is typical that a woman of the theatre like Meredith Monk, who is known for her spatially arranged poems of images and sounds, once remarked: 'I came to theatre from dance but it has been theatre that brought me to music.'[48]

The consistent tendency towards a musicalization (not only of language) is an important chapter of the sign usage in postdramatic theatre. An independent *auditory semiotics* emerges; directors also apply their sense of music and rhythm, which is influenced by pop music, to classical texts (Jürgen Kruse); Wilson calls his works 'operas'. In the course of the dissolution of dramatic coherence the actor's speech becomes musically overdetermined through ethnic and cultural peculiarities:

> It has been an intentional and systematic practice of important directors since the 1970s to bring together actors from totally different cultural or ethnic backgrounds because what is of interest to them is precisely the diverse speech melodies, cadences, accents, and in general the different cultural habitus in the act of speaking. Through the different auditory peculiarities the enunciation of the text thus becomes the source of an independent musicality. The works of Peter Brook and Ariane Mnouchkine are world famous examples for this. What some French critics consider a problem – namely that Japanese or African actors were missing the particular musicality of the French language – interested Brook precisely as a

discovery of *another*, richer music: namely the sound figures of an intercultural polyphony of voices and speech gestures.[49]

This also includes the music that already migrates into theatre through the ubiquitous polyglossia:

> What at first appears as a provocation or as a rupture: the emergence of incomprehensible, foreign language sounds, beyond the immediate level of linguistic semantics gains its own quality as musical richness and as the discovery of unknown sound combinations.[50]

In a conversation conducted in 1996 on the occasion of 'Theater der Welt' in Dresden,[51] Paul Koek declared: 'Hollandia is situated in a kind of tradition similar to that of Kurt Schwitters. We analyse modern music, too, like that of Stockhausen.' And about Hollandia's production of *The Persians*:

> We absolutely wanted it to approximate the Greek rhythms as closely as possible. The choruses, too, were developed rhythmically, that is determined by the tonality or the melody . . . I called one of the actors into my studio and asked him to give his monologue, but as in Japanese Bunraku theatre: crazy sounds, tone pitches from all the way up to very low.

In electronic music it has become possible to manipulate the parameters of sound as desired and thus open up whole new areas for the musicalization of voices and sounds in theatre. While the invidividual tone is already composed of a whole array of qualities – frequency, pitch, overtones, timbre, volume – which can be manipulated with the help of synthesizers, the combinations of electronic sounds and tones (sampling) result in a whole new dimension of 'sound' in theatre. Heiner Goebbels' 'conceptional composing', as he calls it, combines the logic of texts and the musical and vocal material in many variations. It is becoming possible to manipulate and structure the entire sonic space of a theatre in a targeted fashion. Just like the progression of actions, the musical level is no longer constructed in a linear fashion but rather, for instance, through simultaneous superimposition of sonic worlds, as for example in the dance piece *Roaratorio* (1979) by John Cage and Merce Cunningham. Significantly, when this piece was performed in Avignon, Cage read text from James Joyce's *Finnegans Wake*, a text that opened up a new era of ways of dealing with language material: transgressions of the boundaries between national languages, condensations and multiplications of possible meanings, and musical-architectonic constructions. Postdramatic theatrical signs are situated in the tradition of such textures.

Even where great directors use dramatic texts but emphasize the non-dramatic, purely theatrical aspects about them, it is not least of all the musicalization which most strikingly manifests the otherness *vis-à-vis* the dramatic theatre. 'The staging of *Hamlet* (1999) by the Lithuanian director Eimuntas Nekrosius, shows how the musicality that already stood out in his earlier productions, for example in *Three Sisters*, here reaches its apogee', notes Eleni Varopoulou.

> Almost throughout the entire duration of three hours music can be heard, the protagonist is played by a famous Lithuanian rock star, and on the level of sounds and noises a rich repertoire of musical forms is utilized: the regular dripping of melting ice is a leitmotif of the whole production, the rhythms of stomping feet and clapping hands, the noise of swishing poles that functions as a chorus during the duel between Hamlet and Laertes. Even the only noticeable pausing of music – it occurs in Ophelia's madness scene – is interpreted as a music of silent dance. In Nekrosius' work musicalization manifests itself especially in the relationship between humans and objects on stage. The latter undergo a perversion of their function, they are used as musical instruments and interact with the human bodies to produce music.[52]

From a methodological point of view it is crucial to consider such phenomena not merely as (perhaps thoroughly original) extensions of dramatic theatre. The analytical perspective must 'switch over', so to speak, and recognize even in such stagings of drama the new and no longer dramatic language of theatre.

6 Scenography, visual dramaturgy

As the example of musicalization shows, within the paratactical, de-hierarchized use of signs postdramatic theatre establishes the possibility of dissolving the logocentric hierarchy and assigning the dominant role to elements other than dramatic logos and language. This applies even more to the visual than to the auditory dimension. In place of a dramaturgy regulated by the text one often finds a *visual dramaturgy*, which seemed to have attained absolute dominance especially in the theatre of the late 1970s and 1980s, until in the 1990s one could observe a certain 'return to the text' (which had, however, never quite disappeared). Visual dramaturgy here does not mean an exclusively visually organized dramaturgy but rather one that is not subordinated to the text and can therefore freely develop its own logic. What is of critical interest about the 'theatre of images' from our point of view is not whether it is a blessing or a catastrophe for the art of theatre, or whether it is the last resort for theatre in a civilization of images; neither is it important, in a historiographical sense, whether its time has run its course and whether neo-Naturalist or narrative forms of theatre are perhaps going to make a come-back. Rather it is a question of what is symptomatic about it for the semiosis of theatre. Sequences and correspondences, nodal and condensation points of perception and the constitution of meaning communicated through them (however fragmentary it may be) in visual dramaturgy are defined by optical data. A *theatre of scenography* develops. Mallarmé already contemplated such scenic 'graphism' when he considered dance as a physical writing ('écriture corporelle'):

> A savoir que la danseuse *n'est pas une femme qui danse*, pour ces motifs juxta-posés qu'elle *n'est pas une femme*, mais une métaphore résumant un des aspects élémentaires de notre forme, glaive, coupe, fleur, etc., et *qu'elle ne danse pas*, suggérant, par le prodige de raccourcis ou d'élans, avec une écriture cor-porelle ce qu'il faudrait des paragraphes en prose dialoguée autant que descriptive, pour exprimer, dans sa rédaction: poème dégagé de tout appareil du scribe.[53]

Instead of a translation, which is especially problematic in the case of Mallarmé, let us try to interpret these formulas. What we have to see, or rather read on stage, according to Mallarmé, is what the multiple falsity of the expression 'a woman who dances' makes us misconceive. The one who dances does not rep-resent an individuated human form but rather a multiple figuration of her body parts, of her form in figures that change from moment to moment. What we should actually 'see' is the invisible of the different 'aspects', of the human body in general – just like a flower in a frame no longer shows a certain flower but *the* flower as such. It is not a matter of 'a' woman, but neither is it of a 'woman'; rather the gaze will be directed at an ostensibly 'invisible' body that transcends not only gender but also the sphere of anything human – as a form of a sword, bowl, flower, etc. In this sense the gaze in turn is a reading gaze, the scene a writing (graphy), a poem, written without the writing implements of a writer. Scenography, naming a theatre of complex visuality, presents itself to the con-templating gaze like a text, a scenic poem, in which the human body is a metaphor, its flow of movement in a complex metaphorical sense an inscription, a 'writing' and not 'dancing'.

Theatre is catching up on an aesthetic development that other art forms went through earlier. It is no coincidence that concepts which originated in visual arts, music or literature can be used to characterize postdramatic theatre. It was only under the influence of reproductive media like photography and film that theatre became conscious of its specificity. Important contemporary theatre practitioners often have a background in visual arts. There is little reason to be surprised that it is only in the theatre of the recent decades that we have seen trends that can be described with keywords such as self-referentiality, non-figural, abstract or concrete art, autonomization of the signifiers, seriality, or aleatoric art. Since theatre as an expensive aesthetic practice necessarily had to think of ways to survive in bourgeois society through substantial income – and that means through popularity with a wide audience – new risky innova-tions and important transformations and modernizations have emerged with a characteristic delay compared to the state of affairs in less costly art forms, such as poetry or painting. In the meantime, however, even in the land of theatre the above mentioned tendencies have provoked considerable and lasting bewilder-ment. It is still hard to accept for a wider theatre audience, however, that the innovations of the so-called modern theatre, which they have just become used to and which are partially already passé, demand newly changed attitudes from its spectators.

7 Warmth and coldness

For an audience brought up in the tradition of text-based theatre, the 'dethroning' of linguistic signs and the de-psychologization that goes with it are especially hard to accept. Through the participation of living human beings, as well as through the century-old fixation with moving human fortunes, the theatre possesses a certain 'warmth'. Even though the classical avant-gardes, epic theatre and documentary theatre have already largely put an end to this, the formalism of postdramatic theatre is a qualitatively new step and still causes perplexity. For someone who expects the representation of a human – in the sense of psychological – world of experience, it can manifest a *coldness* that is hard to bear. It is especially alienating because in the theatre we are dealing not just with visual processes but with human bodies and their warmth, with which the perceiving imagination cannot avoid associating human experiences. Hence, it is provocative when these human appearances are captured in visual grid pattern or when, for example, a war scene in Wilson's *The Civil Wars* presents a thoroughly choreographed collective death with terrifying coldness (and beauty). Conversely, the autonomization of the visual dimension can lead to an *overheating* and a flood of images. In his adaptation of Dante, Tomaz Pandur aspired to an 'infernal' intensity and through visual 'overkill' came close to circus. In the 1980s the Serapionstheater in Vienna was taking on impulses from Wilson, Mnouchkine and others to create a visual dramaturgy that exerted an enormous attraction. Especially famous was *Double & Paradise: Ein Visuelles Gedicht, Kataphrasen zu Edgar Allen Poe und Buster Keaton* by Erwin Piplits, which by March 1983 had been performed 120 times in Vienna and toured in several other cities. Here, it was a matter of a plethora of visual effects, cruelty and 'stimulus overload'.[54]

8 Physicality

Despite all efforts to capture the expressive potential of the body in a logic, grammar or rhetoric, the aura of physical presence remains the point of theatre where the disappearance, the fading of all signification occurs – in favour of a fascination beyond meaning, of an actor's 'presence', of charisma or 'vibrancy'. Theatre conveys meaning that cannot be named, or at least is always 'waiting' to be named, to use an expression by Lyotard. This is why a shift in the understanding of sign production overall is at work when in postdramatic theatre an immediately imposing, often shocking physicality occurs. The body becomes the centre of attention, not as a carrier of meaning but in its physicality and gesticulation. The central theatrical sign, the actor's body, refuses to serve signification. Postdramatic theatre often presents itself as an *auto-sufficient physicality*, which is exhibited in its intensity, gestic potential, auratic 'presence' and internally, as well as externally, transmitted tensions. In addition there is often the presence of the *deviant body*, which through illness, disability or deformation deviates from the norm and causes an 'amoral' fascination, unease or fear.

Possibilities of existence that are generally repressed and excluded come to prominence in the highly physical forms of postdramatic theatre and repudiate all perception that has established itself in the world at the expense of knowing how narrow the sphere is in which life can happen in some 'normality'.

Postdramatic theatre again and again transgresses the pain threshold in order to revoke the separation of the body from language and to reintroduce into the realm of spirit – voice and language – the painful and pleasurable physicality that Julia Kristeva has called the semiotic within the signifying process. As its presence and charisma become decisive, the body also becomes ambiguous in its signifying character, even to the point of turning into an insoluble enigma. The intensity and turbulence of the theatre can open out into 'tragic' as well as hilarious and enjoyably ecstatic configurations. The persistent boom of a *dance theatre* carried by rhythm, music and erotic physicality but interspersed with the semantics of spoken theatre is not by chance an important variant of postdramatic theatre. If in 'modern dance' the narrative orientation was abandoned, and in 'postmodern dance' the psychological orientation as well, the same development can also be observed in postdramatic theatre – with a delay compared to the development of dance theatre. This is so because the spoken theatre was always, incomparably more so than dance, the site of dramatic signification. Dance theatre uncovers the buried traces of physicality. It heightens, displaces and invents motoric impulses and physical gestures and thus recalls latent, forgotten and retained possibilities of body language. The directors of spoken theatre, too, often create a theatre with considerable or continuous choreography of movement, even when there is no actual dance in evidence (Michael Thalheimer). Yet conversely, the notion of what is meant by the term dance has become broadened to such an extent that categorical distinctions are becoming increasingly meaningless. In the works of the Greek director Theodoros Terzopoulos, for example, movement theatre and movement chorus come so close to dance that the gaze becomes indecisive, no longer knowing to which parameter it should adjust its perception.

As postdramatic theatre moves away from a mental, intelligible structure towards the exposition of intense physicality, the *body is absolutized*. The paradoxical result is often that it appropriates all other discourses. What happens is an interesting volte-face: as the body no longer demonstrates anything but itself, the turn away from a body of signification and towards a body of unmeaning gesture (dance, rhythm, grace, strength, kinetic wealth) turns out as the most extreme charging of the body with significance concerning the social reality. The body becomes the *only subject matter*. From now on, it seems, all social issues first have to pass through this needle's eye, they all have to adopt the form of a physical issue. Love appears as a sexual presence, death as AIDS, beauty as physical perfection. In their relationship to the body theatre works become obsessed with fitness, health and – depending on the point of view – the either fascinating or uncanny possibilities of the 'techno-body'. The body becomes the alpha and omega – at the danger, however, that weaker theatre works that are thus focused on the body only lead to the 'Ah!' and 'Oh!' of the viewer and not to the echo of reflection, which after all remains an implied telos even in the theatre of pure presence that refuses meaning.

While in other visually organized styles of theatre the framing *demarcation* and *distancing* of images dominate over the presence of the actors, in Einar Schleef's theatre the theatrical images seem physically to push over the edge of the stage. Cross forms of the stage and catwalks into the auditorium contribute to a spatial dynamic that runs from the depth of the stage towards the audience (while Wilson, for example, favours the form of movement parallel to the edge of the stage). Through the frontal and direct arrangement, the peculiar 'frontality' of Schleef's theatre produces a physical effect on the spectators. They often have to experience very directly the players' sweat or physical exertion; they feel the pain and extreme demands on the voice in an awkwardly direct manner; they have to watch the dangerously aggressive choruses stomping towards them in a peculiar rhythm; they also experience, however, the ironically reconciliatory 'feedings' of the audience (tea, potatoes boiled in their skins, chocolate chips . . .). The physicality of the theatrical event stands out in the hard, even physically dangerous actions of the players. Echoes of discipline in sports and paramilitary exercises charge the movements with memories of collective German history. In the latter, the themes of militarily steeled physical discipline, physical strength, control and self-control, collective drill and merging into a community play an important role. Consequently, Einar Schleef was surrounded by controversy from the start. Some overhasty critics chose not to see the artistic or political qualities in this theatre and even associated Schleef with neo-fascist tendencies. Certainly this says more about the level of the reviews in question than about these theatre pieces. As happens so often, since his untimely death Schleef is being accepted as an important, even towering figure of German theatre. It is worthwhile to stay with this topic for a moment, however, because it poses the more fundamental question as to the political and ethical dimensions of the aesthetic use of signs. The latter eludes the yardstick of political correctness. If one were to commit it to this, one would have to draw consequences and reduce any aesthetic representation to its 'message', which is clearly an absurd enterprise. For example, what the bodies in Schleef's theatre did when they tested their strength and stamina, naked and drenched in sweat, did not 'demonstrate', 'show' or 'communicate' the presence of a past political catastrophe or the possible future of a thoughtless and unscrupulous sportive, virile or military body, but instead manifested all this. Precisely because Schleef knew that historical memory does not operate simply via consciousness but through physical innervation, his images refused the simple moral or political interpretation. They were all the more deeply troubling and compelled reflection: as a physical memory combined with an attack on the sensory apparatus of the spectator. The physical body, whose gestic vocabulary in the eighteenth century could still be read and interpreted virtually like a text, in postdramatic theatre has become its own reality which does not 'tell' this or that emotion but through its presence *manifests* itself as the site of inscription of collective history.

9 'Concrete theatre'

In what is often called 'abstract' theatre, in the sense of a theatre without action/plot, or 'theatrical' theatre, the preponderance of formal structures is so radical that a reference to reality can hardly be spotted as such any more. One should speak here of *concrete theatre*. Just as Theo van Doesburg and Kandinsky preferred the term 'concrete painting' or 'concrete art' over the commonly used term 'abstract art' because it positively emphasizes the immediately perceivable concreteness of colour, line and surface instead of (negatively) referring to its non-representational nature, in the same way the non-mimetic but formal structure or formalist aspects of postdramatic theatre are to be interpreted as 'concrete theatre'. For here *theatre exposes itself* as an art in space, in time, with human bodies and in general with all the means included in the entire art work, just as much as in painting colour, surface, tactile structure and materiality could become autonomous objects of aesthetic experience. In this sense, Renate Lorenz in her study of Jan Fabre's *The Power of Theatrical Madness* proposed 'concrete theatre' for this performance, with reference to Theo van Doesburg's concept.[55]

When theatre discovers the possibility to be 'simply' a concrete treatment of space, time, physicality, colour, sound and movement, it is in turn catching up on possibilities that were already anticipated in concrete poetry and on the level of text in theatre by authors of the Vienna Group, such as Konrad Bayer and Gerhard Rühm, or in the punning 'wordtheatre' of H. C. Artmann (*tod eines leuchtturms* or *how lovecraft saved the world*). The time of concrete poetry in the narrow sense is over but elements of a concrete writing practice can still be found everywhere in contemporary poetry. What remained a marginal experiment in theatre at the time has become a central possibility of theatre aesthetics thanks to the new possibilities of combining media technology, dance theatre, spatial art and performing practice. Thus, in theatre – which is a place of the gaze – it became possible to realize an extreme of the principle of 'visual dramaturgy'. The latter becomes the 'concrete' realization of formal visual structures of the scene. In this way, a kind of sign usage is introduced to the theatre which like no other challenges traditional conceptions. As long as signs, as discussed above, still include some material 'content' (references) – even if they no longer offer a synthesis – they can still be assimilated through labyrinthine associative work. If, however, these references cease almost entirely, then reception faces an even more radical refusal: the confrontation with a figuratively 'silent' and dense presence of bodies, materials and forms. The sign merely communicates itself, or more precisely: its presence. Perception finds itself thrown back onto the perception of structures.

Thus the scenic elements in Fabre's work are employed in a similar manner as in the 'non-relational art' of Frank Stella, according to the principles of simplicity and non-hierarchical sequencing, symmetry and parallelism. Actors, lights, dancers, etc. are given over to a purely formal observation; the gaze finds no occasion to detect a depth of symbolic significance beyond the given, but instead – either with pleasure or boredom – remains stuck within the activity of seeing the 'surface' itself. An aesthetic formalization without compromise here becomes a mirror, in which the indeed empty formalism of everyday perception recognizes itself – or at least could recognize itself. It is not the content but the formalization itself that constitutes the challenge: the tiring repetition, emptiness, pure mathematics of what is happening on stage, which forces us to experience the very symmetry we are dimly afraid of because it brings with it nothing less than the threat of nothingness. Bereft of its usual crutches of comprehension, the perception of this theatre fails and is forced to engage in a difficult mode of seeing – namely one that is simultaneously formal and sensorially exact. This mode of seeing might produce a more easygoing, more 'negligent' attitude, if it were not for the provocative coldness of the geometry here and the dissatisfied craving for meaning there. Both become particularly acute in Fabre's work and are experienced by the spectator as a dialectic of form and aggression.

What is carried to the extreme in Jan Fabre's theatre in an exemplary manner, shows distinctly what has taken the place of the dramatic centre in postdramatic theatre. In a frame of meaning that has become porous, the concrete, sensuously intensified *perceptibility* comes to the fore. This term, 'perceptibility', captures the virtual and incompletable nature of the theatrical perception that is produced or at least intended here. While mimesis in Aristotle's sense produces the pleasure of recognition and thus virtually always achieves a result, here the sense data always refer to answers that are sensed as possible but not (yet) graspable; what one sees and hears remains in a state of potentialiaty, its appropriation postponed. It is in this sense that we are talking about a *theatre of perceptibility*. Postdramatic theatre emphasizes what is incomplete and incompletable about it, so much so that it realizes its own 'phenomenology of perception' marked by an overcoming of the principles of mimesis and fiction. The play(ing) as a concrete event produced in the moment fundamentally changes the logic of perception and the status of the subject of perception, who can no longer find support in a representative order. Waldenfels remarks in a commentary on Max Imdahl's conception of the 'seeing seeing' (*das sehende Sehen*):

> Strictly speaking, nothing is represented or transmitted here because in such situations of upheaval there is nothing that could be either represented or transmitted. *The seeing seeing experiences the emergence, the birth of what is seen and of the subject who is seeing* – a birth that is at stake in each event of seeing, of becoming and making visible.[56]

10 Irruption of the real

The traditional idea of theatre assumes a closed fictive cosmos, a 'diegetic universe', that can be called thus even though it is produced by means of mimesis,

which normally is contrasted with diegesis. Even if theatre has a number of conventionalized disruptions of its closure (asides, direct audience address), the play
on stage is understood as diegesis of a separated and 'framed' reality governed
by its own laws and by an internal coherence of its elements and which is
marked off against its environment as a separate 'made up' reality. While
arguably 'real', the occasional disruption of the theatrical frame has traditionally been treated as an artistically and conceptually negligible aspect of theatre.
Shakespeare's characters often communicate vehemently with the audience and
the lamentations of tragic victims of all historical periods have always been
directed at the present audience, too, and not just at the gods. It was not unique
to Lessing's times that the spectators took the maxims pronounced on stage to
be instructive precepts addressed to themselves. Nevertheless the artistic task
consisted in integrating all this into the fictive cosmos as inconspicuously as possible, so that addressing the real audience and speaking outside the play would
not be noticeable as a disturbing element. In this respect, one can draw a parallel between the drama in theatre and the 'frame' of a picture that closes the
picture off to the outside and at the same time creates an internal cohesion. The
categorical difference, however – and with it the systematic virtuality of the
rupture of the frame in theatre – resides in the fact that the latter, unlike the
framed picture (or the finished film or the written story), takes place *in actu*. An
especially long pause in speech may be due to an actor involuntarily 'drying' (at
the level of the real) or it may be intentional (at the level of the staging). Only
in the latter case does it systematically belong to the aesthetic condition of
theatre (of the staging); in the former case we are dealing with an accidental
'goof-up' in this one performance that does not belong to it any more than a
typo belongs to the novel.

So much for the state of affairs as it applies to dramatic theatre, in which the
'intentional object' of the *staging* has to be distinguished from the empirically
accidental *performance* (notwithstanding our love for the real, fallible theatrical
play). The postdramatic theatre is the first to turn the level of the real explicitly
into a 'co-player' – and this on a practical, not just theoretical level. The irruption of the real becomes an object not just of reflection (as in Romanticism) but
of the theatrical design itself. This operates on a number of levels, but in an
especially revealing way through a strategy and an *aesthetics of undecidability* concerning the basic means of theatre. In Fabre's *The Power of Theatrical Madness* the
houselights come on in the middle of the performance after an especially
exhausting action by the performers (an endurance exercise *à la* Grotowski).
Out of breath, the actors take a smoking break while looking at the audience. It
remains uncertain whether their unhealthy activity is 'really' necessary or
staged. The same holds true for the sweeping up of shards and other stage
actions that are necessary and meaningful from a pragmatic point of view but
which, in the light of the theatrical signs' lack of reference to reality, are perceived on an equal footing with the more clearly staged events on stage.

The experience of the real, of the fact that no fictive illusions are created,
is often accompanied by disappointment about the reduction, the apparent

'poverty'. The objections to theatre of this kind concern, on the one hand, the boredom of a purely structural perception. These complaints are as old as modernism itself, their reason being above all the reluctance to engage with new modes of perception. On the other hand, one criticizes the triviality and banality of purely formal games. But ever since the Impressionists offered banal meadows instead of grand subjects and Van Gogh featured simple chairs, it has been evident that the trivial, the reduction to the greatest simplicity, can be an essential prerequisite of the intensification of new modes of perception. Here, too, theatre aesthetics lags behind literary aesthetics. It has been acknowledged by now that the trivial occurrences in Beckett's works are anything but trivial, that their radical reduction rather lets the simplest things shine as for the first time; it has likewise been acknowledged that the pure word collages and everyday scenes in contemporary literature represent an aesthetic quality in their own right. It still proves difficult to accept that only a too limited notion of theatre creates the expectation that it should always present us with a heightened representation of human affairs, that theatre is just as much an art of the body, of space, of time as sculpture or architecture.

More serious is the objection that any strategy of an irruption of the real into the play not only robs it of its 'higher' artistic quality but is morally reprehensible and dishonest. Schechner places the self-mutilations of performance artists on the same level as the infamous 'snuff films' and as gladiator fights, inasmuch as in all these cases 'living beings are reified into symbolic agents. Such reification is monstrous, I condemn it without exception.'[57] Later we shall return to the problem of the reification of the body into signifying material in performance art. Here we continue our reflection by considering that in the postdramatic theatre of the real the main point is not the assertion of the real as such (as is the case in the mentioned sensationalist products of the porn industry) but the unsettling that occurs through the *indecidability* whether one is dealing with reality or fiction. The theatrical effect and the effect on consciousness both emanate from this ambiguity.

Aesthetically and conceptually the real in theatre has always been excluded but it inevitably adheres to theatre. It usually manifests itself only in mishaps. It is only in the form of embarrassing mistakes (related in theatre anecdotes and jokes, the analysis of which would be tempting in this light) that this image of trauma and desire of the theatre, the irruption of the real into the performance, is normally thematized. Theatre is a practice, however, which like no other forces us to realize 'that there is no firm boundary between the aesthetic and the extra-aesthetic realm'.[58] To varying degrees art always contains extra-artistic admixtures from the real – just as, inversely, there are aesthetic factors in the extra-artistic realm (e.g. in crafts). Here a peculiar quality of the aesthetic in general makes itself felt: the somewhat surprising observation that, on closer inspection, the work of art – every work of art, but especially so the theatre – presents itself as a construct made of non-aesthetic materials. Mukařovský states that the work of art:

ultimately presents itself as an *actual accumulation of extra-aesthetic values* and as *nothing but precisely this accumulation*. The material elements of the artistic product and the way in which these are used as creative means appear simply as conductors of the energies embodied in the aesthetic values. If we ask at this moment where the aesthetic value resides, it turns out that it has been dissolved into the individual extra-aesthetic values and is actually nothing but the summary designation for the dynamic totality of its reciprocal relations.[59]

If, in this sense, the 'real' is embedded into the aesthetic to such a degree that the latter can only enter perception 'as itself' through a continuing process of abstraction, then it is not trivial to state that the *aesthetic* process of the theatre cannot be separated from its extra-aesthetic materiality in the same manner as one can distinguish the intentional aesthetic object, the ideatum of a literary text from the materiality of paper and ink. (No, we have not forgotten the insight into the materiality of writing here – not Mallarmé's 'un coup de dés', not the necessary 'espacement' of all signs. But the more specific differences between the materiality of theatre signs and of written signs is not the topic here.) While a written chair is also a material sign, it is precisely not a material chair. By contrast (and this drastic statement has to suffice here) theatre is *at the same time* material process – walking, standing, sitting, speaking, coughing, stumbling, singing – and 'sign for' walking, standing, sitting, etc. Theatre takes place as practice that is at once signifying and entirely real. All theatrical signs are at the same time physically real things: a tree is a cardboard tree, sometimes also a real tree on stage; a chair in Ibsen's Alving house is a real chair on stage that the spectator locates not only in the fictive cosmos of the drama but also in its real spatio-temporal situation onstage.

The potentiated abstractness of the theatrical sign, its characteristic that it is – as is often forgotten – always 'a sign of a sign' (Erika Fischer-Lichte), has two interesting consequences. In a complex manner the signifying nature of theatre points to the *constitution* of meaning in general. For,

> by using the material products of [the respective] culture as its own signs, theatre creates an awareness of the semiotic character of these material creations and consequently identifies the respective culture in turn as a set of heterogeneous systems of generating meaning.[60]

But at the same time theatre thus always reminds us of the space for *new* ways of producing meaning that diverge from the officially licensed rules. It implicitly invites not only performative acts that confer new meanings but also such performative acts that bring about meaning in a new way, or rather: put meaning itself at stake.

This potentiated signifying nature of theatre corresponds to its no less confusing 'uninterpretable' concrete nature. Only through the latter does the aesthetics of the irruption of the real become possible. It is inherent to the constitution of theatre that the real that is literally being masked in and by the theatrical semblance can resurface in it at any moment. Without the real there is no staging. Representation and presence, mimetic play and performance, the represented realities and the process of representation itself: from this structural split the contemporary theatre has extracted a central element of the postdramatic paradigm – by radically thematizing it and by putting the real on equal footing with the fictive. It is not the occurrence of anything 'real' as such but its *self-reflexive* use that characterizes the aesthetic of postdramatic theatre. This self-referentiality allows us to contemplate the value, the inner necessity and the significance of the extra-aesthetic *in* the aesthetic and thus the displacement of the concept of the latter. The aesthetic cannot be understood through a determination of content (beauty, truth, sentiments, anthropomorphizing mirroring, etc.) but solely – as the theatre of the real shows – by 'treading the borderline', by permanently switching, not between form and content, but between 'real' contiguity (connection with reality) and 'staged' construct. It is in this sense that postdramatic theatre means: theatre of the real. It is concerned with developing a perception that undergoes – at its own risk – the 'come and go' between the perception of structure and of the sensorial real.

At this point we witness a displacement that all questions of morality and behavioural norms undergo through theatre aesthetics, in which there is a deliberate suspension of the clear line between reality (where, for instance, the observation of violence leads to feelings of responsibility and the need to intervene) and 'spectatorial event'. For, if it is true that solely the *type of situation* decides about the significance of actions, and that it becomes an essential moment of the experience of theatre that the spectators *themselves* define their situation, then they each also have to take responsibility for the manner of their participation in the theatre. By contrast, the prior *definition* of the situation as 'theatre' (or not) cannot define the status of the actions that is at stake here. Theatre scholars have nevertheless attempted to define theatre from the start and categorically as a 'spectatorial' event, for which the only applicable criterion is whether it takes place before and for an audience. Rightfully, critics have objected to this (overly orderly) attempt at classifying theatre as an event 'for watching' in that it was only valid for as long as one assumed that watching is 'socially and morally unproblematic'.[61] For postdramatic theatre it becomes crucial, however, that this security is removed, and thus also the security of its definition. When in the Vietnam revue *US*, staged by Peter Brook, an apparently live butterfly was burnt, this caused a furore. By now playing with the real has become a widespread practice of new theatre – most of the time not as an immediately political provocation but as a theatrical thematization of theatre – and thereby the role of ethics within it.

When fish are dying on stage, or frogs are (seemingly) squashed, or when it deliberately remains uncertain whether an actor is really being tortured with electric shocks in front of the audience (as was the case in Fabre's *Who Speaks My Thoughts?*), the audience possibly reacts to it as to a real, morally unacceptable incident. Put differently: when the real asserts itself against the staged on stage, then this is mirrored in the auditorium. When the staging practice forces the spectators to wonder whether they should react to the events on stage as fiction (i.e. aesthetically) or as reality (for example, morally), theatre's treading of the borderline of the real unsettles this crucial predisposition of the spectators: the unreflected certainty and security in which they experience being spectators as an unproblematic social behaviour. The question of where exactly the moveable border between 'theatre' and everyday reality runs in the course of a performance appears often enough as a *problem* and thus an object of theatrical design in postdramatic theatre – it is far from being a known factor secured by the definition of theatre. The aesthetic distance of the spectator is a phenomenon of dramatic theatre; in the new forms of theatre that are closer to performance this distance is structurally shaken in a more or less noticeable and provocative way. Wherever this unsettling blurring of boundaries happens in postdramatic theatre, it is invaded by the qualities of a *situation* (in the emphatic sense of the term), even in cases where all in all it seems to belong to the genre of classical theatre with its strict division of stage and theatron (auditorium).

11 *Event/situation*

By analysing a theatre that retracts its signifying character and tends towards a mute gesture, towards exhibiting processes as if to make enigmatic occurrences known for an unknown purpose, we have reached a new level of interrogating the postdramatic use of theatrical signs. Now it is no longer a question of their possible combinations, nor only of the indecidability between signified (the real) and signifier, but a question of the metamorphosis that happens when the signs can no longer be separated from their 'pragmatic' embeddedness in the *event* and the *situation* of theatre in general, when the law that governs the use of signs is no longer derived from representation *within* the frame of this event or from its character as presented reality but from the intention to produce and render possible a communicative event. In this postdramatic theatre of events it is a matter of the execution of acts that are real in the here and now and find their fulfilment in the very moment they happen, without necessarily leaving any traces of meaning or a cultural monument.

There is no need to explain in detail that theatre in this way is in danger of getting close to the insignificant 'event' [English in the original] of advertising and PR talk. This problem will not concern us here as much as its consequent affinity with happenings and performance art. Both are characterized by a loss of meaning of the text and its literary coherence. Both work on the physical, affective and spatial relationship between actors and spectators and explore possibilities of participation and interaction, both highlight presence (the doing in the real) as opposed to re-presentation (the mimesis of the fictive), the act as opposed to the outcome. Thus theatre is defined as a process and not as a finished result, as the activity of production and action instead of as a product, as an active force (energeia) and not as a work (ergon). In this a motif of modernism lives on. The transition of theatre into feast, debate, public action and political manifestation – in short: into the event – was realized by the classical avant-gardes in manifold ways. Yet, the function and meaning of processes that at first glance may seem to be equivalent change deeply with the historical context. If in Russian revolutionary theatre there were political discussions before the performance and dancing afterwards, such expansions of the limits of the 'theatre experience' were a logical conclusion of the total politicization of all areas of life at the time. In their conception of action art, Futurism, Dada and Surrealism were motivated by the desire for a radical 'revaluation of all values' of civilization and for a fundamental revolution of all social conditions. In the context of a different 'logic of its being produced' ('Logik ihres Produziertseins', Adorno), the significance of the 'same' stylistic trait towards an art of the event has to be understood quite differently in postdramatic theatre than in the superficially similar procedures in the avant-garde aesthetic at the beginning of the twentieth century. Nowadays action art has its energetic centre no longer in the demand for changing the world, expressed by social provocation, but instead in the production of *events, exceptions* and moments of *deviation*.

In its American version especially, the happening, too, was initially not an act of political protest, but, as the name indicates, simply a disruption of the everyday, which was perceived as routine, by the fact 'that something happened': theatricalization as a disruption and/or deconstruction – 'Sought after: the gap in the procession.'[62] In the 1960s and 1970s a number of American theatre groups led the way in this direction, political appeals and intentions of cultural revolution still playing a part, however. The Living Theatre, Performance Group, The Wooster Group, Squat Theatre and many others explored happening-like forms of theatre, in which presence and chances of communication were favoured over represented actions. We could think of the performances by Squat Theatre, in which the audience was placed in a shop with large shop windows, the performers combining their presentation of spoken text with all sorts of activities while another audience curiously observed actors and audience through the shop windows from the street. Certainly there always was an element of war against the audience at stake in these forms of theatre, against its 'automated' perception – every form of art that produces new modes of perception wages this war. Yet these forms of theatre also heralded the possibility of separating the new theatre from those political forms that had dominated the experimental scene from the historical avant-gardes until the 1960s: theatrical communication not primarily as a *confrontation* with the audience but as the production of situations for the *self-interrogation, self-exploration, self-awareness* of all participants. The question of whether this represents a depoliticization, a resignation only effective for a short term, or a changed understanding of what politics in theatre can be will, of course, not be settled here.

People often talk about an 'event' as something not to be missed. The philosophical term 'event' (*Ereignis*), however, suggests not so much the sense of appropriation and self-affirmation but the moment of incommensurability. The late Heidegger captures the meaning of the concept of '*Ereignis*' with the pun that it was in essence an '*Ent-eignis*', a kind of dis-appropriation. The event removes certainty and permits the experience of a certain 'indisponibility'. As theatre brings into play its real 'event-ness' for and against the audience, it discovers its capacity to be not only an exceptional kind of event but a provocative situation for all participants. This is why we place the term 'situation' next to the more common term 'event'. This notion is intended to bring into play the context of the thematization of the situation in Existential philosophy (Jaspers, Sartre, Merleau-Ponty). Here the term 'situation' designates an unstable sphere of simultaneously possible and imposed choice, as well as the virtual transformability of the situation. Theatre playfully puts us in a position where we can no longer simply 'face' the perceived but are participating in it, thus accepting, as Gadamer emphasized about the 'situation', that we are in it in such a way that 'we are unable to have any objective knowledge of it'.[63] Apart from the elaboration of the concept by Sartre, the term situation, however, also calls to mind the Situationists. They were concerned with a practice that had at its heart the 'construction of situations' (Guy Debord). In place of artificially manipulated illusory worlds, a situation constructed of concrete materials from everyday life was meant to arise, a challenging environment created for a certain time, in whose context the visitors could become active themselves and discover or develop their creative potential. Last but not least, a higher level of emotional life was meant to be attained in this way.[64] Like the forms of theatre that have the character of an event and like the actions of the Surrealists before them, the procedures of the Situationists – for example, in addition to the constructed situations, the *dérive* (drifting) or *urbanisme unitaire* (unitary urbanism) – attempted to provoke the spectators' own activity with the political aim of revolutionizing social life.

Erving Goffman defines:

> By the term social situation I shall refer to the full spatial environment anywhere within which an entering person becomes a member of the gathering that is (or does then become) present. Situations begin when mutual monitoring occurs and lapse when the penultimate person has left.[65]

A theatre that is no longer spectatorial but instead is a social situation eludes objective description, because for each individual participant it represents an experience that does not match the experience of others. A reversion of the artistic act towards the viewers takes place. The latter are made aware of their own presence and at the same time are forced into a virtual quarrel with the creators of this theatrical process: what is it they want of them? In this way a movement within visual arts reaches the theatre: the reversion from the work to the process, as inaugurated by Marcel Duchamp with the 'real' of the urinal. The aesthetic object hardly has any substance any more but instead functions as a trigger, catalyst and frame for a process on the part of the viewer. Barnett Newman's title *Not There, Here*, which thematizes the presence of the viewer facing the picture, enters the theatre. Only in the sense of the traditional theatre of 'dramatic illusion' is Susanne K. Langer right to consider breaking the 'fourth wall' as 'artistically disastrous' in principle, since, as she points out, 'each person becomes aware not only of his own presence, but also of other people's, too, and of the house, the stage, the entertainment in progress'.[66] For post-dramatic theatre this is precisely where the chance of a change in perception resides.

Theatre becomes a 'social situation' in which the spectator realizes that what s/he experiences depends not just on him/herself but also on others. Inasmuch as the spectator's role comes into play, the basic model of theatre can virtually be turned around. The director Uwe Mengel, for example, rehearses a story with his performers in such a way that the action itself is not performed at all, but instead its 'result' is exhibited in a shop window functioning as the theatre. After a process of intense engagement with the social problems of a particular part of the town, a 'story' is invented that refers to them. The performers intensively familiarize themselves with their role. In the fiction someone is killed, and the shocked friends, mourning relatives, the murderer and all other participants in this fictive story are present in the shop like witnesses, one performer taking on the part of the corpse. The shop door is open and the performance itself consists of the spectators entering and *asking* the players individually about their story, their opinions and feelings, and involving them in conversation. Logically, the spectators get the theatre they 'deserve' individually through their own activity and willingness to communicate. Following visual art, the theatre turns back to the viewer. If some people no longer want to give the name theatre to such a practice situated between 'theatre', performance, visual art, dance and music, we should not hesitate to turn to Brecht, who proposed ironically that when people no longer wished to call his new forms 'theatre', they could call them 'thaetre' instead.

Examples

1 An evening with Jan and his friends

Like many other contemporary theatre practitioners, the Belgian artist Jan Lauwers thinks of himself not simply as a 'director' but as an 'artist' who among other things also happens to make theatre. In 1980 the 'Epigonentheater zlv' ('zonder leiding van' – or 'without guidance of') was founded in Brussels. Jan Lauwers, one of the initiators, was originally a painter; another co-founder of the collective, André Pichal was a musician. Dancers, too, joined the group. The first performances were *Night-illness* in 1981, *Already Hurt and Not Yet War* in 1982, *Simonne la puritaine* in the same year, the demonstration *Vogel Strauss* in 1983, *Boulevard ZLV* in 1984, and *Incident* in 1985. After the foundation of the Needcompany under the direction of Jan Lauwers, *Need To Know*, presented in 1988 at the Frankfurter TAT, was the first work that took up classical text (fragments from Shakespeare's *Antony and Cleopatra*) in a collage of scenes about love and death. This was followed by *Ça va* in 1989, and then in 1990, to the general surprise of critics, by *Julius Caesar*, a production in which, unlike in the previous works, the text played a dominant role. In 1991 Lauwers showed *Invictos* based on texts by Ernest Hemingway, especially *The Snows of Kilimanjaro* (a story in which Hemingway is in turn writing about the writer Scott Fitzgerald), and on E. Hotchner's biography *Papa Hemingway*. As Lauwers confirmed, in his work before *Julius Caesar* the theatre was based mainly on images. And after *Julius Caesar*, too, he again sought a non-dramatic text that he could 'construct' on stage himself, instead of being reduced to the rather dissatisfying role of the director and staging an already created work – which would allow him to do only '50 per cent of the creative work'. Interviewing him, the journalist Gerhard Fischer expressed his utter surprise at the 'conventional', 'linear' representation in *Invictos*, at what he saw as the outmoded method of having a narrator.[67] But a narrator in the context of the postdramatic aesthetic cannot simply be understood as a traditional epic-literary function. His narrating here manifests the direct contact with the audience.

In this theatre of *postepic narration*,[68] one observes often enough that the action (already fragmented and riddled with other materials anyway) appears only in the form of an account being given: narrated, reported, casually communicated. The extent to which the dramatic has disappeared is especially striking whenever death is being staged in Lauwers' work. One of the strongest moments of this theatre is when actors who have just died in the fiction, are very calmly led off the stage by fellow players the next moment: a stage life has finished, the actor remains joined to the others in friendship – one of the recurrent motifs in Lauwers' work. In Hemingway's *The Snows of Kilimanjaro*, a sick man is waiting for his death in the African expanse without resisting it. His leg is gangrenous, the rescue plane is a long time coming, but the man does not want to be rescued anyway. With the woman who wants to keep him alive he leads a conversation punctuated by hatred, tiredness, despair and disgust. The short story is atmospherically dense and heavy with the pathos of an Existentialist coldness; the performance of the Needcompany is relaxed, casual, friendly and full of humour, virtually contenting itself with only citing the hard edges of the story. All elements of action that drive the personal in Hemingway's work into the typically 'Spanish' drama are omitted (ironically, at the beginning a model of a mighty Spanish fighting bull is rolled from centre stage to the margins). Despite a calculated and rehearsed staging, the (seeming) relaxedness of the performers, the abandoning of a closed action, and the disruption of spoken and read dialogue through the insertion of little dance numbers mean that the isolation of the stage process is continually prised open. When theatre presents itself as a sketch and not as a finished painting, the spectators are given the chance to feel their own presence, to reflect on it, and to contribute to the unfinished character themselves. The price for this is the consequent depreciation of suspense. The spectator concentrates all the more on the physical actions and presence of the players. As almost always in Lauwers' works, the described evening speaks of death, of its terror, and of loss – but it does so mildly, as if from the other side of death. The model: we are watching a party, but the door is not quite open. We therefore look in on it as though on a party of distant acquaintances, without really participating. One could say: the spectator spends an evening at Jan's and his friends (not 'with' them).

2 Narrations

The principle of *narration* is an essential trait of postdramatic theatre; the theatre becomes the site of a narrative act. (Occasionally this can also be observed in film: *My Dinner with André* consists of almost nothing else but André Gregory talking about his work with Jerzy Grotowski over dinner.) One often feels as though one is witnessing not a scenic representation but a narration of the play presented. Here the theatre is oscillating between extended passages of narration and only interspersed episodes of dialogue; the main things are the description and the interest in the peculiar act of the *personal* memory/narration of the actors. This is related in a form of theatre that is categorically different from epic theatre and the epicization of fictional events, even though it shows some similarity to those forms. Since the 1970s, performance and theatre practitioners have found the meaning of theatre work in giving preference to *presence* over representation, in as much as it is about the communication of *personal experience*. In *WYSIWYG* (what you see is what you get), a theatre project conducted in 1989 by Frankfurt students under the direction of Renate Lorenz and Jochen Becker, the everyday reality of the participants – going shopping, making their way to the university, visiting the dentist, meeting with friends, etc. – was 'made present' in all manner of different forms (picture, diary, photo, film, played dialogue). In this way, an anti-media-effect was achieved through mediated presentation and a highly conscious use of media: the presence of the actors keeps theatre in the proximity of the personal encounter, unlike the arbitrary exhibitions of biographical 'realities' in the confessional shows of television. It was therefore part of the conception of this project that the evening of narration was concluded with a collective celebration in the same room that had been used for performance.

Lost in the world of media, narration finds a new site in theatre. It is no coincidence that performers rediscover the telling of fairy tales in the process. Bernhard Minetti realized a memorable evening (directed by Alfred Kirchner) in which he performed all alone as a storyteller of Grimms' fairy tales on the.stage of the Schillertheater. In a performance by the Danish company Von Heiduck – famed for works exploring eros, its uncannyness and potential for anxiety by means of dance, gesture and scenic design – the dancing suddenly stops and for about half an hour a man retells Hans Christian Andersen's *The Metal Pig* in a monotonous, calm and undramatic voice. This is a surprising coup in an evening of theatre which, through a mixture of Hollywood film music quotes and provocative erotic gestures of self-staging, tells with 'silent' means of the seduction and loneliness of sexualized bodies. The moment of narration returns to the stage and asserts itself against the fascination of bodies *and* of media.[69]

The works of the Societas Raffaello Sanzio by the Castelucci siblings not only let tragedy become a scary fairy tale (*Oresteia*) that also has space for motifs from *Alice in Wonderland*, but in *Buccetino* (Tom Thumb) also place the spectators in children's cots where they listen to the amplified voice of a female narrator situated in the middle of the room (as well as to all sorts of noises from outside). Political theatre like that of the company Bread and Puppet narrates the great stories, the parables of the Bible and the allegories, with the help of schematizations in the vein of the Commedia dell'Arte and with the use of puppets. It takes the narrator figure from epic theatre and therefore keeps to the narration of a world. Yet, while epic theatre changes the representation of the fictive events represented, distancing the spectators in order to turn them into assessors, experts and political judges, the post-epic forms of narration are about the foregrounding of the *personal*, not the demonstrating presence of the narrator, about the self-referential intensity of this contact: about the closeness within distance, not the distancing of that which is close.

3 Scenic poem

Lauwers' work reintroduces the fictive reality of the play or narration into the reality of the stage; the players, often behaving in a seemingly private, informal way, 'inhabit' the stage. Even inhabiting their role, they do not create the illusion of being fictional characters. Time and again, they interrupt their play addressing their gaze directly to the audience, who thus find themselves included into the theatre moment. This takes over the whole stage process. As in Jan Fabre's work, what is originally a performance impulse is captured in a theatrical form that undermines the categorization narrative/non-narrative. Lauwers injects into the theatre an especially heightened sense for that which is ephemeral and destined to die. Theatre to him is an irretrievable moment of communication. Accentuating the momentary, his works are united by an independent stage aesthetic brought to the theatre by the visual artist: the visual details, gestures, colours and light structures, the materiality of things, costumes and spatial relations, together with the exposed bodies form a complex web of allusions and echoes. In spite of its seemingly accidental nature and accepted imperfection, this web forms a deliberate *composition*.

In the course of Lauwers' artistic development we can discern a progression or at least a bipolarity of his works: here the works that are more focused on the creation of a contact situation, there the ones in which the autonomous stage reality is more pervasive. The configuration of the elements text and body, which is rich in tension, at the same time forms manifold reflections in conjunction with the objects: light and object, ice, water and blood; splinters, wounds and 'hashed up' language. In this postdramatic stage space, bodies, gestures, movements, postures, timbre, volume, tempo and the pitch of voices are torn from their familiar spatio-temporal continuum and newly connected. The stage becomes a complex whole of associative spaces composed like 'absolute poetry'. One could read Lauwers' theatre, in the sense of Rimbaud and Mallarmé, as a new kind of aesthetic alchemy, in which all staging means join into a poetic 'language'. Texts are combined with the gestures and physicality of the performers. At the same time the fragmentation and collage of different moments of action ensure that instead of the (epic) attention on the course of actions (narrated and played out), the focus is entirely on the presence of the performers and the mutual reflections and analogies. Thus a lyrical dimension develops, in the sense of Mallarmé's famous comparison: in the poetic formation the words are meant to reinforce each other through their mutual reflections and analogies as in a diamond that sparkles because the rays of light in it are refracted over and over again.

An example: in the context of texts and scenes that refer back to the time around 1900, the following aesthetic and highly significant action happens in Lauwers' *Snakesong Trilogy III*: downstage a young woman, being anxiously observed by the audience and by other actors, is very slowly and very systematically building an insecurely balanced, fragile and dangerous looking pyramid of delicate pieces of glass. The danger of injury, the seemingly 'decadent' eroticism and the extreme self-referentiality of the process are attuned in form and content to the utilized 'aestheticist' texts by Mallarmé, Huysmanns and Wilde. The spectator believes himself to be looking at an unknown 'text' in enigmatic hieroglyphs. The human being, the physical gesture, flesh and glass, matter and space form a purely scenic figuration, the spectator taking on the role of a reader who gathers the human, spatial, tonal signifiers scattered across the stage. Such formations/processes situated in between poetry, theatre and installation are best characterized as *a scenic poem*. Like a poet, the director composes fields of association between words, sounds, bodies, movements, light and objects.

4 Between the arts

Heiner Goebbels' creations of '*scenic concerts*' and the multiform theatre pieces he realizes as a composer, director, arranger and 'collagist of texts' are about the interaction of complex spatial arrangements, light, video and other visual material with musical and linguistic practices such as song, recital, instrumental performance and dance. This takes place partly in gigantic dimension (*Surrogate Cities*), partly in small forms, as for example the combination of one speaker, one musician (Goebbels himself) and a vocal artist in *The Liberation of Prometheus* (based on Heiner Müller). In these forms of play the reflection onto the possibility of the interaction of different artists in the frame of a performance is central. The actual theme, however, is the bringing together of different theatre languages (acting, making music, installation, light, poetry, singing, dancing, etc.) that have otherwise become disintegrated. Goebbels' theatre contains the dream of another theatricality that would rather risk the proximity to artistic forms of entertainment than to heavyweight *Bildungstheater* (highbrow cultural theatre). It is postdramatic not only through the absence of drama but especially through the emphasized autonomy of musical, spatial and theatrical levels of creation. On stage the latter first develop their intrinsic value and only then their function in combination with other elements. Goebbels reports, for example, that in the production of *Newton's Casino*, a collaboration with Michael Simon, many impulses for the theatrical work came from a spatial conception by Simon, and that in *Or the Hapless Landing* the diagonal designed by Magdalena Jetelovà became a formative principle of composition for the whole staging by the way in which the perspectives, vanishing lines and angle of the space reflected on the scenic work. In *Black and White*, in *The Repetition* and in other works it can hardly be decided any more what the driving force for the staging is: whether thematic (or philosophical) impulses, stage installations (Erich Wonder), successions of movement or the personalities of certain actors, singers or musicians.

A number of other works are closely related to these experiments, as for example the stage installations with text and music by Michael Simon (with whom Goebbels collaborated on a number of productions), *Narrative Landscape* for instance, whose title doubly indicates the non-dramatic character of the work: by stressing the visual openness of a field and the narration instead of the representation. Here one could witness the interaction of a singer, a horse and glass props in a space whose expansion and structure became virtually indefinable through a clever lighting design. While the stage here comes close to a painting, Goebbels' installation in 1997 for the Documenta X in Kassel proceeded from the 'stage' of an urban architectural 'scene', an unfinished bridge in Kassel's city centre. Pictorial signs, actions, gesture, text and music were used here – a combination which the audience (placed under the bridge) experienced with a certain insecurity as to where the staged work began and ended: environment, installation, open air concert and theatre in one. A title like *Actor, Dancer, Songstress* (by Gisela von Wysocki), for which Axel Manthey created a staging, exemplarily expresses the 'between' of postdramatic theatre: it is about the interaction of the performers and not that of the abstract artistic principles; about the 'between' as a mutual reaction of the different modes of representation, not their addition; not about multi media sensations but an experience that cuts across these effects. In 2003 Heiner Goebbels' stage- and video work *Eraritjaritjaka* found an especially broad resonance worldwide. Here the audience assumes for a long time that scenes from a house in the city are transmitted by video until they discover that all is taking place just in front of them on stage behind the façade of a house front.

5 Scenic essay

Works that offer a public reflection on particular themes instead of a dramatic action are symptomatic for the landscape of postdramatic theatre. 'Theoretical', philosophical or theatre aesthetic texts are dragged out of their familiar abode in the study, university or theatre studies course and presented on stage – by no means without an awareness of the fact that the audience might tend to think that the actors ought to devote themselves to such occupations *before* the performance. Companies and directors use the means of theatre to 'think aloud' publicly or to make theoretical prose heard. In works that use theatre texts one can also find that the actors seem to be more engrossed in the debate about their subject and its representation than in the actual presentation of it. In the works of the company Matschapij Discordia, for example, one witnesses a public debate among the actors about their subject rather than its staging. Such transitions to a form that could be described as a theatrical or *scenic essay* incidentally represent the reverse of the noticeably increased attempts to theatricalize the teaching processes in schools and universities. The reminder that the use of the stage for such purposes, which at first sight seem alien to it, can also widen the possibilities for theatre tempers our consternation at such attempts.

The mention of the genre of the scenic essay may call to mind Bazon Brock (*Unterstoberst* and *Pfingstpredigt*), *Shakespeare's Memory* at the Berliner Schaubühne or *Elvire Jouvet* by Giorgio Strehler. As a mixture of theatre and essay two works by Peter Brook are interesting in this context: *The Man Who . . .?* (based on Oliver Sacks' bestseller *The Man Who Mistook His Wife for a Hat*) and *Who Is There?* The former presented examples of pathological dysfunctions of perception, the latter the maxims of famous theatre teachers, their anecdotes, mini treatises and descriptions. In both cases the performers acted in a cheerfully relaxed atmosphere, agreed on certain scenes in front of the audience, conversed and debated as in a seminar, addressed themselves directly to the spectators and interspersed the theory with scenes of demonstration or exemplary speeches of dramatic figures. In Christoph Nel's *About the Gradual Elaboration of Thoughts while Speaking* based on Kleist, the theatre was the topic of a playfully theoretical, scenic exploration of Kleist's ideas. Philosophy was playfully and scenically explored in performances like *Symposium* and *Phaidros* at the Berliner Schaubühne. The staging of Plato's texts in the 1990s, the essay *The Night* (by Hans Jürgen Syberberg and Edith Clever) created from a montage of quotes, the realization of theatre projects with texts by Freud or Nietzsche (notably Einar Schleef's last grand performance of Nietzsche's *Ecce Homo* in 2000) – all these demonstrate the obvious establishment of a genre of the scenic essay at the end of the twentieth century, at the beginning of which Edward Gordon Craig had conceived of a performance, never realized at the time, of all of Plato's *Dialogues*.

One can place this 'genre' of scenic theatre essays in the 'tradition' of Molière's *Impromptu de Versailles* and Brecht's *Messingkauf*, in so far as they revolve around the theatre itself. If one wanted to emphasize their seemingly effortless, sketch-like nature and provisional construction instead of laborious commentary, one should also mention the works of Jean Jourdheuil, many in collaboration with Jean-François Peyret and with set designs by Gilles Aillaud (who also created many spaces for Grüber). Jourdheuil earned himself a reputation with his – literary and scenic – translations of works by Heiner Müller into French and as a director can be credited with a number of elegant, witty and precise productions of Müller's texts (*Hamletmaschine/Mauser*, *Description of a Picture . . .*, *La Route des chars* and others). Some of these were situated in between a production of and a theatre essay about Müller due to their ironic, reflective character. To these we have to add the Müller evenings organized by Jourdheuil at the Odéon theatre in the presence of the author, who read from his texts. As in Jourdheuil's other productions (e.g. *Robespierre* or *Shakespeare, the Sonnets*), there was no pathos and no unbroken identification here. Its quoting and demonstrating mode characterizes Jourdheuil's theatre as post-Brechtian. Even though his playful elegance contrasts with Müller's toughness, severity and apodictic laconism, this theatre aesthetic combines surprisingly well with that *écriture* because it accentuates the non-dramatic, scenic potential for reflection: emblematic and contemporary 'thought-images' ('Denkbilder', to quote Walter Benjamin) in the theatrical form of scenic essays.

6 'Cinematographic theatre'

That a distinct formalism is one of the stylistic traits of postdramatic theatre does not require extended demonstration. There are the theatre works of a Wilson and a Foreman, the forms of dance theatre modelled on the geometric, machinic structuralism of 'postmodern dance' (Merce Cunningham), or the tendency of younger directors to play with reduced formal structures. Language is offered in a quasi-mechanical manner, gesture and kinesis are organized according to formal patterns beyond meaning, the performers seem to exhibit distanced (but not alienating) techniques of the gaze, of movement and stasis, techniques that capture the gaze but frustrate the hunger for meaning. An epitome of 'formalist theatre', as Michel Kirby has aptly baptized this wide field of the new theatre, is the concrete theatre of Jan Fabre, with its coldness and purely geometric structure unthinkable even in Wilson's work. Another example is the theatre of the Puerto Rican, New York based director, playwright and designer John Jesurun, which critics have baptized 'cinematographic theatre'. Stage space here mostly lacks any sets, as it is cleverly structured by surfaces of light between which the individual sequences switch in rapid succession. We can speak of 'sequences' here because this theatre explores the relationship between theatre and film. Slightly modified, film dialogues are imported into the theatre, the principle of cut and montage is radicalized. One can hardly follow the strand of an action, even though rudiments and fragments of stories flash up time and again. A quasi-robotic, rapid manner of speaking leaves no place for dramatic concepts of individuality, character and story. One faces a kaleidoscope of visual and verbal aspects of a story which is only very partially known. The impression of a collage and montage – videographic, filmic, narrative – blocks the perception of dramatic logic. The texts written by Jesurun himself correspond to this style. They are rapid, rich in punch lines, and often allude to the model of film dialogues. In *Rider without a Horse*, which revolves around the absurd situation that one member of a family has unfortunately turned into a wolf, there is a long dispute about the aggressiveness of wolves. In fact it is a dialogue from Hitchcock's thriller *The Birds*, in which an ornithologist vehemently denies that birds can attack people (while this is already happening) – Jesurun's text has just replaced the birds with wolves.

Jesurun originally trained as a sculptor before he came to the theatre via the desire to make films. For him theatre is like making a film without actually shooting it. With the help of rapid switches between the 'locations', marked out through lighting and props within even the tightest of spaces, the tempo of film cuts is introduced into the theatre. Jesurun worked in television for years, and this experience is even more noticeable in his theatre than the model of film. He partially models the performance mode on the television serial, too: in 1982 he started presenting theatre in weekly 'episodes', a peculiar series of sequels with the Hitchcock inspired title *Chang in a Void Moon* – an ongoing enterprise that has produced more than 50 often 'feature-length' sequels with more than 30 different actors. The tendency towards the filmic and the mediated is also accentuated through the technical reproduction of the performers through video images with whom they seem to be communicating. When their own, sometimes overly large image is involved, the speech acts addressed to the images inevitably thematize the 'self' of the performers. They speak with their image, with 'themselves' as if with a larger than life, controlling figure. Since they have to time their own speaking exactly with the previously recorded text of the video tapes, the body becomes strangely machinized, and at the same time the technological image becomes strangely alive. Along the way, the classical theatre ideology of presence and liveness is dismantled through the perpetual interweaving of mediated and personal presence. In *White Water* (1986) this structure serves to bring into play the ghostly dimensions of the virtual in a theatrical way. It revolves around a boy who claims to have had a mystical apparition; in his description he gets embroiled in unsustainable contradictions but, unmoved by the rational incompatibilities of his representation, he keeps insisting on his 'version' of his experience. While 'dramatic' situations do appear in the dialogues of Jesurun's theatre, these remain fragments the spectator has to spin out. The figures appear as de-psychologized speaking machines and thus negate the conventions of both theatre and cinema, which is formally cited. Through the cinematographic procedure this theatre without drama paradoxically becomes all the more 'theatre'. Despite the interweaving of many levels, the 'rhizome' of media images, apparatuses, structures of light and performers does not fall apart. It is kept together by the formal rigour and by the spoken text. Thus the spoken language, which is devalued as individual psychological characterization, assumes the role of a constitutive, connecting element binding the whole performance together.

7 Hypernaturalism

The economic and ideological power of the cinematographic and electronic industry of images has succeeded in making the most platitudinous idea of what art can or ought to be prevail – namely perfect reproduction or 'simulation'; it has allowed the trivial attraction of the illusion of realities to assume theoretical dignity. Art defends itself against this atrophy with deliberate manoeuvres of esoterism, provocation, refusal and 'negativity', as Adorno has most pointedly argued. Since their massive spread the photographic media have promoted the Naturalist ideology as the most natural thing, so to speak, while the interest in stylization, alienation (*Verfremdung*), distancing or heightening – in short, interest in the peculiarity of the *forms* of art as ways of reflecting and/in presenting – has dwindled. Art forms and genres are hardly perceived as realities in their own right any more but merely as different modes of consumption ('the book accompanying the film'), as vehicles for the only interesting thing – the story. In a letter written to Schiller in 1797, Goethe remarked that as soon as people had read a novel they wanted to see it in the theatre (today it would be on television or in the cinema), likewise they instantly wanted to see literary descriptions as images – 'etched in copper'.[70] He complained that all this was also promptly delivered, 'because the artists, who actually ought to create the works of art within their pure conditions, give in to the desire of the spectators and auditors to *find everything completely true*'. And 'just so that there is no effort left to their imagination, everything is meant to be true to the senses, entirely present; everything is meant to be dramatic, and the dramatic itself is meant to stand side by side with the real reality'.[71]

With respect to Naturalistic reproduction, there is a fundamental difference between film, on the one hand, and theatre and literature, on the other. What becomes crucial for the theatre is a trait it shares with literature: that it does not represent/reproduce but signifies. The theatre image has a low 'density', so to speak; it exhibits lots of gaps where the photographic image is without gaps. Here the same difference applies that Adorno observed between film and text: 'The less dense reproduction of reality in Naturalist literature left room for intentions: in the unbroken duplication achieved by the technical apparatus of film every intention, even that of truth, becomes a lie.'[72] In other words: 'Radical naturalism to which the technique of film lends itself would dissolve all surface coherence of meaning and finish up as the anti-thesis of the familiar realism.'[73] For commercial reasons, film in the tradition of Lumière began to contradict its own Naturalist premises at the moment that it brought meaning, perspective, intention to the reproduction of reality.

In postdramatic theatre there is now a return to *Naturalist* stylistic traits, which after epic, absurdist, poetic and formalist theatre seemed to have the least chance of a future. (If one wanted to follow Baudrillard's radicalism, the old question of original image and represented image would by now be altogether obsolete. If only the 'simulacrum' remains, which can be understood as an artificial production of original images, then the real cannot be differentiated from a perfectly functioning simulacrum in any way, Naturalism is no longer an issue.) Naturalism can be found in theatre forms where, at first glance, nothing more is being offered than a more or less entertaining reproduction of everyday life. However, the new forms of a heightened and reflected Naturalism have to be distinguished from the 'pseudo-realism of the culture industry' (Adorno). What may have seemed to be Naturalistic in the theatre since the 1970s – probably also under the impression of photorealism – actually represents a form of *derealization*, not of the perfection of reproduction. Werner Schwab wrote plays in

which the milieu of depravity, small-mindedness and petty bourgeois parochial-
ism in an everyday life described with caricaturistic precision gives birth to
meaningless violence as a ritual of horror. Realism once 'discovered' drama in
the seemingly uneventful everyday life of normal citizens, in conversation, in the
humdrum existence of the lower classes. Theatre, including the realist and Naturalistic theatre, was defined not only by representing that which had been
repressed by 'respectable society' but also by elevating and surpassing real life
through the form of drama. The new Naturalism of the 1980s and 1990s offers
situations that exhibit a grotesque decay and absurdity. Certainly, there is also a
heightening of reality in the new theatre works, but this time the heightening
occurs downward: where the toilets are, the scum, that is where we find the
figure of the scapegoat, the pharmakos. The lowest is not, as in the earlier Naturalism, the truth, the real that has to be revealed because it has been hidden and
repressed. Rather the lowest is now the new 'sacred', the proper truth, that
which explodes norms and rules: 'dépense' (Georges Bataille), *going for broke* in
drugs, dereliction and ridicule. The misdeeds that happen in the banality of
parochial everyday life here take on the significance of the 'other', of the exception, of the monstrous and unheard of, of ecstasy. Because of this 'charging' of
banal and trivial reality it would be misleading to see in this only a new Naturalism. Rather, the term *hypernaturalism* is preferable, as it makes reference to the
concept of 'hyperrealism' that Baudrillard used to designate a non-referential,
media produced, heightened resemblance of things to themselves, not the ade-
quacy of images to the real.

In the hypernaturalist scene modelled on TV scenes of everyday life a *phan-
tastic vision* can break forth without commentary or interpretation. Trivial,
utopian images of desire of great intensity emerge. In *Moeder en Kind*, a performance by the Belgian theatre company Victoria, the confined lodgings of the
sub-proletarians transform into a fairytale-like and crazy pop dreamland where
the individual figures express their deepest longings in pop songs and rock
music. In *81 Minutes* Lothar Trolle stages the everyday life of shop assistants in a
department store, in such a way that their tales and little conflicts suddenly give
rise to utopian desire. The sudden change from everydayness into the *absurd*
occurs frequently in these more-than-realistic forms of theatre: the narrated
experiences or events become increasingly improbable and are marked by
grotesque comedy, as in the texts by René Pollesch that are inspired by the style
of television. From everyday scenes bizarre events emerge (Werner Schwab).
Similar tendencies can be observed in plays by Wolfgang Bauer, Kroetz, Fass-
binder (*Katzelmacher*, *Bremer Freiheit*), Turrini, Vinaver, Michel Deutsch and
others. In this theatrical hypernaturalism without Naturalist drama, the world
that exists under the surface is not brought to light through a dramaturgy of
revelation and interpreted socially but instead manifests itself in poetic and
visual ecstasies of the imagination.

In other contexts, Jean-Pierre Sarrazac has used the term 'hypernaturalism'.
With critical intention, he states that many theatre pieces cultivate a hypernaturalism in the sense of a Naturalism 'of the second degree'. In the course of it, the

lower worlds take on the attraction of the exotic that is offered for consumption.[74] Indeed Naturalism was, as Brecht criticized most trenchantly, a drama of pity. Although the cult of sympathy has become problematic as an *ersatz* emotion (because social change is called for, not inconsequential tears), ultimately *all* dramatic representation implicitly calls for empathy, sympathy, commiseration and compassion with the simulated fate of the simulated figure embodied by the actor. Now, however, the tragic or grotesque/tragic-comic dramaturgy – as it was still practised by Dürrenmatt or Frisch when they thought only comedy could still cope with the world – is replaced by an astonishing 'de-pathization'[75] in the exhibition of 'the lower life'. The word 'cool' suggests itself for the characterization of a whole genre of theatre forms. *Playing with coldness* constitutes one of the significant traits of postdramatic theatre. We repeatedly come across a tendency towards 'disinvolvement' and ironic, sarcastic distance. Moral indignation does not take place where it would have been expected; likewise dramatic excitation is lacking, even though reality is depicted in ways that are obviously hard to bear. It would be too simple to moralize this observation by concluding that the creators of this theatre are socially insensitive. Likewise it would remain superficial to trace the lack of a precise socially targeted satire in theatre to a blindness associated with the ideological and emotional world of the petty bourgeoisie.[76] Rather the new theatre has to be understood in the context of the comprehensive virtualization of reality and the widespread penetration of all perception by the grid of the media. In the face of the formative power and hardly avoidable mass dissemination of mediatized reality, most artists see no way out other than to 'graft' their own work onto the existing models, rather than to undertake the seemingly hopeless attempt of finding entirely divergent 'personal' artistic formulations in a mediatized world. But as the mediatized clichés creep into any representation, seriousness is on its last legs, too. Cool is the name for emotionality that has lost its 'personal' expression to such an extent that all feelings can be expressed only in quotation marks, and all emotions that drama was once able to show must now pass through the 'irony filter' of a film and media aesthetic.

8 Cool Fun

In the 1980s and 1990s, the new generation of theatre practitioners searched almost violently for a 'real' that could provoke through the renunciation of form and be an adequate expression for a saddened but also desperately psyched-up sense of life. Theatre here mimics and reflects the omnipresent media and their suggestion of immediacy, but at the same time searches for another form of a sub-public. Behind an ostensible exuberance, melancholia, loneliness and despair become perceivable. This conspicuous variety of postdramatic theatre often finds its inspiration in the patterns of television and film entertainment and makes references (irrespective of quality) to splatter movies, quiz shows, commercials and disco music, but also to a classical intellectual heritage. At the same time this theatre registers the state of mind of its mostly young spectators – their feelings of resignation, rebellion and sadness, and their desire for happiness and to live life intensely. These theatre forms – often hardly theatre any more – are probably responding to a basic sense of an infinite lack of future prospects, which cannot be covered up even by the most forcible assertion of 'fun' in the now. It seems that the strangely static state of the social (despite the transformations through world politics since 1989) can hardly be resisted by the arts head on but only through an attitude of deviating and turning away. This lays the foundation for *Cool Fun* as an aesthetically thriving attitude. We will hardly find dramatic actions here but more likely playful imitations of scenes and constellations from crime novels, television series or films. When 'action' does happen, it is in order to show that it lacks interest. Theatre reflects the disintegration of experience into minute bits of time and impulses, as much as the dominance of mediated experience.

Corresponding to the fun, there is a tendency towards parody, which was already noticeable in the Theatre of the Absurd. Parody has always lent itself to the opening of the theatre process in order to return the theatre from the status of an object to the experience of a communal process that ultimately does not allow for an interpreting distance. Parody is one variety of the forms of intertextuality differentiated in detail by Genette.[77] The *audience is theatricalized*, as the awareness of other texts (images, sounds) is evoked and the appropriation of parody is confirmed through laughter – cabaret and comedy thrive on this form of interaction just like Cool Fun. Moreover, in parody the degree of its distance towards the quoted remains open. Of course references to the lived world are already inscribed in the simplest act of reception – I only recognize that for which I can find an analogous schema within my horizon of experience. Yet what counts from the point of view of theatre aesthetics is whether this fact is being 'actualized', whether the inclusion of the personal horizon in the aesthetic intention and in the spectators' perception is explicit or merely latent. The spectator follows a course of allusions, citations and counter-citations, insider jokes, motifs from cinema and pop music, a patchwork of rapid, often minute episodes: ironically distanced, sarcastic, 'cynical', without illusion and 'cool' in tone. Even the most obvious corny joke is preferable to the intolerable and dishonest 'seriousness' of public and official rhetoric. Réné Pollesch, Stefan Pucher or the company Gob Squad are German and English examples of the attempt to search tenaciously for contemporary connections of media technology and live actors in this spirit. They articulate dreams in 'speeding standstill' (Paul Virilio) that operate without a dramatic context in a rather associative or pop-lyrical manner. (Texts by the beat and pop influenced poet Rolf Dieter Brinkmann have repeatedly been translated into scenic works by Stefan Pucher.)

Part of this theatre is a new boom of *club culture*: in new forms of living room theatre (the announcement circulates among friends and acquaintances, the spectators are invited directly into one's own living room), in theatre arrangements that produce direct contact with the audience.

In tenement blocks, backyards and deserted industrial parks there are spaces that are transitory zones: actually dwelling places but at the same time galleries, bars and happening sites. These clubs and meeting places are ephemeral installations, afraid of the mainstream, idylls off the beaten track. They last as long as the fun in them lasts.[78]

The expressive forms of 'club culture' unite 'the trivial culture of the tasteless majority, the mass commodity, socialist advertising art and postwar baroque, superman and candlelight'.[79] Ostentatious kitsch, solidarity with the taste of the masses, rebellion and a thirst for fun are combined here. Most of the time there is hardly any action on the level of scenic realization. More often, the accent is on incidental and insignificant situations: parties, TV shows, encounters in a club. From within these situations fantasies, experiences, anecdotes, jokes are told. With the help of slide projectors, photos, acted out scenes, re-enacted dialogues, videos and sound recordings, show elements and narration, all manner of things falling between aggressive triviality and marginalized intelligence are presented.

The company Gob Squad from Nottingham plays not in theatres but in offices, galleries and car parks. The youthful, urban aesthetic here reflects the closeness and distance between people in often baffling ways. In *Close Enough To Kiss*, the actors are locked in a long room behind one-way mirrors, in which they exhibit themselves in a desperate, and at the same time hilarious manner, to the audience outside. It is a matter of 'radically epic theatre', if one wants to use this term. Except that there is no author, only a number of sometimes hardly individually characterized 'average people' who through a 'role' in a fictive stage world display themes and gestures that are largely fed and mediated by secondary media perception. In the course of the performance the relentless fun tends towards the sarcastic, ironic exhibition of obscenity, everyday violence, loneliness and sexual desire, combined with the ironic citation and use of popular culture. We could also cite here the projects of young theatre practitioners from the Institute for Applied Theatre Studies (Angewandte Theaterwissenschaft) in Giessen, projects where collective work and a basic 'cool' atmosphere come together. The combination of theatre situations with youth club culture happens for example in the work of groups like Showcase Beat Le Mot. Theatre is outbid or undercut by forms of contact, as in the collective She She Pop's *Warum tanzt ihr nicht?* (*Why Don't You Dance?*) where audience and actors negotiate what is to be played; or as in Felix Ruckert's *Hautnah* where the audience initially gather in a place with the atmosphere of a bar from where each spectator is led to 'choose' one of the dancers who then performs '*hautnah*', up close and personal, just for them in separated rooms, involving them in interactive communication.

The relaxed evenings with BAK-Truppen from Bergen (Norway), in turn, create an atmosphere of intense and cordial participation because the company makes theatre nearly 'invisible'. The audience hardly glimpses what it is about but the personal habitus of the work creates a situation of theatrical communication *between* the public and the private. Moments of seemingly improvised dilettantism (hopping more than dancing), eye contact with the spectators, interruptions in the performance, proximity with the spectators created through an (apparent) lack of professionalism, and the almost complete lack of a structure enfolding the actions all let a *feeling of community* come about. Literature here provides the cues: in 1989 Heiner Müller's *Germania. Death in Berlin*, in 1990 Ibsen's *When We Dead Awaken*, in 1991 *Peer, du lügst. – Ja* based on *Peer Gynt*. Most of the time a playful self-alteration or risk is built into the performances: for example, all players are wearing defamiliarizing, overly blue ('true') contact lenses (in the production about the liar Peer Gynt) or they suck helium into their lungs, thereby temporarily altering their voices grotesquely, or they set off small explosives attached to their own bodies (as worn by movie actors to simulate the impact of bullets).

Especially in the Netherlands and in Belgium a vital theatre culture of companies has emerged who also perform in big theatres and cultural centres and are seen as equal to the established traditional theatres. It is mostly young actors and spectators who gather around companies like Dito, Dito, t'Barre Land, Toneelgezelschap Dood Pard or Theater Antigone. The performances are characterized by a peculiar mixture of school theatre atmosphere, party mood and folk theatre. The players saunter in leisurely fashion onto the stage, chatting, glancing at the audience, muttering things to each other, seemingly agreeing on something. Then it may gradually become clear that they are in the middle of allocating roles. Jokes, within the play or outside of it, private conversations and a mode of acting that does not want to cover up the lack of professionalism: all this converges into scenes that can in turn be interrupted again. The use of props, the attitude, the manner of speaking: everything remains at once relaxed, defamiliarized and epic (all performers 'demonstrate' their figures and only rarely insert stylized identificatory scenes); throughout, the performance is addressed to the audience. The dramatic text, fragmented and played in a manner adapted to the experiential world of young people, is rigorously used as material for representing one's own worries and concerns – for example a conflict between king and prince (Shakespeare's *Henry IV* has been chosen purely as a characteristic example) to represent the conflict between parents and children. The objective is not the quality of the appropriation of a classical text but *unthreatening theatre* as a social event. We can recognize laboratories of an enormous vitality here: theatre without drama (even if it is made use of) and without the overwhelming burden of a tradition rich in dramatic literature (as in Germany). Perhaps we should ask why this kind of phenomenon should be discussed here at all when there can be no doubt that much of it cannot live up to higher artistic demands of depth and form. The answer is: because this search for modes of expression and behaviour beyond established practices is still superior to most routinized productions – even taking into account the frequent failure of its artistic means. For apart from the noticeable pleasure in theatrical play, these performances vividly communicate sadness, compassion and anger at social and political conditions, and a desire to communicate in new ways. Even as 'bad' *art* they are often better *theatre* than the artistically and technically 'good' theatre. It is from these theatre moments situated somewhere between pop and seriousness, rather than from the polished routine of the presentation of classics, that we can in the future expect new modes of theatre practice and new ways of dealing with literature.

Looking at the established theatre most comparable to this 'scene', the Berliner Volksbühne, one realizes that, even for a theatre fully resourced with all artistic competences, one must not underestimate how much there is to be gained by deliberately lowering standards. Through obvious provocation it becomes possible here to assert theatre not at its cultural or 'dramatic' high level but as a live moment of public debate. The work of the Berliner Volksbühne is surrounded by an atmosphere of politicized discussion and formations of like-minded people. Frank Castorf remarked in the programme notes to his production *Golden fließt der Stahl* at the Berliner Volksbühne that it was a special characteristic of artists from the former GDR, unlike their West European postmodern counterparts, that they considered themselves, 'however ironically', as 'failed politicians' making a contribution to ideology. (In this context we should not forget to mention the phenomenon of Christoph Schlingensief, whose actions, located somewhere between pop, Dada, Surrealism, politics and media theatre, were able to achieve a remarkable public and media presence.) In a clever mode of triviality, Frank Castorf's productions relate theatre to colportage and banality and in this way articulate a witty – though occasionally simply silly – rebellion, which is, however, becoming increasingly artistically weak and hollow as the distance from its 'origins' in the former GDR grows.

9 Theatre of 'shared' space

A particular radicalization of the non-mimetic principle in postdramatic theatre can be found in the work of Angelus Novus. The well-documented works of this company[80] and – after its break-up – the productions and workshops by Josef Szeiler (e.g. in Berlin, London, Tokyo, and Argos in Greece) took place *with* the audience: ways of speaking and reading worked on in improvisation, the simple and intensive physical presence of performers in a situation where the difference between stage and auditorium does not exist at all. At the performances, considered to be a public extension of the rehearsals (in principle the rehearsals themselves are public, too), the audience can come and go as they see fit. What is important is the *shared space*: it is experienced, used and, in this sense, shared equally by performers and visitors. A ritual space without a rite develops through the palpable concentration. It remains open, no one is excluded, passers-by can look in, visitors, journalists and interested people come and go. During the work on *Hamlet/Hamletmaschine* (1992) in Tokyo, which took place in a film studio, the gates towards the street remained wide open. Because the threshold could constantly be crossed during rehearsals and then during performances, the sense of inside and outside was intensified; entering and leaving the studio space became noticeable as an act, even a decision of the spectator. The light that penetrates into the space and changes with the time of day begins to enter consciousness, filling the space with a concrete light-time: open theatre which, owing to the lack of assigned roles, staging means and actions, makes it almost impossible to say where it is actually taking place and which nevertheless unfolds a strange intensity.

For the performers the 'action' of speaking, reading, improvising without a plot, role or drama represents a challenge. In this arrangement they are not afforded the protection of the stage, being open to all sides, including the back, to the gaze, the de-concentration, perhaps also the disturbance and aggression of impatient or annoyed visitors. The patience of the Japanese audience, totally surprised by the lack of expected theatre plots and trying to make sense of this highly peculiar event, was amazing. People clad in black who did not 'play', did not use sets, had no 'roles' but spoke the text of Heiner Müller's *Hamletmaschine* with the disciplined freedom of improvisation. They interspersed their text with German (and thus incomprehensible) passages, spoke individually, in chorus, as women or as men, turned in on themselves, gave a general address, or addressed particular spectators. They were '*disseminating*' *the text over the space*. It is a postdramatic *theatre of speech*, also of readings of text, of voices, of theatrical minimalism. It comprises a kind of concentration on the text that is 'behind the times' – corresponding to the 'out of time-ness' of theatre itself – and a strange reduction. The minimal motifs of voice, body, space and duration reject illusory magic but proceeding from this zero-point engender a different kind of theatricality. Here, the secret love of the theatre belongs to *architecture*. With only a minimal amount of exaggeration the theatre of Josef Szeiler can be understood as an intricate mechanism for dragging spaces out of their muteness and state of neglect with the help of voices, bodies and choreography, making them sounding and emphatically visible for a kind of vision that operates with the whole body, with one's movement and positioning in the space, not just with the optical apparatus of one's eyes.

Action occurs only as the content of the texts that are spoken or read, epic texts such as Homer's *Iliad*, plays by Beckett and Müller, Brecht and Aeschylus. What happens in a real and physical way is a repertoire of gestic events. There is no stage world that seeks to comment on, let alone illustrate, what the text is saying. In order to erase the division between playing space and auditorium, theatre discards one toy after another that is usually seen as necessary for, if not constitutive of, theatre: especially dramatic action, role play and drama – favouring instead improvised actions aimed at a specific experience of presence and ideally the equal co-presence of actors and spectators. The character of a 'situation', in the sense described above, here comes about through the following factors: first of all, by entering the theatrical space the spectator cannot help but become a 'participant' for the other visitors. Every individual becomes the *only spectator* for whom the performers and the rest of the audience produce 'his' or 'her' theatre. Secondly, a heightened awareness for one's *own presence* develops: for the sounds one gives off, for one's position in relation to the other people present, etc. Thirdly, the physical proximity to the actors involves entering into *direct contact* (looks, eye contact, possibly fleeting body contact) and experiencing a peculiarly 'underdefined' sphere – neither completely public nor completely private. This immediate sensation of a 'questionable' communication, initiated physically and spatially, produces reflections on forms of behaviour and interpersonal communication. Finally, these actions leave room not only for 'automatic' but also for purposeful personal participation: spectators may decide to follow a performer in their slow-motion walk; sometimes there are texts that allow spectators to join in the reading or speaking, etc. Text, body and space produce a musical, architectonic and dramaturgical constellation that results from predefined as well as 'unplannable' moments: everyone present senses their presence, sounds, noises, position in space, the resonance of steps and of words. It induces them to be careful, circumspect and considerate with respect to the whole of the situation, paying attention to silence, rhythm and movement. As theatre is thus understood as a 'situation' it simultaneously takes a step towards the dissolution of theatre *and* to its amplification. It links up with the attempts of the 1960s and 1970s, in which the roles of the spectators and the actors had already begun to merge, and it quietly radicalizes the *responsibility* of the spectators for the theatrical process, which they can co-create but also disturb or even destroy through their behaviour. The vulnerability of the process becomes its *raison d'être* and inquires into the norms of everyday behaviour. In Fabre's work the constitutive responsibility of all participants – including the spectators – for the theatre remains a virtual dimension. One remains a spectator and has to account only to oneself for one's participation in the events taking place. Here, by contrast, the theatre gives practically every spectator the opportunity to interfere with it, or even render it impossible through insensible or aggressive acts.

The aesthetic distance reached a new minimum in the earlier performances of the company La Fura dels Baus. While in Madrid state-subsidized and private theatres played a dominant role, in Catalonia a lively culture of independent companies could be observed even under the dictatorship. Els Joglars, Els Comediants and La Fura dels Baus became internationally famous. Certainly La Fura dels Baus is an extreme case, but in the extremes we can also read the hidden dialectic of more moderate theatre forms. This theatre involves the spectator not just on a voluntary basis: herd-like, people repeatedly dash to the sides when clunky big wagons rapidly roll through the crowd who are huddled together in a tent. One moment the audience is shoved together into a tight space, the next it is abandoned without orientation. A claustrophobic atmosphere arises in the theatre, reminiscent of situations during violent street protests. One is roughly jostled aside in order to make space for the next action, pushed on several sides by the performers and the crowd of other visitors. Deafeningly loud music and drums, glaring lights and noises, as well as pyrotechnic effects, surround the spectators; one begins to fear for the safety of the performers during seemingly brutal actions.

After a while, however, the sense of threat lessens: one begins to observe that even the breakneck and risky-looking actions, such as the wagons being driven directly among the visitors, are precisely controlled. In this theatre situation the whole idea of the theatre space of former times has been abandoned. The body of the spectator becomes a constitutive part of the staging. There can be no doubt that we are dealing here with theatre, not with a demonstration or the beginnings of a street battle. Even a kind of theme is discernible in the enigmatic events of a Fura production: power, domination and subordination, terror and violence. An evening like *MTM* is structured in a very precise manner: prologue, four scenarios of power, epilogue. In each scenario there is a climax and each ends in so-called 'nexus cataclysms', catastrophes that create an empty space for the following scenic image. The theme is treated in a mythical or poetic but hardly explicitly political way. This was still entirely different in the works of The Living Theatre where the interaction with the audience was direct and obviously political. They involved people in discussions, which – like the brawls staged by the Futurists – could also lead to fisticuffs. While Esslin regarded this already as a problematic 'manipulation of reality' and a 'borderline case' with respect to whether or not it was still theatre,[81] theatre has since increasingly turned borderline cases between performance and situation into the rule.

10 Theatre solos, monologies

A number of directors have translated classical dramas or narrative texts into monologies. We can think of Klaus-Michael Grüber's monologue version of *Faust* (with Bernhard Minnetti) in Goethe's anniversary year 1982, Hermann Broch's *Story of the Maidservant Zerline* (with Jeanne Moreau and Hanns Zischler as the silent auditor in half-shade) or Robert Wilson's *Hamlet – A Monologue* in 1994 and *Orlando* by Virginia Woolf (with Jutta Lampe in Berlin and Isabelle Huppert in Paris). Numerous attempts to theatricalize for example the monologues of Arthur Schnitzler's 'Fräulein Else' or James Joyce's Molly Bloom attest to the desire to win texts from the literary tradition for a monologic form of theatre. Or else one finds actors who single-handedly play or speak all the roles of a play or text – not a monologue in the strict sense of the word but a theatre form constructed like a monologue. Examples of the latter would be Edith Clever's *Penthesilea* or her *Marquise of O* (directed by Syberberg) or Marisa Fabbri in Euripides' *Bacchae* (directed by her mentor Luca Ronconi over several years from 1976 to 1979). Finally it is not to be overlooked that certain innovators of the theatre, such as Jan Fabre, Jan Lauwers or Robert Lepage, apart from their preference for the tableau form, also repeatedly seek out the structure of the monologue in order to stage 'solos' for certain performers. We could think of Robert Lepage's *The Needle and the Opium* or his *Four Hours in Chatila* by Genet, where the form becomes the medium of direct political address. In 1992 Jan Lauwers staged *Schade/schade*, the self-presentation of his actor Tom Jansen. In this piece, Jansen (who wrote the text himself) tells the audience about his life: in a simplicity devoid of theatricality he talks about his childhood, his first sexual experiences, his family, and at the end the death of his brother. An extreme example is the radical performance *Flaming Creatures/Roy Cohn/Jack Smith* by Ron Vawter, an evening described as a 'Theatre Solo', in which this brilliant actor of The Wooster Group – already marked by AIDS of which he would die shortly thereafter – presents in succession the American reactionary

Roy Cohn and then a gay artist famous in the San Francisco community. The Wooster Group's preference for Eugene O'Neill's texts, too, is striking, as they already have a monodramatic tendency (*The Emperor Jones, The Hairy Ape*). One could also refer to Heiner Goebbels' Müller versions, for example *Prometheus, Or the Hapless Landing*, and countless works by young theatre practitioners all over Europe. To round off the picture it may suffice, however, to point out that the dialogue, even where it still exists, is often deprived precisely of that which the art of the theatre author was traditionally meant to produce with its help: namely the electric suspense towards the response and progression.

One of the newer works by Robert Wilson, *Hamlet – A Monologue* (premiered in 1994) is instructive in terms of the complete interference between new theatre languages close to performance and the textual level of a drama rearranged into a monological structure. This performance is situated in a long tradition of monodramatic interpretations of *Hamlet*. The prevalence of monologues in *Hamlet* has often been noted and related to the reflective character of the protagonist. Mallarmé saw *Hamlet* as an exemplary possibility of a lyrical, monological theatre; Müller's *Hamletmaschine* dissected the drama into monologues. Wilson himself plays Hamlet as well as some of the main figures of the play. The newly arranged text begins with one of Hamlet's last utterances – probably chosen as the beginning because it characterizes Wilson's theatre: '*Had I but time* – as this fell sergeant, Death, Is strict in his arrest – O, I could tell you – But let it be . . .' Wilson's monologue reveals itself as Hamlet's reflection and memory on the verge of death, organized like a flashback. A poetic-epic reconsideration of his story has taken the place of the dramatic development. The rearrangement of the text by Wolfgang Wiens makes it patently clear that it is not actually about the deeds and non-deeds of Hamlet. Rather it is a matter of a process of reflection and questioning dressed up as a monological narration. (This is not the place to discuss whether the *Hamlet* drama itself could not be read precisely in this light, the postdramatic adaptation thus corresponding very precisely to its subject.) In the process of the text, Hamlet's sentences from different stages in the drama come together and illuminate each other in a new light; the texts of different figures are mixed and combined, too. All this is held together by the voice of Wilson/Hamlet and the music by Hans Peter Kuhn. Wilson's performance is so uninhibitedly and obviously *verfremded* (defamiliarized), his intonation of different voices, especially the female ones, is so clearly 'exhibited', that the production might as well be called *Robert Wilson – Performance in the Mirror of the Hamlet Figure*. He speaks with constantly changing pitch of voice, by turns croaking and overrefined, in a falsetto voice and growling. Comic moments, too, are not missing: a declamatory tone to the point of parody, quoting the acting styles of former generations, alternates with natural rhythms of speech. At each moment one is aware of the quotation of the Hamlet text as a material for the person of the performer Wilson – who also declared that this presentation of Hamlet was a very personal affair for him. (This is why he deliberately accepted the risk of appearing 'too old' for the role.) The 'formalism' of his theatre incidentally receded somewhat in the 1990s in favour of a more personal expression of emotions, incorporating psychology and poetry and leaving space also for the person Robert Wilson to show and stage himself. But then again what does formalism mean if one speaks of it like Wilson? 'Formalism means looking at things from a distance; like a bird who looks into the vastness of the universe from a branch of its tree – in front of it spreads infinity, whose temporal and spatial structure it can nevertheless recognize.'[82]

In an illuminating and at the same time misleading way Jan Kott compares the great monologue in Shakespeare's dramas to the close-up in film.[83] Yet, what at first sight indeed looks like an analogous function – namely the isolation of the protagonist – actually has an almost diametrically opposite significance. It is true that the theatrical monologue offers a look inside the protagonist, as does the cinematic close-up in its own way. But what happens above all in the perception of the enlarged face is the removal of spatial experience. As Deleuze shows, the gaze of the cinema spectator experiences an *espace quelquonque*, an *any-space*. The close-up ruptures the realistic impression of a space continuum. While the any-space of the close-up leads us away from reality and deeper into *phantasm*, by contrast the monologue of figures on stage reinforces the certainty of our perception of the dramatic events as a *reality* in the now, authenticated through the implication of the audience. It is this *transgression of the border of the imaginary dramatic universe to the real theatrical situation* that leads to a specific interest in the text form of the monologue, as well as in the specific theatricality attached to the monologue. It is not by coincidence, therefore, that one aspect of postdramatic theatre revolves essentially around the monologue. It offers monologues of diverse kinds; it turns dramatic texts into monological texts and also chooses non-theatrical literary texts to present them in monologue form.

It is possible to differentiate in theatre an intra-scenic axis of communication from an orthogonal axis of communication between the stage and the (really or structurally) distinct place of the spectators. Mindful of the fact that the Greek word 'theatron' originally designated the space of the spectators, not the whole theatre, we call the latter axis the 'theatron axis'. All the different varieties of monologue and apostrophe to the audience, including solo performance, have in common that the *intra-scenic axis recedes compared to the theatron axis*. The actor's speaking is now accentuated above all as a 'speaking to' the audience; his/her speech is marked as the speech of a real speaking person, its expressiveness more as the 'emotive' dimension of the performer's language than as the emotional expression of the fictive character represented. Thus a *latent split* of all theatre is actualized: theatrical discourse has always been doubly addressed: it is at the same time directed *intra-scenically* (i.e. at the interlocutors in the play) and *extra-scenically* at the theatron. Proceeding from this well-known duality of *all* theatre, postdramatic theatre has drawn the conclusion that it has to be possible in principle to make the first dimension almost disappear in order to reinforce the second dimension and to raise it to a new quality of theatre. With this move, the conception of theatre semiotics, according to which drama as a theatre text is always based on two communication systems, becomes problematic. It becomes unavoidable to realize that theatre as an 'external communication system' can exist almost without the construction of a 'fictional internal communication system'.[84] All too hastily such theatre is dismissed with the remark that 'typologically speaking . . . it can only be related to the dramatic genre if it is called a "metadrama" or "metatheatre"',[85] which in turn is only possible by misleadingly and wrongly conceiving of 'drama' as staged drama. In postdramatic theatre, the theatre situation is not simply added to the autonomous reality of the dramatic fiction to animate it. Rather, the theatre situation as such becomes a matrix within whose energy lines the elements of the scenic fictions inscribe themselves. Theatre is emphasized as a situation, not as a fiction.

An obvious method for letting the representational aspect of language recede in favour of its theatrical reality is to reinforce its character as *apostrophe* on the theatron axis. This can take the form of lamentation, prayer, confession or rather 'self-accusation' (see Handke's play by the same name), or of 'offending the audience' (Handke). Not only the speech and voice but also the body, gesture, or idiosyncratic individuality of an actor or performer in general are 'isolated', in Mukařovský's sense, i.e. within the frame of the stage they are exhibited through an additional special framing. Because this is not simply a matter of a continuation of the monologue as a textual form, it is preferable to use a neologism for this tendency of postdramatic theatre: it creates *monologies* that can be considered as a symptom and index for the postdramatic displacement of the concept of theatre. Where the presence of the performers is conceptually, and not just accidentally, determining for the staged events, we can speak of monology as a basic model of theatre. It exists outside the area of drama, which Northrop Frye has defined as 'mimesis of dialogue'.

Most studies of monologue proceed from the polarity of dialogue and monologue inherent to the analysis of drama, and because of their text-centred approach do not recognize the theatrical subtlety of monologies. Distinctions such as the one between 'soliloquies[86] that are actional and those that are non-actional, or reflective'[87] or the thesis that the convention of the soliloquy 'stylises a pathological extreme', talking to oneself, 'into a normal form of communicative behaviour'[88] are informed by the schema of the more or less realistic representation of a dramatic action. They may serve a useful function in the analysis of drama but are misleading for an analysis of *theatre*. The monologue also seems to lead to rash interpretations of form. For example, the common thesis that monologue (or 'soliloquy', as Pfister calls it) 'expresses themes such as the disruption of communication and the isolation and alienation of the individual'[89] is unproductive for the theory of theatre. From the point of view of theatre aesthetics it could be claimed that, conversely, only in the system of dialogue does the failure of speaking as communication between people become visible, while a monologue as a speech that has the audience as its addressee intensifies communication – namely the communication taking place in the here and now of theatre. Conversely, a theatre that has, in the words of Szondi, 'absolutely' withdrawn behind the fourth wall and which lets smoothly functioning dialogical communication take place there, could be said to prevent the communication *in the theatre*. From the perspective of theatre another valency of the theatre comes to prominence than from the point of view of the dramatic text. This analysis does not mean to imply that monologues or 'soliloquies' can under no circumstance represent the absence of communication. We could think here of the ghostly monologue of the old thresher at the deathbed of his wife in Herbert Achternbusch's *Gust*, premiered in 1984 in French at the Théâtre de l'Est de Paris and played in the Munich production in 1985 by Joseph Bierbichler. In the tradition of his monologue *Ella*, Achternbusch here shows by means of the loneliness of monologizing how everyday people become 'biblically terrifying' (Benjamin Henrichs).

11 Choral theatre/theatre of the chorus

Apart from disturbed communication, monologue theory has rightfully observed another reason for the '*monologization of dialogue*' in drama: not only an unbridgeable rift of conflict but also an excessive *consensus* of the speakers can prevent the expression of dialogue. In this case, the figures talk not so much at cross-purposes but rather in the same direction, so to speak. Such a non-conflictuous, additive language causes the *impression of a chorus*. Szondi observed this, for example, in Maeterlinck's work. For postdramatic theatre, it is symptomatic that monological *and* choral structures supersede the dialogical structure. Initially the assertion of a choral dimension for contemporary theatre may come as a surprise considering that modern theatre very obviously seemed to have taken leave of the chorus a long time ago. Yet, the disappearance of the chorus is perhaps only a superficial reality masking a choral theme at a deeper level. At any rate, it is irrefutable that the chorus is making a resurgence in postdramatic theatre. We can see choruses being staged directly. In 1995 Gerardjan Rijnder and Anatoli Vassiliev in separate projects both took the lamentations of Jeremia as their subjects. A chorus of speech and movement, lamenting and singing incantation often takes the place of drama and dialogue. From Servan to Grüber the occupation with ancient tragedy emphasizes the choral dimension. The parallel of chorus and monologue becomes strikingly apparent in the case of the company Theatergroep Hollandia, who, on the one hand, stage ancient tragedies in the spirit of the chorus (*The Persians*, *The Trojan Women*) and, on the other hand, under the title *Twee Stemmen* (Two Voices) combine two solos based on texts by Duras and Pasolini. Here two parallel motifs of theatre are obviously conjoined: the reduction to the choral and monologic lamentation and the resurrection of the ancient subject matter.

The parallel interest in chorus and monologue is explicable. The 'tendency of the monologue to cross over into chorus-like speaking' was observed early on.[90] From Schiller's *Wallenstein Camp* to Büchner's *Danton's Death*, a choral line runs through classical drama. Bauer demonstrates that in contrast to 'bound dialogue', which maintains an 'antithetical' character even in the presence of several speakers, in Act IV of *Danton's Death* (the last scene in the Conciergerie) a polyphony rather than a dialogue develops: the individual speakers contribute only stanzas, so to speak, to a collective chorus of lamentation. Whenever the drama mobilizes a multitude of figures for depicting a world, it tends towards the chorus, in so far as the individual voices add up to a general chant, even if there is technically no choral speaking. In the age of media, it is precisely such forms of speaking that rupture the dialogic unity of the dramatic universe, namely the monologue and the chorus, that move into the centre of theatre.

Just like the 'monology', the chorus (owing to its character as a crowd) is able to function scenically as a mirror and partner of the audience. A chorus is looking at a chorus, the theatron axis is put into play. Furthermore, a chorus offers the possibility of manifesting a collective body that assumes a relationship to social phantasms and desires of fusion. It is obvious that it hardly takes any directorial effort to make the audiences associate choruses on stage with masses of people in reality (of classes, the people, the collective). The chorus formally negates the conception of an individual entirely separated from the collective. Simultaneously it displaces the status of language: when texts are spoken chorally or by dramatis personae who are not individuals but raise their voices as part of a choral collective, the independent reality of the word, its musical sound and rhythm, is newly experienced. The choral voice means the manifestation of a not-just-individual sound of a vocal plurality and, at the same time, the unification of individual bodies in a crowd as a 'force'. It is perhaps less apparent that the fusion of voices in a chorus can also lead to the experience of an alienated and literally purloined voice. The chorus raises a voice in whose sound waves the individual voice does not disappear entirely but it also no longer participates in its unadulterated peculiarity, instead becoming a sonic element in a new choral voice that has uncannily taken on a life of its own, neither individual nor only abstractly collective. If the individual voice can no longer be detached from the resonant space of the whole choir (even if it can often still be distinguished in it), inversely the chorus speaks in every individual speaker. The sound estranged from the individual body hovers above the whole chorus like an independent entity: a ghostly voice belonging to a kind of liminal body. This brings about an interesting parallel between the chorus and the *mask*. Looking at an individual speaker one experiences intensely that the sound belongs to the individual face. By contrast, listening to someone wearing a mask (or to oneself speaking from under a mask), the voice appears strangely detached, separated from the self, belonging only to the persona (the mask) and no longer to the person speaking.

Einar Schleef has related the history of modern drama in general to the fate of the chorus. According to him, classical drama displaced the ancient chorus, above all the female chorus. The eviction of woman and of the chorus, the disappearance of the female chorus, for Schleef is 'intimately related to the expulsion of tragic consciousness'. This consciousness could only be regained through the 'reintroduction of woman into the central conflict', while in bourgeois theatre, which only knew the male bond and the male chorus, the woman was condemned to 'exclusion'.[91] Indeed it is cause for thought that in Heiner Müller's texts the woman and the female chorus actually move into the centre (Elektra/Ophelia/Chor; the Angel of Despair, Betrayal pictured as a woman;

Dascha, Medea, etc.). They balance out the scenic male 'I' that could not even constitute itself without its ambivalent relationship to woman. According to Schleef, the modern drama broke with the ancient chorus because it wanted to forget the interdependence of the collective and the individual. The birth of the bourgeois individual severed the umbilical cord to collective reality in order to erect the bourgeois subject in its full grandeur. A new theatre form must reconnect with the relics and displaced figures and forms, in which the basic model of the axis chorus/individual survived. Thus, many classical German dramas could basically be read as choruses: *The Soldiers, The Weavers, The Robbers*.[92] 'The German plays', according to Schleef, 'vary the motif of the Last Supper, the necessity of the drug, its use by a chorus and the individualization of a chorus member through betrayal.'[93] Against this background, he reads in drama the coexistence of an obvious suppression and a secret persistence of the choral motif, reading *Faust* and *Parsifal* as the symptomatic works in which the 'drug' works as a catalyst (the blood of the Last Supper in *Parsifal*; magic potions, lethal poisons, sexual stimulants in *Faust*). In Schleef's choral staging of Brecht's *Puntila*, only the 'Master' remains a single figure. Just as Kantor appeared on stage as a director, Einar Schleef here appears on stage as a director and as Puntila. On the other hand, Matti, Brecht's 'positive hero', becomes a choral mass. The dramatic play axis between father Puntila and daughter Eva (Jutta Hoffmann) is preserved merely as a reminiscence of one of the favourite themes of bourgeois drama, the difficult and ambiguous father–daughter relationship. Schleef's choral productions have been discussed widely and controversially. His theatre is the most explicitly choral theatre within the postdramatic spectrum: the artful rhythmic stagings that create a distanciation, as well as the combination of speaking chorus, movement chorus and space, have created a particular theatrical idiom that demands a detailed analysis. This would go beyond the scope of this survey, however, which is intended to indicate the most important aspects of choral aesthetics, not to appreciate their individual realizations in detail.

In a different manner, the 'evenings' staged by Christoph Marthaler – for example, *Murx den Europäer . . .* and *Stunde Null oder die Kunst des Servierens* – are also symptomatic for a drama-less, choral presence of the performers. Apart from the absence of drama, one is struck here by the number principle as it works in variety theatre or the circus. The interest is sustained through continual surprise and change of perspective. Marthaler stages musical and lyrical structures. Poetry and songs punctuate the performances. Rather than a dynamic of sequence and consequence, the evening is dominated by a mosaic-like, continually renewed revolving around the main topic. It is already 'contra-dramatic' in that the performances focus on the everyday behaviour among the petty bourgeoisie, on inconsequential moments of jealousies, unsatisfied sexual desires, periodically erupting aggressions and tearful reconciliations. They revolve around a cosmos of averageness, a state that can become recognizable through little actions but which cannot be changed through dramatic collisions. The means to its representation is the form of the *social chorus* which, although it is made up of individual voices, not only repeatedly unites in choral singing but also maintains a continuous choral quality through the constant alternation of voices. On the level of the text, there are hardly any dramatic texts but instead songs, speeches and lectures. The numerous choral songs in Marthaler's work show the collective longing for harmony. The scenes, by contrast, consist of nothing but small acts of malice, cruelties big and small, anxieties and boastings. In the folk songs that Marthaler loves to insert, the tensions are harmonized and the choral singing allows their beauty to be heard in spite of all quarrels. Through the chorus the scene thus becomes a kind of musical 'enlightenment' and cogent ideological critique. The continuous presence of all performers on stage contributes greatly to this effect in Marthaler's work. A system of entries and exits constitutes a characteristic of the dramatic theatre. If, by contrast, a 'choral' presence of all participants is chosen, in which even the performers who are not active at the moment remain on stage, then all together appear as a social chorus. This staging strategy could be traced in many works of the new theatre from, for example, Otomar Krejca's Chekhov productions, via Peter Stein's *Summer Guests*, to Marthaler.

12 Theatre of heterogeneity

In every epoch, theatre is also defined through the manner in which the heterogeneity that is systematically immanent to it is foregrounded and thematized. Theatre as such embraces the whole scale of human work, activity and possibilities of expression 'in a nutshell', as a microcosm. Theatre practice unites sound technology and feast, dance and debate, set construction and philosophy. Thus a scenic idea may arise from the combination of a theoretical idea, a technical condition, the physical expression of a performer and a poetic image, from a discussion between lighting technician, dramaturg, actor and author. This is its heterogeneously structured 'rhizomatics'. In every one of its elements it points outside of theatre into 'real life'. As theatre is simultaneously an artistic act and part of the everyday life of a community, existing in a multitude of urban and political contexts, its relation to the everyday can become one of its basic themes. Since the 1970s the theatre has sought out spaces of working life in order to find points of contact where theatre as art can join the worlds of life and work and become inspired by them. In the 1980s and 1990s one could observe a growing tendency, not so much of bringing the everyday into the art of theatre, but rather of occupying public spaces with theatre, pushing the limits of where it was still possible to perceive its aesthetic character and often going beyond these limits. Thus texts from Brecht's *Lehrstücke* were being read at the social services department in order to provoke debate. Thus in Münster an action usually reserved for the sphere of social welfare, namely providing free food for hundreds of needy people, was staged as a theatre performance. In this manner theatre becomes involved in processes of socialization, pedagogy and therapeutic pedagogy, making theatre, for example with disabled people, without it always being clear whether art is being inspired by that which is foreign to it or whether it inscribes itself into the heterogenic practice of other social areas. In fact, in the course of these and other similar actions serious debates can develop among the participants as to whether the events observed were 'part of it' or not. Through its own tendency, postdramatic theatre is a 'theatre at the vanishing point' (Herbert Blau).[94] It realizes the character of a feast that is immanent to it as a genre anyway, a gathering and prominent social, even political event; but it also realizes its character as an entirely real doing, treating this character with theatre aesthetic means. The staged, temporal, dynamic formation 'theatre' thus presents itself rather as an 'occurrence'.

Performance

Theatre and performance

A field in between

The changed use of theatre signs leads to a blurred boundary between theatre and forms of practice such as Performance Art, forms which strive for an experience of the real. With reference to the notion and practice of 'Concept Art' (as it flourished especially around 1970), postdramatic theatre can be seen as an attempt to conceptualize art in the sense that it offers not a representation but an intentionally unmediated experience of the real (time, space, body): *Concept Theatre*. Since the immediacy of a shared experience between artists and audience is at the heart of Performance Art, it is obvious that the closer theatre gets to an event and to the performance artist's gesture of self-presentation, the more a common borderland between Performance and Theatre develops – especially since in the Performance Art of the 1980s a counter trend towards theatricalization could be observed. In this context, RoseLee Goldberg cites artists like Jesurun, Fabre, LeCompte (of The Wooster Group), Wilson and, following him, Lee Breuer (*The Gospel at Colonus*, 1984). In addition, a new amalgamation of opera, performance and theatre emerges. Goldberg further mentions the Italian groups Falso Movimento and La Gaia Scienza, the Spanish La Fura dels Baus, and Arianne Minouschkin (*sic!*) and others.[1]

Performance approaches theatre in its search for elaborate visual and auditive structures, its extension through media technologies, and its use of longer spaces of time. Inversely, experimental theatre becomes 'shorter' under the influence of accelerated rhythms of perception: with pieces no longer being oriented towards the psychological unfolding of action and character, performance durations of an hour or less can often suffice. From the point of view of visual arts, Performance Art presents itself as an expansion of pictorial or object-like presentations of reality through the addition of the *dimension of time*. Duration, momentariness, simultaneity and unrepeatability become experiences of time in a form of art that no longer restricts itself to presenting the final outcome of its secret creative process but instead valorizes the temporal process of becoming a picture as a 'theatrical' process. The task of the spectators is no longer the neutral reconstruction, the re-creation and patient retracing of the fixed image but rather the mobilization of their own ability to react and experience in order to realize their participation in the process that is offered to them.

The actor of postdramatic theatre is often no longer the actor of a role but a performer offering his/her presence on stage for contemplation. Michael Kirby has coined the terms 'acting' and 'not-acting' for this, including an interesting differentiation of the transitions from 'full matrixed acting' to 'non-matrixed acting'.[2] Beyond the technical differentiation, his analysis is valuable because it brings to prominence the vast terrain 'below' classical acting. 'Non-acting', the one extreme, refers to a presence in which the performer does nothing to amplify the information arising from his/her presence (for example, the stage servants in Japanese theatre). Not being integrated into a play context, the performer is here in a state of 'non-matrixed acting'. For the next stage, 'symbolized matrix', Kirby refers to an actor who as Oedipus has a limp. He is not acting the limp, however, because a cane shoved down his trousers is forcing him to limp. Thus, he does not mime limping but only executes the action. When the context of signs being added from *outside* increases without the performers themselves producing them, we can speak of 'received acting' (e.g. in a bar scene some men are playing cards in a corner; they do nothing else but are perceived as actors and seem to be acting). When a clear emotional participation is added, a desire to communicate, the stage 'simple acting' is reached. (Performers of The Living Theatre walk through the audience and passionately explain: 'I'm not allowed to travel without a passport', 'I'm not allowed to take my clothes off' and so on; the pronouncements are true, not fictional, but a simple acting has set in.) Only when *fiction* is added can we speak of 'complex acting', acting in the normal sense of the word. The latter applies to the 'actor' while the 'performer' moves mainly between 'not-acting' and 'simple acting'. For performance, just as for postdramatic theatre, 'liveness' comes to the fore, highlighting the provocative presence of the human being rather than the embodiment of a figure. (To analyse how the profile of demands on the performers of new theatre forms has changed compared to that of dramatic theatre would deserve a study in its own right. In the course of the present study a number of aspects of this problem have already been mentioned, for example the technique of presence or the duality of embodiment and communication, but these cannot be further pursued within the scope of this book.)

The positing (Setzung) *of performance*

Performance in the wider sense has aptly been described as an 'integrative aesthetic of the live'.[3] At the centre of the performance procedure (which includes not only artistic forms) is a 'production of presence' (Gumbrecht), the intensity of a 'face to face' communication, that cannot be replaced by even the most advanced interface mediated communication processes. And just as in Performance Art the criteria of a 'work' are no longer applicable, in the new theatre, too, the staging practice itself claims a previously unknown aesthetic importance: the right to posit through a performative act a reality without the justification of something 'real' being represented. The importance of the theatre is not derived from a literary master copy, even if it may actually correspond to one. This has led to considerable confusion in literary studies. Wolfgang Matzat may serve as an illustration: with considerable concern, he speaks of 'theatrical theatre' in cases where the theatrical playing takes precedence over the represented dramatic process because the 'theatrical perspective' here dominates; but apart from farce and *Commedia dell'Arte*, he gives no further examples other than the Theatre of the Absurd (writing in 1982 after all!). Moreover, for the latter he already diagnoses the danger that an 'extreme emphasis on the theatrical presentation' lets the theatre appear 'strangely empty': 'The presented actions become signifiers without signifieds, symbols without meaning, because they cannot be filled with an emotional substance.'[4] Why a performance in its own particular reality should not exhibit any emotional substance remains in the dark. Yet such misjudgments call even more attention to the necessity for analysing the displacement of sites and structures of theatrical communication in postdramatic theatre with precision.

The split between presence and representation, the represented and the mode of representation, that was introduced in anti-illusionist and epic forms of theatre certainly contained new proposals for perception but the position of the viewer (situated 'opposite' the stage) remained in essence unchanged – even when the audience were meant to be provoked, awakened, socially mobilized and politicized. In the eyes of modernists, the degree of the 'real' had not been sufficient in the old theatre of dreamlike illusion, and thus strategies of disillusionment had emerged. Yet, this argument of a lack of realness could structurally return and be turned against the modern theatre itself. While the audience may have received it more consciously, this theatre did not focus on the real of the theatre situation itself, i.e. on the process between stage and audience. This precisely, however, becomes the core of the performance concept. This implies a further step towards the loss of artistic criteria that could be enforced and controlled more easily by making reference to a 'work' (*Werk*). When it is not the 'objectively' appraisable work but a process between performers and audience that constitutes the artistic value, then the latter depends on the experience of the participants itself, i.e. on a highly subjective and ephemeral reality compared to the permanently fixed 'work'. The definition of what can be termed performance and where, for example, the borderline to a merely exhibitionist, conspicuous behaviour can be drawn becomes impossible, too. The definitive information can now be none other than the self-conception of the artists: performance is that which is announced as such by those who do it. The performative positing (*Setzung*) cannot be measured by previously determined criteria but above all by its *communicative success*. It is inevitable that it is now the audience – no longer just an unaffected witness but a participating partner – that determine the communicative success. In this way, an unavoidable proximity to the *criteria of mass communication* has come about. This is the downside of theatre's liberation towards a performative positing, which at the same time opens up a wide leeway for new styles of staging. Systematically inserted between a pre-text and a reception, the performance (*Aufführung*) shifts its emphasis towards the latter. Previously considered a work of representation, a reified product (even if it was composed as a process), theatre has to become an act/moment of communication. It has to become a communicative exchange that not only admits to its momentariness (the transitoriness traditionally regarded as its deficit compared to the lasting work) but asserts it as indispensably constitutive of the practice of communicative intensity.

Self-transformation

This study can only aim to name the area of overlap between theatre and Performance Art because this area belongs to the discourse of postdramatic theatre. It can in no way provide an adequate analysis of Performance Art itself. What is under consideration is the following shift: theatre implied that the artists represent an artistically transformed reality through materials and gestures. In Performance Art, the action of the artists is designed not so much to transform a reality external to them and to communicate this by virtue of the aesthetic treatment, but rather to strive for a 'self-transformation'.[5] The artist – in Performance Art noticeably often a female artist – organizes, executes and exhibits actions that affect and even seize her own body. If one's own body is thus used not as the subject of action but at the same time as its object, as signifying material, then this procedure annuls all aesthetic distance – for the artists themselves as much as for the audience. Chris Burden who in *Shoot* (1971) had someone fire a shot at him, Iole de Freitas, and Gina Pane who in *A Hot Afternoon* (1977) cut into the tip of her own tongue with a razor blade, provoke questions about the status of aesthetic difference and above all about the position into which the *spectator* is put. At the point where transformation becomes the principal value, the theatre draws a different consequence than Performance Art. In theatre, too, the moment of self-transformation can be reached but theatre stops short of turning it into an absolute. While actors want to realize unique moments, they also want to *repeat* them. They may refuse to be doubles of a character, may appear as 'epic' players who 'demonstrate', or as self-performers, as 'performers' who use their own presence as their primary aesthetic material. But they want to repeat the process the next day as themselves. An irrevocable manipulation of one's own body may occasionally occur but is not the aim.

Whether the performers create an image of themselves as 'victims', whether the spectators are made culpable through the experience of their participation and thus get into the role of the victim themselves,[6] or whether the performance turns into self-manipulation at the limit of what is bearable – in all these cases there is repeatedly an analogy with archaic rituals that cannot be unproblematic now that they are being executed outside of their former mythical and magic spiritual context. Indeed the concept of self-transformation may invite us to consider the performance of public suicide as the most radical perspective of performance, an act which would be unclouded by any compromise through mere 'theatricality' and representation and which would represent a radically real, present (and unrepeatable) experience. This reflection is not meant either sarcastically or polemically. The personal and artistic authenticity of the performance concept is not put into question. It has not only produced extraordinary live moments but has also lastingly transformed our understanding of art. We only want to mark here the difference in the point of departure, the option with respect to the relationship between real life and art: does aesthetic distance, even if radically reduced, remain the principle of aesthetic action or not? Underlying the question of virtual radical self-transformation in performance and theatre is the question of *ethical choice*. RoseLee Goldberg quotes a phrase from Lenin (!), 'Ethics is the aesthetic of the future',[7] which in 1976 inspired the title of a performance by Laurie Anderson, *Ethics is the Aesthetic of the Few(ture)*. In theatre, too, the body can be exposed to risk: as the body is always used as a material in a material practice, theatre is always already a pollution of the border between the showing and the shown. This is the case for classical ballet which requires a torturous drill; and it can also be discussed as a radical (and also questionable) practice in the work of Schleef, Fabre and others. The differentiation between performance and theatre (we know there is no completely clear border) would have to be made not only where the exposure of the body and the self-inflicted injury introduce the body as signifying material into a situation, in which it is 'absorbed' by the signifying process, but where the situation is brought about expressly for the purpose of self-transformation. In principle, performers in theatre want to transform not themselves but a situation and perhaps the audience. In other words, even in theatrical work oriented towards presence, the transformation and effect of catharsis remains (1) virtual, (2) voluntary, and (3) in the future. By contrast, the ideal of performance art is a process and moment that is (1) real, (2) emotionally compulsory, and (3) happening in the here and now.

It would lead us too far off the track to work out the details of the dividing lines between transformation and self-transformation in various uses of ritual. Performance as ritual, as for example in the work of the Vienna Actionists (Nitsch, Mühl), is meant to transform the viewer. The ethics of catharsis – aggressiveness repressed in civilization is being reintroduced into the space of consciousness and the experiential – demands participation and transgresses the 'splendid isolation' of the spectator through the arousal of uncontrollable affective reactions (fear, disgust, fright). Nevertheless, the self-identity of the performers is maintained here, and the event remains theatre, as much as Arnulf Rainer's paintings remain art. Since I am not concerned with an anthropological study here, I have throughout resigned myself to emphasizing the ritual or quasi-ritual aspects of forms of theatre and of performance. One might concede that it remains questionable to transplant modes of behaviour associated with magical and mythical modes of imagination into a modern world. But it is obvious that the recourse to archaic elements, the reflection on the limits of civilized codes of behaviour, and the adaptation of ceremonial forms of behaviour (even if superficial) have objectively become productive for art, sup-

porting especially the resistance against pressing radical art into the frame of traditional aesthetic rules. Johannes Lothar Schroeder rightly turns against a
'generalized rejection that withdraws from the challenge of actions by means of
an "enlightened" aversion to the religious'.[8] Ritual in contemporary theatre and
performance practice interrogates the possibilities of the human being at the
border of its taming through civilization. That the artist – and certainly the
especially marginalized performance artist – cannot really function as a shaman,
i.e. as a socially recognized and admired outsider who transgresses boundaries
for the others, is all too apparent. In today's society, every artist executes the
ritual at his/her own expense.

   'So wherever we look and no matter how far back', Schechner writes, 'theatre
is a mixture, a braid of entanglement of entertainment and ritual. At one
moment ritual seems to be the source, at another it is entertainment. They are
Gemini acrobats tumbling over one another, neither one always on top, neither
one always first'.[9] It would be inaccurate to limit the infiltration of ritual impulses
to the theatre of the 1960s and 1970s. What was then developed has established
itself in the theatre of the 1980s and 1990s in multifaceted forms. In the theatre
of the real as much as in styles of staging that are aggressively addressed to the
audience, in performance as much as in numerous para-theatrical activities, there
is an area between theatre and ritual. The theatre anthropological thesis states
that the actual basic polarity is not between ritual and theatre (Performance Art)
but in the parameters 'efficacy' (which is at stake in ritual) and 'entertainment' (in
art).[10] It remains to be seen how far this distinction, which is central for cultural
anthropology, can also be applied to the analysis of the new theatre. The difficulty arises in the fact that aesthetic behaviour in general, as Schechner's image
of the twins suggests, indeed consists of the 'entanglement' of both motifs. Thus
theatre can strive for a variation of 'efficacy' that has little connection with the
ritual procedures of, say, African societies, and that nevertheless represents far
more than entertainment.

Aggression, responsibility

It is conspicuous that body- and person-centred Performance is very often a
'woman's domain'. Among the best-known performance artists are Rachel
Rosenthal, Carolee Schneeman, Joan Jonas and Laurie Anderson. The female
body as a socially coded 'projection screen' for ideals, wishes, desires and humil-
iations has become especially thematized as feminist criticism has made the
male-coded images of woman, and increasingly also gender identity, recognizable as constructs, raising consciousness about the projections of the male gaze.
We should cite here, for example, performances like the *Kitchen Shows* by Bobby
Baker, who started out as a painter. For this performance she regularly invited
two dozen spectators into her large private kitchen (or into 'guest kitchens'
around the world) and there, from up close, presented a surrealistically heightened monologue about the enslavement of women in the kitchen ('marking'
every one of her dozen actions with a physical mark on her body). In other

performances, the reality of the endangered body takes precedence above all other themes. When Marina Abramowicz presented herself to the visitors stipulating that they were allowed to do anything to her, perception had to turn into the experience of a responsibility. In the performance mentioned, naked aggression came to the fore among some of the visitors who allowed themselves to be provoked by the absence of limits, so that the performance had to be stopped when someone put a loaded gun into the artist's hand and pointed it at her temple. Here danger and pain are the result of deliberate passivity, everything is unpredictable because it is left to the behaviour of the visitors.

The performance artists of the 1960s and 1970s sought the transgression of socially repressive norms through the experience of pain and danger. In Chris Burden's performance *Shoot*, the risk of self-harm, pain and even real danger to his life also came about through an act inflicted by someone else but it was initiated by Burden himself. Here, too, unpredictability was part of the game, a limitation of one's own control. The victim role is clear in both cases but it proceeds from an individual subjective *will*. What happens, however, when we become aware that the 'personal' will is itself conditioned, that it is the victim and result of social structures? A new degree of uncannyness can be found in the work of Orlan whose publicly staged cosmetic surgery operations according to the ideals of Western culture (the forehead of Mona Lisa, the nose of Nefertiti and so on) beautify, distort and dissimulate her body and especially her face, thus withdrawing any 'natural' identity. Traditionally, the face is regarded as the expression of unmistakable individuality – here, by contrast, it is repeatedly changed over several years and is thus exhibited precisely not as unprecedented identity but as the result of a choice, a 'personal' decision of the will. The subjective will here *seems* even more increased compared to the 'self-sacrifice' of the performance artists mentioned before. But at the same time, a new problem becomes manifest. As the subject voluntarily disposes of her body, on the one hand, an apotheosis of the 'self-willed' individual develops who does not resign herself any more to a predestined reality, for example her physical appearance. Orlan proves her tendentially absolute freedom to choose 'herself'; and this gives us a glimpse of a future 'multi-optional society', in which virtually nothing need still be regarded as naturally given but in which the individual will also increasingly have to bear the burden of choice and responsibility. On the other hand, however, Orlan's performances reveal with frightening clarity that the 'will' – where it seems to be at its most powerful and courageous – has basically already abdicated: it reveals itself as thoroughly conditioned by cultural norms, ideals of beauty and models of representation. In Orlan's work the 'self-will' of the personal body stylizations informed by art becomes a mutilation to attain 'beauty', an abysmal and scary materialization of the nothingness of the 'I', the transformation not only of the personal 'self' but of the image of the human being. The localization of responsibility becomes uncertain to an unbearable degree – especially since Orlan has avoided making her performances more palatable with the help of theses of ideology critique (e.g. a feminist critique of cosmetic surgery).

The present of performance

Hans Ulrich Gumbrecht has demonstrated the extent to which the 'elementary gesture' of a 'production of presence' that 'seems to have taken away a lot of space from the forms, genres and rituals of representation'[11] is responsible for our fascination with sport (as a real event). According to this argument, it is a matter of 'moving things within reach so that they can be touched'.[12] This is a rewording of Benjamin's thesis that the indomitable desire of the masses to move things closer was the basis for the de-auratization of the arts. For the hermeneutics of the production of presence, Gumbrecht draws on nothing short of the Eucharist, in which bread and wine are not the signifiers for Christ's body and blood but real presence in the act of communion, not something designated but substance: the model of a 'presence' that refers to itself and joins the gathered congregation in a ritual ceremony. In this sense, Gumbrecht compares the sports event to the medieval stage: here as there, it is not a hermeneutic attitude that is demanded. Unlike in modern theatre (according to Gumbrecht), the players on stage do not pretend that they do not notice the audience but instead interact with it.

The thesis that in sports we are dealing with the phenomenon of a performance (*Performanz*) symptomatic for the cultural development trend, and which does not function according to the registers of representation and hermeneutic interpretation, makes good sense. It indeed seems to be the case 'that the increasing importance of sports events is possibly part of a larger shift within contemporary culture',[13] in which the cultural phenomenon of the 'production of presence' (*not* mimesis or representation) is gaining in importance. It is another question, however, whether especially in sports the 'realistic' dimension of victory and defeat, (monetary) gain and loss, does not repress the epiphany of presence, so that in the end sport is still entirely dissimilar to theatrical rituals – a question that cannot be further discussed here. In any case, the combination of a naïve or blasphemous execution of a magic ceremony, interactive performance, and production of presence is an illuminating motif for post-dramatic theatre. It explains the latter's insistence on presence, the ceremonial and ritual tendencies, and the tendency to put it on a footing with rituals prevalent in many cultures. Gumbrecht does not ignore that such a presence can never be completely 'there' or 'fulfilled', in the full sense of the word, that it always retains the character of the 'longed for' and the 'alluded to', and always disappears when it enters into the reflected experience. He goes back to Schiller's idea of a reference which is not naïve but merely 'sentimental' in order to think of it as the 'birth of a presence' (Nancy), as a coming, an advent, a simply *imaginable* presence.[14]

Meanwhile, what is important for the theatre is not only the insight into the merely virtual mode of being of presence but also its ethically overdetermined quality of *co-presence*, i.e. the mutual challenge. If there is a paradox of the actor (Diderot), then there is all the more a paradox of his presence. There is the gesture, the sound that he gives to us – but not simply as an emanation from this actor there, from the plenitude of his reality, but as an element produced by the complex situation of the theatre as whole, as a situation, which in turn cannot be summed up in its totality. What we encounter is an obvious presence but it is of a different kind than the presence of a picture, a sound, a piece of architecture. It is objectively – even if not intentionally – a co-presence referring to ourselves. Hence it is no longer clear whether the presence is given to us or whether we, the spectators produce it in the first place. The presence of the actor is not an ob-ject, an objectifiable present but a co-presence in the sense of an unavoidable implication of the spectator. The aesthetic experience of theatre – and the presence of the actor is the paradigmatic case here because as the presence of a living human being it contains all the confusions and ambiguities related to the limit of the aesthetic as such – this aesthetic experience is only in a secondary manner reflection. The latter rather takes place *ex post* and would not even have a motivation had it not been for the prior experience of an event that cannot be 'thought' or 'reflected' and which, in this sense, has the character of a shock. All aesthetic experience knows this bipolarity: first the confrontation with a presence, 'sudden' and in principle this side of (or beyond) the rupturing, doubling reflection; then the processing of this experience by an act of retroactive remembering, contemplating and reflecting.

The aesthetics of fright (*Ästhetik des Schreckens*) of Karl Heinz Bohrer proves helpful in analysing the presence we are dealing with in performance and in those forms of theatre that abandon the paradigm of dramatic theatre. 'Aesthetic time is not metaphorically translated historical time. The "event" situated within aesthetic time does not refer to the events of real time.'[15] What we consider the specific temporality of performance itself – as distinguished from the represented time – for Bohrer is an aspect of shock and fright. Inversely, we are exploring the question of fright as an element of the theatre aesthetic. Here it is worthwhile to look at Bohrer's elucidations on fright. Considering Caravaggio's *Medusa* as an example, he explains that aesthetic fright is distinguished from real fright through a stylization that turns the frightening into an ornamental form. Hence, only an 'imaginary identification' takes place.[16] The second quality is even more important: 'The face of this Medusa is not actually instilling fright itself but she herself seems to be seeing something frightening (her own mythic destiny, so to speak).'[17] Trembling in itself, the aesthetic appearance is situated beyond the representation of empirical fright. It does not represent something actually frightening. As aesthetic reality, the present 'appearance', therefore, does not invite the explanation, investigation or (for example, 'tragic') interpretation of the frightening but only the 'mimetic' experience of getting frightened. The viewer of the painting goes through the realization of getting frightened that is 'posed' in the picture. Bohrer deduces from this model the qualities of *intensity* and of the *enigma*, which he rightly regards as constitutive elements of 'aesthetic experience', which on its part can be described with the equivalent formulas 'sudden appearance' and 'self-referential epiphany'.[18] It is beyond our present consideration to what extent the aesthetic temporality of this epiphany exclusively or overridingly defines modernity. Bohrer states the existence of a 'Greek and modern "aesthetics of fright"'[19] and considers the epiphany of fright as an 'aesthetic structure . . . that recurs in different phases of European literature and art history'; he regards fifth-century Athens, the late Renaissance and the time around 1900 as especially favourable 'breeding grounds' for the phenomenality of fright (which in itself is not founded historically but aesthetically).

At this point it is fitting, however, to relate Bohrer's reflection to theatre and to vary it. We could say it is perhaps not her own destiny that the head of the Medusa sees. Instead her fright relates to a frightening reality which cannot be named at all. Precisely for this reason, according to the logic of the painting, the object of the fright has to remain *outside of* the represented (representable) world. It is formless. The painted gaze of the severed head does not 'look' but in the logic of the painted picture expresses precisely the gaze of the dead Medusa, i.e. a 'not-seeing'. It is the death of the gaze, its emptiness, its failure that is frightening. Thus, a fundamental motif within contemporary theories of art and theatre enters our context: the idea of the 'shock' (Benjamin), of 'suddenness' (Bohrer), of 'being assailed' (Adorno), of 'being horrified' (*Erschrecken*) that is 'necessary for cognition' (Brecht), the idea of fright (*Schrecken*) as the 'first appearance of the new' (Müller), the 'threat that nothing happens' (Lyotard). Both the de-dramatized forms of theatre, which communicate a kind of empty contemplation, and the immediately terrorizing and uncanny forms of radical pain-performance demonstrate this: a psychological interpretation of the fright which constitutes the experience of presence cannot suffice (and rightly does not interest Bohrer, either). There we would always have to think of fright as triggered by a representable object or circumstance. In the dimension of theatre aesthetics, however, we must recognize the structure of a shock whose arousal is independent of an object – not a fright occasioned by a story or an event but a fright about fright itself, so to speak. It can be illustrated by the experience of being *startled* when we suddenly realize we are missing something or cannot remember something – we cannot say what – and this not-having or not-knowing 'suddenly' enters our consciousness as an experience of emptiness – a signal we cannot interpret but that nevertheless affects us. The present, which in this way is an experience that is not suspended or suspendable, is the experience of a lack or of having missed something. This experience of lack takes place at the seam of time. Contrary to the suspicion of aestheticism, such an *aesthetic of startling* in theatre would be another name for an aesthetic of responsibility. The performance addresses itself fundamentally to my involvement: my personal responsibility to realize the mental synthesis of the event; my attention having to remain open to what does not become an object of understanding; my sense of participation in what is happening around me; my awareness of the problematic act of spectating itself.

Postdramatic theatre is a *theatre of the present*. Reformulating presence as present, in allusion to Bohrer's concept of the 'absolute present tense' ('das absolute Präsens'), means, above all, to conceive of it as a process, as a verb. It can be neither object, nor substance, nor the object of cognition in the sense of a synthesis effected by the imagination and the understanding. We make do with

understanding this presence as something *that happens,* i.e. drawing on an epistemological – and even ethical – category as distinguishing for the aesthetic realm.
Bohrer's formula of the 'absolute present' is incommensurate with all conceptions that regard the aesthetic as an intermediary, a medium, a metaphor, or a
representative of an other reality. Art is not an intermediary either of the real, or
the human, or the divine or the absolute. Art is not 'real presence' in the sense
of Georg Steiner. Instead the 'other' that is strictly without content is 'created in
this moment, not as an aesthetic Pentecost but as an epiphany *sui generis*' in the
presence of the work of art.[20] The variants of such 'epiphanies' can be systematically deduced but can only be analysed and dissected in their respective
concrete forms. This present is not a reified point of time but, as a perpetual disappearing of this point, it is already a transition and simultaneously a caesura
between the past and the future. *The present is necessarily the erosion and slippage of
presence.* It denotes an event that empties the now and in this emptiness itself lets
memory and anticipation flash up. The present cannot be grasped conceptually
but only as a perpetual self-division of the now into ever new splinters of 'just
now' and 'in an instant'. It has more to do with death than with the often
evoked 'life' of theatre. As Heiner Müller states: 'And the specificity of theatre is
precisely not the presence of the live actor but the presence of the one who is
potentially dying.'[21] In postdramatic theatre, the present in this sense of a floating, fading presence – which at the same time enters experience as 'gone' (*fort*),
as an absence, as an 'already leaving' – crosses out dramatic representation.

Perhaps in the end postdramatic theatre will only have been a moment in
which the exploration of a 'beyond representation' could take place on all
levels. Perhaps postdramatic theatre is going to open out onto a new theatre in
which dramatic figurations will come together again, after drama and theatre
have drifted apart so far. A bridge could be the narrative forms, the simple,
even trivial appropriation of old stories, and (not least of all) the need for a
return of conscious and artificial stylization in order to escape the Naturalist
glut of images. Something new is going to come, and to use Brecht's words:

> This superficial rabble, crazy for novelties
> Which never wears its bootsoles out
> Never reads its books to the end
> Keeps forgetting its thoughts
> This is the world's
> Natural hope.
> And even if it isn't
> Everything new
> Is better than everything old.[22]

Aspects

Text – space – time – body – media

Text

Chora-graphy, the body-text

The new theatre confirms the not so new insight that there is never a harmonious relationship but rather a perpetual conflict between text and scene. Bernhard Dort talked about the unification of text and stage never really taking place, saying that it always remained a relationship of oppression and of compromise.[1] Being a latent structural conflict of any theatrical practice anyway, this inevitability can now become a consciously intended principle of staging. What is decisive here is not – as is often implied by the popular and unquestioned opposition between 'avant-gardist' theatre and 'text theatre' – the opposition verbal/non-verbal. The wordless dance may be boring and overly didactic while the signifying word may be a dance of language gestures. In postdramatic theatre, breath, rhythm and the present actuality of the body's visceral presence take precedence over the logos. An opening and dispersal of the logos develop in such a way that it is no longer necessarily the case that a meaning is communicated from A (stage) to B (spectator) but instead a specifically theatrical, 'magical' transmission and connection happen by means of language. Artaud was the first to theorize this. Julia Kristeva pointed out that Plato in his *Timaeus* develops the idea of a 'space' that is meant to render a logically unsolvable paradox thinkable in an 'anticipating manner', namely the paradox of having to think of being also as becoming. According to Plato, there was at the origin a conceiving, receptive (maternally connoted) 'space', not logically comprehensible and in whose womb the logos with its oppositions of signifiers and signifieds, hearing and seeing, space and time was differentiating itself in the first place. This 'space' is called 'chora'. The chora is something like an antechamber and at the same time the secret cellar and foundation of the logos of language. It remains antagonistic to logos. Yet as rhythm and enjoyment of sonority it subsists in all language as its 'poetry'. Kristeva refers to this dimension of the 'chora' in all processes of signification as the '*Semiotic*' (as distinguished from the 'Symbolic'). What is emerging in the new theatre, as much as in the radical attempts of the modernist 'langage poétique', can therefore be understood as attempts towards a *restitution of chora*: of a space and speech/discourse without telos, hierarchy and causality, without fixable meaning and unity. In this process the word will resurge in its whole amplitude and volume as sonority and as address, as a beckoning and appeal (Heidegger's 'Zu-sprache'). In such a signifying process across all positings (*Setzungen*) of the logos, it is not the destruction of the latter that is happening but its poetic – and here theatrical – deconstruction. In this sense, we can say theatre is turned into *chora-graphy*: the deconstruction of a discourse oriented towards meaning and the invention of a space that eludes the laws of telos and unity.

A history of the new theatre (and already of the modern theatre) would have to be written as the history of a mutual disruption between text and stage. From this perspective, Brecht's theses on the 'literarization' of theatre, developed in the 1920s, appear in a new light, too: they are equally, although with different intention, aimed at the presence of the written text as an interruption of the self-sufficient imagery of the stage. An interesting example for the theatrical treatment of literary text can be found in the work of Giorgio Barberio Corsetti. Corsetti, one of the most distinguished minds of the Italian avant-garde theatre, worked on Kafka for many years. His thesis, too, is: the theatre needs the *text as a foreign body*, as a 'world outside the stage'. Precisely because theatre increasingly extends its borders with the help of optical tricks and the combination of video, projections and live presence, according to Corsetti, it must not get lost in the permanent self-thematization of the 'opsis' (visual presentation). Rather, it has to refer to the text as a quality that resists the scenic image. Corsetti explicitly refers to Meyerhold, Grotowski and The Living Theatre. In his theatre works the performers do not embody particular persons. A critic described Corsetti's realization of Kafka's *Description of Struggle* as follows:

> Sometimes they – the actors – are one and the same person with three people, sometimes monsters with multiple heads and arms, . . . sometimes only an element, a 'building block' in a complicated body machine, sometimes a projected film 'shadow' of a person takes on a surreal life of its own.[2]

The unreal room evoked in Kafka's text finds its correspondence in tilting boxes, revolving walls, steep staircases the actors are having to struggle up, and the alternation of shadow play and corporeal presence. Interior and exterior intertwine just as in Kafka's text. Theatre here does not interpret individuals and the narrative threads of a text but articulates its language as a disturbing reality on stage, which for its part is inspired by the text's idiosyncrasies.

The *principle of exposition* applied to body, gesture and voice also seizes the language material and attacks language's function of representation. Instead of a linguistic *re*-presentation of facts, there is a 'position' of tones, words, sentences, sounds that are hardly controlled by a 'meaning' but instead by the scenic composition, by a visual, not text oriented dramaturgy. The rupture between being and meaning has a shock-like effect: something is exposed with the urgency of suggested meaning – but then fails to make the expected meaning recognizable.

The idea of an exposition of language seems paradoxical. Nevertheless, since Gertrude Stein's theatre texts – if not earlier – we have the example of a language that loses its immanent teleological temporality and orientation towards meaning and becomes like an *exhibited object*. Stein achieves this through techniques of repeating variations, through the uncoupling of immediately obvious semantic connections, and through the privileging of formal arrangements according to syntactic or musical principles (similarities in sound, alliterations, or rhythmic analogies).

Apart from collage and montage, the principle of polyglossia proves to be omnipresent in postdramatic theatre. Multi-lingual theatre texts dismantle the unity of national languages. In *Roman Dogs* (1991) Heiner Goebbels created a collage made up of spirituals, texts by Heiner Müller in German and by William Faulkner in English (*The Sanctuary*), and French Alexandrine verses from Corneille's *Horace* (performed by the actress Cathérine Jaumiaux). These verses were being sung more than recited, the language perpetually tipping over from beautiful perfection into broken stuttering and noise. Theatre asserts a polyglossia on several levels, playfully showing gaps, abruptions and unsolved conflicts, even clumsiness and loss of control. Certainly the employment of several languages within the frame of one and the same performance is often due to the conditions of production: many of the most advanced creations of theatre can only be financed through international co-productions, so even for pragmatic reasons it seems obvious to bring the languages of the participating countries to prominence. But this polyglossia also has immanent artistic reasons. Rudi Laermans has pointed out that for Jan Lauwers it is not enough to state that his theatre is multilingual. For, this circumstance does not explain why his performers have to use sometimes their mother tongue but sometimes also a foreign language, so that the 'difficulty with language communication' arises not just for the spectators. Lauwers establishes a shared *space of language problems* in which the actors as well as the spectators experience the blockades of linguistic communication.

Frequently we are made aware of the physical, motoric act of speaking or reading of text itself as an *unnatural, not self-evident* process. In this principle of understanding the *speech act as action*, a split emerges that is important for post-dramatic theatre: it provokes by bringing to light that the word does not belong to the speaker. It does not organically reside in his/her body but remains a *foreign body*. Out of the gaps of language emerges its feared adversary and double: stuttering, failure, accent, flawed pronunciation mark the conflict between body and word. In the reading-performances of Theater Angelus Novus, however, the sheer duration of the *Iliad* reading (22 hours) entailed that after a certain time the sensual and vocal sound world of speech seemed to separate from the people reading. The words were floating in space by themselves like the sound of certain Tibetan 'singing bowls' as you circle their rim – like an autonomous sonorous body that hovers above it in the air. Jacques Lacan has advanced the thesis that the voice (just like the gaze) belongs to the fetishized objects of desire that he refers to with the term '*objet a*'. The theatre presents the voice as the object of exposition, of an erotic perception – which produces all the more tension when it contrasts so drastically with the horrifying content of battle descriptons, as in the case of the Homer reading.

Textscape, theatre of voices

A term that could capture the new variants of text should carry the connotation of the 'spacing' understood in the sense of Derrida's 'espacement': the phonetic materiality, the temporal course, the dispersion in space, the loss of teleology and self-identity. I have chosen the term 'textscape' because it designates at the same time the connection of postdramatic theatre language with the new dramaturgies of the visual and retains the reference to the landscape play. Text, voice and noise merge in the idea of a *soundscape* – but of course in a different sense than in classical stage realism (e.g. Stanislavsky's stagings of Chekhov's plays). By contrast to the latter, the postdramatic 'audio landscape' Wilson talks about does not mimetically represent reality but creates a space of association in the mind of the spectator. The 'auditive stage' around the theatre image opens up 'intertextual' reference to all sides or complements the scenic material through musical motifs of sound or 'concrete' noise. In this context, it is illuminating that Wilson occasionally remarked that his ideal of theatre was the union of silent film and radio play. This, he said, was a matter of opening the frame. For the respective other sense – the imaginary seeing in the radio play, the imaginary hearing in silent film – a boundless space opens up. When we are watching (a silent film), the auditive space is boundless, when we are listening (to a radio play) the visual space is boundless. While watching a silent movie, we imagine voices of which we can only see the physical realization: mouths, faces, the facial expressions of the people listening, etc. When listening to a radio play we imagine faces, figures and shapes for the disembodied voices. What we are talking about here is that the space of the stage and the more comprehensive sound space together create a third space that comprises the scene *and* the theatron.

From sense to sensuality is the name of the shift inherent to the theatrical process. And it is the phenomenon of the live *voice* that most directly manifests the presence and possible dominance of the sensual *within* sense/meaning itself and, at the same time, makes the heart of the theatrical situation, namely the *co-presence of living actors*, palpable. Owing to an illusion constitutive to European culture, the voice seems to be coming directly from the 'soul'. It is sensed as the quasi-unfiltered mental, psychic and spiritual charisma of the 'person'. The speaking person is the *present person* par excellence, a metaphor of the 'other' (in the sense used by Emmanuel Levinas) appealing to the responsibility of the spectators – not to a hermeneutics. The spectators find themselves exposed to the 'meaningless' (*sinnfrei*) presence of the speaker as a question addressed to them, to their gaze as corporeal creatures. But often postdramatic theatre does not so much aim to make us hear the one voice of the one subject but rather realizes a *dissemination* of voices, which incidentally is by no means exclusively tied to electronically or otherwise 'technically' arranged fragmentations. We find the *choral* bundling and the *desecration* of the word; the exposition of the *physis* of the voice (in screaming, groaning, animal noises) and the architectonic *spatialization*. Whether we think of Schleef, Fabre and Lauwers, of Matschappej Discordia, Theatergroep Hollandia, La Fura dels Baus or Théâtre du Radeau – simultaneity, polyglossia, chorus and 'scream arias' (Wilson) contribute to the text, frequently becoming a semantically irrelevant libretto and a sonorous space without firm boundaries. The boundaries between language as an expression of live presence and language as a prefabricated material are blurred. The reality of the voice itself is thematized. It is arranged and made rhythmic according to formal musical or architectonic patterns; through repetition, electronic distortion, superimposition to the point of incomprehensibility; the voice exposed as noise, scream and so on; exhausted through mixing, separated from the figures as disembodied and *misplaced voices*.

Traditionally, the vocal sound as an aura around a body, whose truth *is* its word, promised nothing less than the subjectively determined identity of the human being. Hence, playing with the new media technologies that decompose the presence of the actor and especially his/her corporeal and vocal unity is no child's play. The electronically purloined voice puts an end to the privilege of identity. If the voice was classically defined as the most important instrument of the player, it is now a matter of the whole body 'becoming voice'. An explicit experience of the auditive dimension emerges when the tightly sealed whole of the theatre process is decomposed, when sound and voice are separated and organized according to their own logic, when the body-space, the scenic space and the space of the spectator are divided, redistributed and newly united by sound and voice, word and noise. Between the body and the geometry of the scene, the sonic space of the voice is the unconscious of spoken theatre (*Sprechtheater*). The theatre of drama, the *mise en scène* of textual meaning, does not bring the auditive semiotics to prominence in its own right. Reduced to transporting meaning, the word is deprived of the possibility to sketch a sonic horizon that can only be realized theatrically. In postdramatic theatre, however, the electronic and corporeal/sensory disposition newly discovers the voice. As it makes the presence of the voice the basis of an auditive semiotics, it separates it from meaning, conceiving of the sign-making as a *gesticulation of the voice* and listening to the echoes in the dungeons of the literary palaces. This is a *sono-analysis* of the theatrical unconscious: behind the slogans the scream of the body, behind the subjects the vocal signifiers. It is not 'I' but 'it' that is speaking, namely through/as a complex machinized composition (Deleuze's 'agencement'). Thus, in the work of John Jesurun the stage becomes an environment of light structures and auditive structures. From the very first moment, a text machine of voices, words and associations is working at rapid speed with lightning fast responses and connections, practically without pause. Fragments of a plot can be intuited. From the field of indeterminacies individual dialogues, disputes, declarations of love, etc. become discernible. Political and private matters mix. Jesurun's theme – communication, the uncanniness of language – conveys itself through the form more than the content. In his work, too, the voices are often 'purloined' through invisible microphones and heard from elsewhere. Sentences fly back and forth, orbit, or create fields, which produce interferences with what is visually presented. Who is speaking just now? One discovers the moving lips, associates the voice with the image, reassembles the fragmented parts, and loses them again. Just as the gaze moves back and forth between body and video image, reflecting on itself in order to find out where fascination, eroticism or interest attach themselves – i.e. experiencing itself as a video gaze – thus the hearing constructs another space inside the optical space: fields of references, lines crossing the barriers. Beyond the lost sentiment, precisely in the machinism, at points of rupture, the longing for communication suddenly articulates itself, the distress at the impossibility (difficulty, hope) of breaking through the wall, the sonic wall of untranslatable languages. A 'human' moment flares up, the whole subject is momentarily found when the gaze has located the voice and returns it to the body – the moment of the human. Then the mechanism of sounds, reactions, electric particles, image and soundtracks takes over again.

Space

Dramatic and postdramatic space

In general it can be said that dramatic theatre has to prefer a 'medium' space. Tendentially dangerous to drama are the huge space and the very intimate space. In both cases, the structure of the *mirroring* is jeopardized. For the stage frame functions like a mirror that ideally allows a homogeneous world of the viewers to recognize itself in the equally coherent world of the drama. A theatre, on the contrary, in which not the transmission of signs and signals but what Grotowski called 'the proximity of living organisms'[3] dominates perception, runs counter to the distance and abstraction essential to drama. If one reduces the distance between performers and spectators to such an extent that the physical and physiological proximity (breath, sweat, panting, movement of the musculature, cramp, gaze) masks the mental signification, then a space of a tense *centripetal* dynamic develops, in which theatre becomes a moment of *shared energies* instead of transmitted signs. The other threat to dramatic theatre is the vast space with a *centrifugal* effect. This can be a space that outweighs or over-determines the perception of all other elements simply through its enormous dimensions (e.g. the Berlin Olympia Stadion in Grüber's *Winterreise*) or a space that eludes being mastered by perception because actions simultaneously take place in different locations, as in 'integrated' theatre. Common to all open forms of space beyond drama is that the visitor becomes more or less active, more or less voluntarily a co-actor. The solo performance of *K.I. from Crime and Punishment* staged by Kama Ginka (as seen in 1997 in Avignon) turned the space that only had a few fragmentary props into a scene of real address of the present spectators. They were individually contacted, taken by the hand, asked for help and drawn into the playful hysteria of the actress (Okzana Mysina) playing (with) the figure of Katerina Ivanova from Dostoevsky's novel. The blurring of the borderline between real and fictive experience to such an extent has far-reaching consequences for the understanding of the theatre space: it turns from a metaphorical, symbolic space into a *metonymic space*. The rhetorical figure of metonymy creates the relationship and equivalence between two givens by means of letting one part stand in for the whole (*pars pro toto*: he's a bright mind) or by using an external connection (e.g. Washington denies . . .). In this sense of a relationship of metonymy or contiguity, we can call a scenic space metonymic if it is not primarily defined as symbolically standing in for another fictive world but is instead highlighted as a part and *continuation* of the real theatre space.

In classical theatre, the distance covered on stage by an actor signifies as a metaphor or symbol a fictive distance, perhaps the distance Grusha travels through the Caucasus mountains. In a metonymically functioning space the distance covered by an actor first represents a reference to the space of the theatre situation, thus referring as *pars pro toto* to the real space of the playing field and *a fortiori* of the theatre and the surrounding space at large.

By contrast, as a *tableau* the stage space deliberately and programmatically closes itself off from the theatron. The closeness of its internal organization is primary. The theatre of Robert Wilson is exemplary for the effects of the stage as tableau. It has justly been compared to the tradition of the *tableau vivant*. In painting the frame is part of the tableau. Wilson's theatre is a primary example for the use of frames. A bit like in baroque art, everything begins and ends here – with framings. Framing effects are produced, for example, by special lighting surrounding the bodies, by geometrical fields of light defining their places on the floor, by the *sculptural precision* of the gestures and the heightened concentration of the actors that have a 'ceremonial' and thus again framing effect.

Another form of postdramatic space can be found in the works of Jan Lauwers. Here, bodies, gestures, postures, voices and movements are torn from their spatio-temporal continuum, newly connected, isolated, and assembled into a tableau-like montage. The habitual hierarchies of dramatic space (the site of the face, of the meaningful gesture, of the confrontation of the antagonists) become obsolete and with them a 'subjectivized' space, a space arranged by the subject-I. In the face of the playing field that is dissected into individual heterogeneous parts, the viewer has the impression of being led back and forth between parallel sequences as in a film. The procedure of *scenic montage* leads to a perception reminiscent of *cinematic montage*. Here one organizational principle can be highlighted that is also peculiar to classical painting: the actors on stage repeatedly behave *like spectators* watching what other performers are doing. Thus, a peculiar focusing on the observed action develops and it functions analogously to the 'direction of the gaze' (*Blickregie*) in classical paintings, which through the gazes of the represented figures traces in advance the 'optic path' for the viewer.

Yet another strategy can be observed in Pina Bausch's work where the space is an autonomous co-player of the dancers, seemingly marking their dance time by commenting on the physical processes. In *Nelken*, the field of thousands of carnations is trampled underfoot, even though the dancers initially try carefully not to tread on the flowers. In this way, the space functions *chronometrically*. At the same time, it becomes a *place of traces*: the events remain present in their traces after they have happened and passed, time becomes denser. Another possibility of bringing the space to life is the process of 'spatializing' the physical actions with the help of a sonic space created with microphones and loudspeakers. For example, the heartbeat of the dancers becomes audible by means of a heart sound amplifier, or their heavy exhalation and inhalation are amplified through a microphone and fill the space. Charged by physical energy, such immediately spatialized *body-time* aims to communicate directly with the spectators' nervous system, not to inform them. The spectators do not observe but experience themselves inside of a time-space.

Outside of the conventional theatre space there are possibilities described as *site specific theatre*, a term originally used in visual arts. Theatre here seeks out an architecture or other location (in the early works of the company Hollandia it was the flat land) – not so much, as the term 'site specific' might suggest, because the site corresponds well to a certain text but because it is made to 'speak' and is *cast in a new light* through theatre. When a factory floor, an electric power station or a junkyard is being performed in, a new 'aesthetic gaze' is cast onto them. The space presents itself. It becomes a co-player without having a definite significance. It is not dressed up but made visible. The spectators, too, however, are co-players in such a situation. What is namely staged through site specific theatre is also a level of *commonality* between performers and spectators. All of them are *guests of the same place*: they are all strangers in the world of a factory, of an electric power station or of an assembly hangar. Similarly as in visual arts, and above all in Performance Art, we often finds works whose motor is the *activation of public spaces*. This can take on very different forms. The company Station House Opera under the artistic direction of Julian Maynard Smith seeks the connection with everyday life. To this purpose it conceives of theatre as developing awareness of architectural processes (e.g. in their architectural performances using breeze blooks in various locations). Theatre opens up in a different way in a project with the title *Aufbrechen Amerika* that Christof Nel, Wolfgang Storch and Eberhard Kloke realized in 1992 (on the Quincentenary of the 'discovery' of America) in and around Bochum. Spread out over three days, this was a mixture of eccentric 'journeys' by bus, train and ship through the heterogeneous diversity of the industrial landscape between Bochum, Duisburg, Gelsenkirchen and Mülheim. The region and its everyday environment mutated into a vast scene. A theatre that has long found its centre elsewhere than in the staging of a fictive dramatic world also includes the *heterogeneous space*, the space of the everyday, the wide field that opens up between framed theatre and 'unframed' everyday reality as soon as parts of the latter are in some way scenically marked, accentuated, alienated or newly defined.

Time

Postdramatic aesthetics of time

Theatre is familiar with the *time dimension of the staging* peculiar to it. While the text gives the reader the choice to read faster or slower, to repeat or to pause, in theatre the specific time of the performance with its particular rhythm and its individual dramaturgy (tempo of action and speech, duration, pauses and silences, etc.) belongs to the 'work'. It is a matter of the time no longer of one (reading) subject but of the shared time of many subjects (collectively spending time). In this way, a physical, sensual reality of the experience of time is inseparably interwoven with a mental reality, namely the aesthetic 'concretization' of what is indented in the performance (as Pavis says following Ingarden). *L'Age d'Or* by Théâtre du Soleil (1975) was a milestone in post-war theatre history, narrating in individual stations the life of an Algerian immigrant worker (family scenes, conflicts at work, etc.) in the representational style of *Commedia dell'Arte*. The vast hall of the Cartoucherie in Vincennes was divided into four large dells, carpeted in a warm ochre tone, on whose 'slopes' the audience sat looking at the performance in the respective 'valley'. From one scene to another, the audience was led into a different dell, a transition that caused the formation of ever new groups and seating arrangements. The intensity and fictional density of the play, which transported the audience into the 'other time' in spite of and because of its epic techniques, also came about through numerous stunning inventions. One example: the worker, who despite a heavy storm has to work on a high scaffold, falls off it to his death. The way the performer, simply standing there, managed to make the position of the body high up above the abyss 'visible' by the way he spread his legs and anxiously looked down; the way he showed the storm by rhythmically pulling on his trouser legs so that they appeared to be fluttering terrifyingly as in a heavy storm; the way his long fall took place as a great run through the hall with outstretched arms; this was one of the moments of great theatre magic. At the end of the performance a remarkable thing happened: as the curtains were pulled aside, a very bright light shone in from outside. It was actually superbly imitated daylight, yet the fact that the spectators had lost all sense of time caused many of them to look at their watches – as if it could already be early morning without them having realized the passing of so many hours. For one precious moment of confusion, one could really believe this to be possible: the 'other' time of the staging had asserted itself against the reality of people's inner clock.[4]

Fictive action *and* staging are familiar with another dimension that cuts across the temporal levels mentioned here, namely *historical time*. It is significant for all dramatic theatre working with older texts and feeding on the realization of past figures and stories. For theatre reception, however, this differentiation remains theoretical, for here an amalgamation develops that merges the heterogeneous levels of time into *one and only one* time of theatre experience. Even sophisticated structures such as the 'play within a play', anachronism and time-collage are of far less importance for the theatre than for the text. The real time of live performance comes into play to such an extent that it overdetermines all theoretically distinguishable levels of time. Compared to the historical time represented in the drama, the time of drama (story and plot) and the temporal structure of the staging, we have to emphasize the *time of the performance text*.[5] Following Schechner, we designate the total real and staged situation of the performance as 'performance text' in order to emphasize the impulse of presence always inherent to it, an impulse that also motivates Performance Art in the narrower sense. Included in this are so-called 'external factors' (which in fact they are not) such as long journeys to get to the performance, late, e.g. nocturnal, performance times, performance durations over several days or throughout a whole night until daybreak (e.g. Peter Brook's *Mahabharata* in a quarry near Avignon, which lasted from late afternoon until morning). It is thus generally important to analyse the 'real time' of the theatre process in its entirety, its fore and after play and its accompanying circumstances: the circumstance that its reception in a very practical sense 'takes up' time, 'theatre time' that is life time and does not coincide with the time of the staging.

The core of drama was the human subject in conflict, in a 'dramatic collision' (Hegel). This essentially constituted the self through an intersubjective relationship with the antagonist. We can say the subject of dramatic theatre only exists in the space of this conflict. In this respect, it is pure intersubjectivity and through conflict constituted as a *subject of rivalry*. The time of intersubjectivity, however, has to be a homogeneous time, one and the same time unifying the enemies in conflict. Dramatic theatre requires one time in which the opponents, agonist and antagonist, can meet at all. The temporal perspective of the individual, isolated subject (as in lyricism or monology) does not suffice here, and neither does the comprehensive time of a world context in which the collision takes place (as in the epic). One recognizes the perspective of our description: once the kind of intersubjectivity we are discussing – let's call it the duel – does not work, the binding intersubjective temporal form becomes obsolete, too. And inversely: inasmuch as the shared homogeneous time becomes confused or disintegrates, the duellists can no longer find each other, so to speak; they get lost in particles acting on different plateaux unrelated to each other. The 'crisis of drama' (Szondi) around the turn of the century was essentially a crisis of time. The transformations in the scientific image of the world (relativity, quantum theory, space-time) contributed to this as much as the experience of a chaotic mixture of the different speeds and rhythms of the metropolis and new insights into the complex temporal structure of the unconscious. Bergson distinguishes experienced time as 'durée' from objective time ('temps'). The increasingly apparent divergence of the time of social processes (mass society, economy) from the time of subjective experience intensified the 'dissociation of world time and life time' Blumenberg observed about modernity. Blumenberg sees this dissociation caused by the expanded historical perspective onto past and future and the subject's concomitant new experience of 'an image of history of such spaciousness and expansiveness that the individual life no longer seems to have any significance in it'.[6] Louis Althusser has turned the irreducible 'alterity' between the time of the social dialectic and the subjective experience of time into the basic model of any 'materialist' and critical theatre, whose task would be to shake 'ideology' in the sense of a subject-centred perception and miscognition of reality.[7] In Kant's work, the function of the 'inner sense' was to guarantee the unity of self-consciousness through the form of a 'temporal order' (*Zeitordnung*). He defined time as the 'form of the inner sense'; this form backs the coherence of the changing representations – which would otherwise pulverize conscious-ness – with the persistent continuum of time that Kant represents in analogy to the line. This linear continuum ultimately supports the unity of the subject because it lends direction and orientation to the experiences, which are radically discontinuous among themselves. However, at the latest since Nietzsche and since Freud theorized the discourse of the unconscious, identity as an immemo-rial familiarity of the continuous subject with itself has come under the suspicion of being a chimera. In modernity, the subject – and with it the intersubjective mirroring through which it could continually enhance itself – loses its ability to integrate the representations into a unity. Or, to put it the other way round: the disintegration of time as a continuum proves to be a sign of the dissolution – or at least subversion – of the subject possessing the certainty of its time.

At the end of the 1950s, one began to observe parallel developments in Infor-mel painting, Serial music and dramatic literature, which amounted to a rejec-tion of traditionally constructed totalities. We can diagnose the loss of the *time frame*. When Stockhausen in the 1960s envisioned that visitors to a concert could arrive later and leave earlier or when Wilson caused a stir by stipulating 'inter-missions at your discretion', this epitomized an essential tendency of the new dra-maturgies of time. They suspend the unity of time with beginning and end as the *enclosing frame* of the theatre fiction in order to gain the dimension of the *time 'shared'* by the performers and the audience as a processuality that is on principle open and has structurally neither beginning, nor middle, nor end. Aristotle had demanded precisely these, however, as a basic rule for drama, so that a whole ('holon') could come about. The new concept of *shared* time regards the aestheti-cally shaped and the real experienced time as a single cake, so to speak, shared by visitors and performers alike. The idea of time as an experience shared by all constitutes the centre of the new dramaturgies of time: from the diverse distor-tions of time to the assimilation of the speed of pop; from the resistance of slow theatre to theatre's convergence with Performance Art and its radical assertion of *real time* as a situation people live through together.

The basis of dramatic theatre was the demand that the spectators leave their everyday time to enter a segregated area of 'dream time', abandoning their own sphere of time to enter into another. In epic theatre the 'filling in of the orches-tra pit' (Benjamin) signifies a shared level of reflection. Brecht wanted the thinking and the smoking spectator, where smoking was meant to be a sign of the spectators' distanced dispassionateness, precisely not a manifestation of *one* shared temporal space. Brecht's spectators precisely do not immerse themselves into a 'being in the here and now' that is emotionally merged with the events on stage (this would be the identification with the dramatic events) but they lean back and smoke, distanced in 'their own time'. While it does not seek illusion either, the postdramatic aesthetic of real time signifies, however, that the scenic process cannot be separated from the time of the audience. Again the contrast between the epic and the postdramatic gesture is clearly apparent. If time becomes the object of 'direct' experience, logically it is especially the techniques of time distortion that come to prominence. For only an experience of time that deviates from habit provokes its explicit perception, permitting it to move from something taken for granted as a mere accompaniment to the rank of a theme. Thus, a new phenomenon in the aesthetics of theatre is established: the intention of utilizing the specificity of theatre as a mode of presentation to turn *time as such* into an object of the aesthetic experience.

Consciously noticeable duration is the first important factor of time distortion in the experience of contemporary theatre. Elements of a *durational aesthetic* can be witnessed in numerous contemporary works of theatre. The *prolongation of time* is a prominent trait of postdramatic theatre. Robert Wilson created a 'theatre of slowness'. Only since Wilson's 'invention' can we speak of a proper aesthetics of duration. The visual object on stage seems to store time in it. The passing time turns into a 'Continuous Present', to use the words of Wilson's role model Gertrude Stein. Theatre becomes similar to a kinetic sculpture, turning into a *time sculpture*. This is true in the first instance for the human bodies, which turn into kinetic sculptures through slow motion. But it is also for the theatrical tableau as a whole, which owing to its 'non-natural' rhythm creates the impression of having a time of its own – midway between the achronia of a machine and the traceable and palpable lifetime of human actors, who attain here the gracefulness of marionette theatre.

Alongside the durational aesthetic, an *aesthetic of repetition* has developed. Hardly any other procedure is as typical for postdramatic theatre as repetition – we only need to mention Tadeusz Kantor, the extreme repetition in some ballets by William Forsythe, the works of Heiner Goebbels and of Erich Wonder where repetition is an explicit theme. As in duration, a crystallization of time occurs in repetition, a more or less subtle compression and negation of the course of time itself. Certainly rhythm, melody, visual structure, rhetoric and prosody have always used repetition: there is no musical rhythm, no composition of an image, no effective rhetoric, no poetry and, in short, no aesthetic form without purposefully employed repetition. In the new theatre languages, however, repetition takes on a different, even opposite meaning: formerly employed for structuring and constructing a form, it is now used for the destructuring and deconstructing of story, meaning and totality of form. If processes are repeated to such an extent that they can no longer be experienced as part of a scenic architecture and structure of organization, the overtaxed recipient experiences them as meaningless and redundant, as a seemingly unending, unsynthesizable, uncontrolled and uncontrollable course of events. We experience the monotonous noise of a surge of signifiers that have been drained of their communicative character and can no longer be grasped as a part of a poetic, scenic or musical totality of a work: a negative postdramatic version of the sublime. On closer inspection, however, even in theatre, there is no such thing as true repetition.[8] The very position in time of the repeated is different from that of the original. We always see something different in what we have seen before. Therefore, repetition is also capable of producing a new attention punctuated by the memory of the preceding events, *an attending to the little differences*. It is not about the significance of the repeated events but about the significance of repeated perception, not about the repeated but about repetition itself. *Tua res agitur*: the temporal aesthetic turns the stage into the arena of reflection on the spectators' act of seeing. It is the spectators' impatience or their indifference that becomes visible in the process of repetition, their paying attention or their reluctance to delve deeper into time; their inclination or disinclination to do justice to and make space for differences, for the smallest thing, and for the phenomenon of time by immersing themselves into the self-alienating act of seeing.[9]

The static effect of theatre beyond dramatic movement, which is produced through duration and repetition, thus has the remarkable consequence that *the focus on 'image-time'*, i.e. the disposition of perception peculiar to the viewing of images, enters the perception of theatre. Just like theatre, the visual arts had earlier taken the step of turning their factual, material reality into the dominant factor of their constitution and consequently also 'imposed' the temporality of the image onto reception: what emerged was the demand on the viewer to realize not simply the temporality of the represented but the temporal aspects of the image itself. Following Gottfried Boehm, let us assume that the image as a 'form of relations' exhibits an 'image time' (*Bildzeit*) that is specific only to it. It appeals to the temporal sense of the viewers to retrace, resense, continue, and in short to 'produce' the movement that is immobilized and *latent* in the image. The image initially appears to be 'without time'. Yet through their own sense of time, imagination, empathy and the capacity to relate physically to sequences of movements, the viewers come to know the temporal movement in the image. It 'supplements' their own seeing (in the case of realistic representations of moving object or figures), repeats it, or rather produces it in the first place (in the case of non-representational or heavily abstracted imagery). Under the banner of visual dramaturgy, the perception of theatre no longer simply prepares for a 'bombardment' of the sensory apparatus with moving images but, just as in front of a painting, activates the dynamic capacity of the gaze to produce processes, combinations and rhythms on the basis of the data provided by the stage. As the visual semiotics seems to want to stop theatre time and to transform the temporal events into *images for contemplation*, the spectators' gaze is invited to 'dynamize' the durational stasis offered to them through their own vision. The result is a hovering of perceptional focus between a 'temporalizing' viewing and a scenic 'going along', between the activity of seeing and the (more passive) empathy. In this way, postdramatic theatre effects a displacement of theatrical perception – for many provocative, incomprehensible, or boring – turning from abandoning oneself to the flow of a narration towards a constructing and constructive co-producing of the total audio-visual complex of the theatre.

By contrast to the strategies of deceleration, immobilization and repetition, other postdramatic forms of theatre attempt to adopt and even surpass the speed of media time. We could mention here the references to the *aesthetic of video clips*, combined with media quotes, a mixture of live presence and recordings or the segmentation of theatrical time as in television series. The works of younger theatre practitioners of the 1990s in particular develop this style, not letting themselves be discouraged by the potential proximity of their work to multi-media spectacles and show business but taking up the media patterns as material they make use of, more or less satirically and mostly at high speed. Thanks to radio, television and the internet, reality from all parts of the world can be integrated into the performance, putting the spectators in contact with people far away from the actual site of performance. What would otherwise remain trivial as a mere demonstration of media communication, in the context of theatre manifests the latent conflict between the moment of life and the surface of virtual electronic time. In the work of Jürgen Kruse the integration of pop and media quotes leads to interesting interpretations of drama, the Danish company Von Heyduck integrates film illusion, and the plays of younger directors like René Pollesch, Tim Staffel, Stefan Pucher or companies like Gob Squad build on the speed of the aesthetic of pop and media. The *simultaneity* that becomes dominant here is one of the major characteristics of the postdramatic shaping of time. It produces speed. The simultaneity of different speech acts and video imports produces the interference of different rhythms of time, bringing body time and technological time into competition with one another (as in the work of John Jesurun or Station House Opera's *Mare's Nest*); and through the uncertainty of whether an image, sound or video is produced live or reproduced with a time delay, it becomes clear that time is 'out of joint' here, always 'jumping' between heteronomic spaces of time. The principle of consciousness to lend continuity and identity to experience through repetition is undermined.

The unity of time

In more than one respect the rule of the unity of time was essential to the Aristotelian tradition of dramatic theatre. Perhaps it referred in the beginning to the unity of a trial and hearing court – Adorno once called ancient tragedy a 'hearing without a judgment'. Even where an external unity of time was not sought (as, for example, in Elizabethan theatre), theatre was governed by the ideal of organic closeness, which had to have consequences for the representation of time. To be distinguished from this are those dramaturgies that transformed the understanding of theatre in the twentieth century. Brecht's concept of 'non-Aristotelian drama', coined in the 1930s, distinguished the epic theatre not so much from the classical rules of dramatic theatre but from the aim of the spectator's 'catharsis' through empathy. Part of the design of epic theatre is a dramaturgy of leaps in time that point to human reality and behaviour as discontinuous:

The modern spectator does not wish to be patronized and violated (namely through 'all kinds of emotional states'), he rather wants to be presented simply with human material *in order to arrange it himself*. This is why he also loves to see the human being in situations that are not self-explanatory; and this is why he needs neither the logical justifications nor the psychological motivations of the old theatre.

And further:

> The relations of people in our time are not clear-cut. Therefore, the theatre has to find a form of representing this lack of clarity in as classical a form as possible, that is in epic serenity.[10]

While Brecht privileges jumps and cuts at all levels, the logical and the temporal, in Aristotle the central importance of the unity of time is to guarantee the unity of action as a coherent totality. No jumps and digressions must occur that could cloud clarity and confuse understanding. Rather, a recognizable logic shall reign without interruption. Important in this context is the already quoted remark in chapters 6 and 7 of Aristotle's *Poetics* that is rarely as appreciated as it deserves to be, namely that the dramatic action has to have a certain magnitude – in the sense of a temporal expansion. Aristotle here uses a strange comparison of the action with an animal (only comprehensible in the light of the idea of the organic unity and totality of action). The beautiful, he says – and it is worth quoting the passage again – depends not solely on the arrangement but also on the right magnitude:

> For this reason no organism could be beautiful if it is excessively small (since observation becomes confused as it comes close to having no perceptible duration in time) or excessively large (since the observation is then not simultaneous [*hama*], and the observers find that the sense of unity and wholeness is lost from their observation, e.g. if there were an animal a thousand miles long).[11]

What is the meaning of this seemingly grotesque comparison of an animal of a length of 1,000 miles, at the extreme limit of perceptibility? What is at stake is the *avoidance of confusion* and the '*at once*' (Greek 'hama'). The form – beauty, organic harmony – has to be perceivable to the intuition without a time delay, in one beat, at one glance. Applied to dramatic action this means that its coherent logic and wholeness (holon) must not elude the spectator. Therefore, the argument goes, the action has to be condensed in such a way that it remains 'eusynopton' – easily surveyable – and simultaneously easy to remember: 'eumnemoneuton'.

A clear overview, the absence of confusion and the reinforcement of logical unity are needed. Without them, nothing beautiful can come about. In the name of this ideal of 'surveyability', the right length of dramatic action is determined according to the time it takes for a reversal, a peripeteia, to take place. A rise and a fall, in other words: *time of the logic of a reversal*. Drama brings logic and structure into the confusing plethora and chaos of being – this is why, for Aristotle, it has a higher status than historiography, which only reports the chaotic events. It is essentially the unity of time that has to support the unity of this logic that is meant to manage without confusion, digression and rupture. One aspect of this concept of the unity of time, that remains only implicit in Aristotle, is this: to the same degree as time and action attain an internal coherence, seamless continuity and totality of surveyability, this same unity draws a distinct line between drama and the external world. It safeguards the closed structure of tragedy. Gaps and leaps in the internal continuum of time, on the other hand, would immediately function as points of intrusion for external reality. Internal coherency and closure towards external reality are complementary aspects of this uniform theatrical time. The aesthetic pleasure must not be without order – to be avoided, for example, are collective ritual ecstasy or excessive 'mimetic' behaviour threatening to lead to affective fusion. The Aristotelian concept of the unity of dramatic time thus seeks (1) to demarcate a sealed off sphere of the aesthetic with its own artistic time, (2) to conceive of an experience of beauty that constitutes it as analogous to rationality. The imperatives of internal continuity, coherency, organic symmetry and temporal surveyability all serve to promote this analogy. In contrast, Aristotle clearly realizes the highly emotional effect of the theatre – eleos and phobos are violent affects. Catharsis is meant to tame them by means of a kind of framing through the logos.

Regardless of its philosophical implications, Aristotle's *Poetics* was a pragmatic and descriptive text. In modern times, however, its observations were reinterpreted as normative rules, the rules as prescriptions, and the prescriptions as laws – description was turned into prescription. During the Renaissance there was still a rivalry between a neo-Platonic notion of art oriented towards the 'poetic furor' and an Aristotelian notion of art oriented towards rationality and rules. The Aristotelian line won out and came to define the ideas of theatre in modern times, above all in classicism. Pierre Corneille's *Discours sur les trois unités* explains in 1660 that the playwright should try to achieve an identity between the represented time and the time of the theatrical representation. This rule, he explains, is dictated not just by Aristotle's authority but simply by 'natural reason'. The dramatic poem ('poème dramatique') is for Corneille without any question an imitation or more precisely a *portrait* of human actions ('une imitation, ou pour en mieux parler, un portrait des actions des hommes'). This comparison is striking. Corneille immediately makes it serve the main argument: the perfection of a portrait, he says, is measured – 'hors de doute' (without a doubt) – by its similarity with the original. As far as the function of the unity of time is concerned, the significant keyword comes up at the point where Corneille argues why after all the represented time must not be longer than the time of the representation, original and 'portrait' having to be as alike as possible in this respect, too. Corneille gives one special reason why we aspire to this identity: namely, for fear of falling into a state without rules ('de peur de

tomber dans le dérèglement').[12] The pragmatic and technical identity of represented time and time of representation is not the real motivation for the unity of
time but rather the *fear of deregulation* and confusion. The reason for the rule is –
the assertion of the rule itself. What is at stake is the prevention of confusion,
the prevention of a free-roaming imagination uncontrolled by the dramatic
process, the prevention of the outbreak of the imagined reception in Lord
knows what other spatial and temporal spheres.

The comprehension of longer time spans in drama, according to Corneille,
should be regulated in such a way that greater lapses in time, if inevitable, be
placed *between* the acts. The thematization of real time is avoided altogether by
not referring to exact dates and times in the spoken text. Likewise, reports
about events occuring prior to the stage action are to be minimized in order not
to overload the spectator's memory and intellectual power.[13] As a preferably
perfect double of reality and, at the same time, as an entity of suggestive rationality and coherence, theatre needs the unity of time, the concentration on the
present and the exclusion of multi-layered spaces of time. The unity creates a
continuity that is meant to make invisible any split between fictive time and real
time. For any rupture in the structure of time, we read, would harbour the
danger that the spectator becomes aware of the difference between original and
copy, reality and image, and is – inevitably – steered towards *his* time, the real
time. Then, without any control, he could let his imagination run wild, reflect,
occupy himself with reasoning or else dream. The temporal structures of the
Aristotelian tradition are not simply an innocent and nowadays outdated framework but rather an essential part of a powerful tradition against whose
normative efficacy the contemporary theatre continually has to assert itself –
even if nobody still adheres to the norm of the unity of time in any formal
sense. The basic aesthetic and dramaturgical conceptions of this tradition can
be deciphered as definitions and containments of reception, as an attempt to
structure the mode of imagination, thought and feeling in theatre. Within it, the
unity of time has the value of a decisively important symptom. We have here
focused on Aristotle and Corneille. Yet in the eighteenth century, too, under the
banner of the so-called 'natural signs' the poetics of theatre continues to be
working on the control and formation of the imagination, including the physical
habitus.

The complementary aspects of the unity of time – continuity on the inside,
isolation from the outside – have been and still are the basic rules not only of
theatre but also of other narrative forms, as a side glance at Hollywood films
with their ideal of the 'invisible cut' would quickly prove. We could conclude
that the Aristotelian tradition of the dramaturgy of time pursued not least of all
this aim: *to prevent the appearance of time as time.* Time as such is meant to disappear, to be reduced to an unnoticeable condition of being of the action. And
the rules for its treatment ultimately served the purpose that it remained unno-
ticed. Nothing was to release the spectator from the spell of the dramatic action.
The true meaning of the Aristotelian aesthetics of time is not aesthetic. Rather
the unity of time in theatre – as a continuity of the fictive time of the drama

and the time of the performance – points to a much more profound *fantasy image, a phantasm of continuity*. Theatre is meant to reflect and intensify the social continuum of interaction and communication, the continuum of a socio-symbolic context of ideals, values and conventions. Inversely: if theatre presupposes the rupture of this deeper continuity, the unity of time will cease, too – not just in drama but also in the reality of the performance text.

Body

Postdramatic images of the body

Cultural notions of what 'the' body is are subject to 'dramatic' changes, and theatre articulates and reflects these ideas. It represents bodies and at the same time uses bodies as its main signifying material. But the *theatrical body* does not exhaust itself in this function: in theatre it is a value *sui generis*. Nevertheless, before modernism the physical reality of the body remained in principle inciden-tal. The body was a gratefully accepted given. It became the manifestation of the 'domination of nature applied to the human being' (Rudolf zur Lippe); it was dis-ciplined, trained and formed to serve as a signifier; but it was not an autonomous problem and theme of the dramatic theatre, where as such it rather remained a kind of *sous-entendu*. This is not surprising considering that drama essentially came about as an abstraction from the density of the material world through the 'dra-matic' concentration on 'spiritual' conflicts – by contrast to the epic's love for concrete detail. Before modernism, physicality was explicitly thematized only in exceptional cases that confirm the rule of its discursive marginalization: the phallus of ancient comedy, Philoctetes' pain, the torture and agony in Christian theatre, Gloucester's hump, Woyzeck's illness. In modernism, however, sexuality, pain and disease, physical difference, youth, old age, skin colour (Wedekind, Jahnn) become 'presentable' themes for the first time. The 'marriage of man and machine' (Heiner Müller) began in the historical avant-gardes with couplings between the organic and the machinic. It continues under the banner of new technologies and takes hold of the human body in a comprehensive manner: wired up to information systems, the body breeds new phantasms in post-dramatic theatre, too. While the spatial organization of Schlemmer's *Triadic Ballet* or the arrangement of the surface in Mondrian's paintings implied the utopian perspective of a rational social organization, the technically mediated machines of desire and terror in contemporary theatre lack this (dramatic) utopian trait. Instead one finds variations of a *technically infiltrated body*: cruel images of the bodies between organism and machinery.

Modernist theatre and postdramatic theatre gain new potentials from over-coming the semantic body. A characteristic factor of the theatre now comes into its own, to which the following formula applies: sensuality undermines sense. It required the emancipation of theatre as a proper dimension of art in order to grasp that the body did not have to content itself with being a signifier but could be an *agent provocateur* of an experience without 'meaning', an experience aimed not at the realization of a reality and meaning but at the experience of potentiality. As such, by pointing only to its own presence in an auto-deixis, the body opens the pleasure and fear of a gaze into the paradoxical emptiness of possibility. Theatre of the body is a *theatre of potentiality* turning to the unplannable 'in-between-the-bodies' and bringing to the fore the potential as a threatening dispossession (as Lyotard theorizes it in the concept of the sublime) and simultaneously as a promise.

The dramatic process occured *between* the bodies; the postdramatic process occurs *with/on/to* the body. The mental duel, which the physical murder on stage and the stage duel only translate metaphorically, is replaced by physical motor activity or its handicap, shape or shapelessness, wholeness or fragmentation. While the dramatic body was the carrier of the agon, the postdramatic body offers the image of its *agony*. This prevents all representation, illustration and interpretation with the help of the body as a mere medium. The actor has to offer himself. Valère Novarina remarks: 'The actor is no interpreter because the body is no instrument.' He dismisses the idea of a 'composition' of a dramatic person through the actor, opposing it with the formula that it is rather the *decomposition of the human being* that is happening on stage.[14] The concept of theatrical communication *qua* body changes drastically. One could say that the dynamic that used to maintain the drama as a form of development has moved into the body, into its 'banal' existence. A *self-dramatization of physis* takes place. The impulse of postdramatic theatre to realize the intensified presence ('epiphanies') of the human body is a quest for *anthropophany*. From this basic position, a series of diverse images of the body arise that all point to the reality that exists only in theatre, namely the *theatrical reality* (*das TheatReale*).

Not by coincidence, it is in dance that the new images of the body are most clearly visible. In dance we find most radically expressed what is true for postdramatic theatre in general: it articulates not meaning but energy, it represents not illustrations but actions. Everything here is gesture. Previously unknown or hidden energies seem to be released from the body. It becomes its own message and at the same time is exposed as the most profound *stranger of the self*: what is one's 'own' is *terra incognita*. This is evident in ritual cruelty exploring the extremes of what is bearable or when phenomena that are alien and uncanny to the body are brought to the surface (of the skin): impulsive gesticulations, turbulence and agitation, hysterical convulsions, autistic disintegrations of form, loss of balance, fall and deformation. Just as the new dance privileges discontinuity, the different members (*articuli*) of the body take precedence over its totality as a *Gestalt*. The renunciation of the 'ideal' body in the work of William Forsythe, Meg Stuart or Wim Vandekeybus is highly visible. There are no heightening costumes, unless they are used ironically. The novel postures do not exclude falling, rolling about, lying or sitting; contortions, gestures like shrugging one's shoulders, the integration of language and the voice, a novel intensity of physical contact (Meg Stuart).

Among the series of images of the body that can be considered as symptomatic for postdramatic theatre is the *technique of slow motion*, which is omnipresent in the wake of Wilson's work. It cannot be reduced to a merely external visual effect. When physical movement is slowed down to such an extent that the time of its development itself seems to be enlarged as through a magnifying glass, the body itself is inevitably *exposed* in its concreteness. It is being zoomed in on as through the lens of an observer and is simultaneously 'cut out' of the time–space continuum as an art object. At the same time, the motor apparatus is *alienated*: every action (walking, standing, getting up and sitting down) remains recognizable but is changed, as never seen. The act of striding along is decomposed, becoming the lifting of a foot, advancing of a leg, sliding shift of weight, careful coming down of the sole. The scenic 'action' (walking) takes on the beauty of a purposeless *pure gesture*.

But what do we mean by gesture? Above all, we have abandoned the sphere of purposive means: walking not as a means for displacing the body but not as an end in itself either (aesthetic form). Dance, for example, is gesture, according to Giorgio Agamben, 'because it consists entirely in supporting and exhibiting the media character of physical movement. *The gesture consists in exhibiting a mediality, in rendering a means visible as such.*' In this description following Walter Benjamin, the body and its gestic essence are articulated as a dimension in which all 'potential' remains in the 'act', in suspense, in a 'pure milieu' (Mallarmé). Gesture is that which remains unsublated in any purposive action: an excess of potentiality, the phenomenality of visibility that is blinding, so to speak, namely surpassing the merely ordering gaze – having become possible because no purposiveness and no tendency to illustrate weakens the real of space, time and body. The postdramatic body is a body of gesture, understood as follows: 'The gesture is a potential that does not give way to an act in order to exhaust itself in it but rather remains as a potential in the act, dancing in it.'[15]

In the work of Societas Raffaello Sanzio the sculptural aesthetic is noticeable. This astonishing company, one of the most important experimental Italian theatre companies, began in 1981. For every project a new ensemble is assembled around the core of the group, the siblings Romeo and Claudia Castellucci. They often integrate people with an 'abnormal' physicality or a physicality modified by disease. 'Every body has its own tale', explains Romeo Castellucci. It is a matter of the return of the body as an incomprehensible and simultaneously unbearable reality. Important productions are *Santa Sofia – Teatro Khmer* (1985), *Gilgamesh* (1990), *Hamlet – the Vehement Exteriority of the Death of a Mollusk* (1992), *Masoch* (1993), *Oresteia* (1995) and *Giulio Cesare* (1997). In *Oresteia* there is an abundance of quotes from visual arts: an actor is chosen because he is long and spindly like a figure by Giacometti. Another is dressed in white with white make-up so that he is reminiscent of the sculptures by George Segal and he sometimes takes on the postures and attitudes of Kafka's drawings. Clytemnestra is played by an actress who literally seems to be a mountain of flesh coloured in red, reclining in a fairytale-like melting immobility. As a corporeal sign her heaviness communicates her power, yet the immediately sensual impression devoid of any interpretation remains dominant. Cassandra is locked into a box-like framework, her features distorted through frosted glass, so that one seems to be looking at a painting by Francis Bacon. Theatre here exists in closest proximity to the visual arts.

The live, trembling human sculpture, the movement sculpture between torpor and vitality, leads to the exposure of the spectator's voyeuristic gaze onto the performer. When the sculptural motif returns in the theatre of the 1980s and 1990s, it is under completely different premises than in classical modernism. The ideal turns into a motif of anxiety. The body is not exhibited for the sake of its closeness to a classical ideal but for the sake of a painful confrontation with imperfection. The attraction and aesthetic dialectic of the classical sculptures of bodies consists not least of all in the sense that the living human being cannot compete with them. In the here and now of the exchange of looks between audience and stage, by contrast, the ageing and degenerating body is subjected to an unsparing exposition. The performer balances on a knife edge between a metamorphosis into a dead exhibition piece and her self-assertion as a person. In a certain way, the performer also presents herself *as a victim*: without the protection of the role, with the fortification of the idealizing serenity of the ideal, the body in its fragility and misery is also surrendered to the tribunal of judging gazes as an offer of erotic stimulation and provocation. From this victim position, however, the postdramatic sculptural body image can turn into an act of aggression and of challenging the audience. As the performer faces him as an individual, vulnerable person, the spectator becomes aware of a reality that is masked in traditional theatre, even though it inevitably adheres to the gaze's relationship to the 'scene': to the *act of seeing* that is voyeuristically applied to the exhibited performer as if she was a sculptural object.

Theatre that rejects the dramatic model can retrieve the possibility of returning to things their value and to the human actors the experience of 'thing-ness' that has become alien to them. At the same time, it gains a new playing field in the sphere of machines, which connects human beings, mechanics and technology – from Kantor's bizarre machines of love and death to high tech theatre. Heiner Müller noticed about Wilson's theatre the 'wisdom of fairy tales that the history of humans cannot be separated from the history of the animals (plants, stones, machines)'. It seemed to anticipate 'the unity of man and machine, the next step in evolution'.[16] It seems indeed that the ever accelerating technologization and with it the tendency of a transformation of the body from 'destiny' to controllable and selectable apparatus – a programmable techno-body – announces an *anthropological mutation* whose first tremors are registered more precisely in the arts than in quickly outdated judicial and political discourses.

Pain, catharsis

Theatre has always been fascinated by pain, even if this traditionally has not had a good press in aesthetics compared to the more ideal suffering. Since antiquity, pain, violence, death and the feelings of fear and pity provoked by them have been at the 'root of the pleasure in tragic objects' (Schiller). In the evocation of the unpresentable that pain constitutes, we encounter a central problem of theatre: the challenge to actualize the incomprehensible by means of the body, which itself *is* 'pain memory' because culture and 'pain as the most powerful mnemonic aide' (Nietzsche) have been inscribed in it in disciplining ways. The mimesis *of* pain initially means that torture, agony, physical suffering and pain are imitated and deceptively suggested, so that painful empathy with the *played* pain arises in the spectators. Postdramatic theatre, however, is above all familiar with 'mimesis *to* pain' ('Mimesis *an* den Schmerz' – Adorno): when the stage is becoming like life, when people really fall or really get hit on stage, the spectators start to fear for the players. The novelty resides in the fact that there is a transition from *represented pain* to *pain experienced in representation*. In its moral and aesthetic ambiguity it has become the indicator for the question of representation: exhausting and risky physical actions on stage (La La La Human Steps); exercises that often appear paramilitary (some dance theatre; Einar Schleef); masochism (La Fura dels Baus); the ethically provocative play with the fiction or reality of cruelty (Jan Fabre); the exhibition of diseased or disfigured bodies. A theatre of *bodies in pain* causes a schism for the perception: here the represented pain, there the playful, joyful act of its representation that is itself attesting to pain.

It is hardly a coincidence that we find in contemporary theatre a persistent return to the metaphor of the world as a hospital or delusional world, a world to which there is no alternative but the equally catastrophic withdrawal into solipsistic isolation. As in the work of Beckett and Heiner Müller, we find people in wheelchairs in the productions of *Dionysus* (1990) and *Elektra* (1995) by the Japanese director Tadashi Suzuki who stages strictly formalized, procession-like images of hell. The Catalonian group La Fura dels Baus places the audience into claustrophobically enclosed, demonic scenarios of agony that seem to be inspired by Dante's *Inferno*: naked bodies submerged in what looks like boiling water and oil, hanged, fallen and maltreated; fire flaring up everywhere, tied up people being flayed and whipped, torturers shouting out orders within a pandemonium of drumming, howling and screaming. While the dramatic theatre conceals the process of the body in the role, postdramatic theatre aims at the public exhibition of the body, its deterioration in an act that does not allow for a clear separation of art and reality. It does not conceal the fact that the body is moribund but rather emphasizes it. When the actor Ron Vawter shortly before his death (he died of AIDS) played two homosexuals in a double portrait, it was impossible to determine whether the sudden pauses in his performance were due to moments of 'acted' or real exhaustion. In the works of Reza Abdoh, who died of AIDS at a young age, the historical, theatrical and mediated ghosts entered into a symbiosis between show and provocation, bloody Grand Guignol and abysmal mourning. His theatre was baroque: displaying a brutal direct sensuality and the search for transcendence, a lust for life and the confrontation with death. Sarajevo, a hospital, and the frightening spectacle of a petty bourgeois interior became the 'writing on the wall' of a world emptied of meaning in which coldness, pain, disease, torture, death and depravity reign.

Media

In the theory of avant-garde theatre it has become commonplace to say that it analyses, reflects and deconstructs the conditions of seeing and hearing in the society of the media. Regardless of the cogency of this statement, it is to be doubted that the self-referentiality of the theatre works in question is really primarily driven by such a pathos of analysis which is more at home in theoretical efforts. Rather it seems realistic that an aesthetic is manifesting itself here that seeks proximity to an artificially changed perception. The often falsely 'dramatized' problem, that the seemingly limitless possibilities of reproduction, presentation and simulation of realities through media information technologies (supported by the universal medium of the computer) were leaving the representational possibilities of the theatre far behind, does *not* constitute the real explosive force of the question of the relationship between theatre and media. Theatre *per se* is already an art form of *signifying*, not of mimetic copying. (A tree on stage, even if it looks very real, remains a *sign* for a tree, not the reproduction of a tree, while a tree in film may mean all sorts of things as a sign but is above all a photographic reproduction of a tree.) Theatre does not simulate but obviously remains a concrete reality of the place, the time, the people who produce signs in the theatre – and these are always signs of signs.[17] What is a real cause of concern for the theatre, however, is the emerging transition to an *interaction* of distant partners by means of technology (at present still in the primitive stages of development). Will such an increasingly perfected interaction in the end compete with the domain of the theatrical live arts whose main principle is *participation?* The point of theatre, however, is a communication structure at whose heart is not the process of a feedback of information but a different 'way of meaning what is meant' (Benjamin's 'Art des Meinens') which ultimately includes death. Information is outside of death, beyond the experience of time. Theatre, by contrast, in as much as within it sender and receiver age together, is a kind of 'intimation of mortality' – in the sense implied by Heiner Müller's remark that 'the potentially dying person' is what is special about theatre. In media communication technology the hiatus of mathematization separates the subjects from each other, so that their proximity and distance become irrelevant. The theatre, however, consisting of a shared time-space of mortality, articulates as a performative act the necessity of engaging with death, i.e. with the (a)liveness of life. Its themes are, to use Müller's words, the terrors and joys of transformation, while film is watching death at work. It is basically this aspect of the shared time–space of mortality with all its ethical and communication theoretical implications that ultimately marks a categorical difference between theatre and technological media.

Media in postdramatic theatre

We can roughly distinguish between different modes of media use in theatre. Either media are *occasionally* used without this use fundamentally defining the theatrical conception (mere media employment); or they serve as a source of *inspiration* for the theatre, its aesthetic or form without the media technology playing a major role in the productions themselves; or they are *constitutive* for certain forms of theatre (Corsetti, Wooster, Jesurun). And finally theatre and media art can meet in the form of *video installations*. Many directors use media on a case-by-case basis – as for example Peter Sellars in his London staging of Shakespeare's *Merchant of Venice* – without this defining their style. Particularly for a director who counts as 'postmodern', it is par for the course. Other theatre forms are primarily characterized not by the employment of media technology but by an *inspiration* through media aesthetic that is recognizable in the aesthetic of the staging. Among these are the rapid succession of images, the speed of conversation in shorthand, the gag consciousness of TV comedies, allusions to the popular entertainment of television, to film and television stars, to the day-to-day business of the entertainment industries and their movers and shakers, quotes from pop culture, entertainment films and controversial topics in the public sphere of the media. In these forms a parodic and ironic refraction of the media is predominant, but sometimes only the themes of the media are adopted. What is postdramatic about these attempts is that the quoted motifs, gags or names are not placed inside the frame of a coherent narrative dramaturgy but rather serve as musical phrases in a rhythm, as elements of a scenic image collage. René Pollesch showed in *Harakiri einer Bauchrednertagung* (*Harakiri of a Ventriloquist Convention*) and *Splatterboulevard* (1992) how entirely without drama the continually churned out dialogue punch lines form a text for which screwball comedy and sitcom serve as models. Accomplished tastelessness, perpetual circling in a state of desolate listlessness and parodic media appropriations here produce their own *pop-theatre* atmosphere. In 1996 Stefan Pucher collaborated with the English company Gob Squad to produce the performance *Ganz nah dran* (*Close up*) at the Frankfurt TAT. Here the media repertoire, which influences the speech, gestures and emotional patterns of everyday life, was theatrically exhibited. A large part of the performance consisted in the self-presentations of the performers, which made it difficult to discern the 'real' biographical elements.

The work of The Wooster Group can serve as an example of the use of media as *constitutive* for certain forms of theatre. As a means of problematizing self-reflection, the electronic images in their 'post-epic' theatre refer directly to the everyday reality and/or the theatre process of the *players*. At most, they quote visual material – in *Hairy Ape*, for instance, a boxing match in which a white guy is fighting a black guy – as a *mental* extension of the stage, not as a document. It is therefore logical that video technology tends to be used for the co-presence of video image and live actor, functioning in general as the technically mediated *self-referentiality* of the theatre. It is a central element in the work of The Wooster Group, a company that originally emerged from Schechner's Performance Group and was named after the group's home in the Performance Garage located in Manhattan's Wooster Street. Theatre here demonstrates its technical possibilities dissected into individual components. The theatre machinery is clearly visible. The technical workings of the performance are openly exhibited: cables, apparatus, instruments are not shamefully hidden or masked by lighting but integrated like props or almost like actors in their own right. The performers often imitate the affectations of television moderators. In *Brace Up!* based on Chekhov's *Three Sisters* a narrator (Kate Valk) guides us through the performance but also speaks text by figures who are not at that moment represented by other performers, introduces actors (for example the very old performer Beatrice Roth playing the youngest of the three sisters), and gives stage directions. During the performance debates may develop over whether a certain passage should be skipped or not – in short: what is shown is somewhere between a rehearsal and a performance, making the *production* of theatre visible and repeatedly addressing itself to the audience as in television. Particularly characteristic is the use of video in order to integrate absent performers, according to the motto: Michael Kirby can't be here tonight but we show him as a video image; one performer is too old to take part in the tour, we show her in the video. Very casually the illusions of the theatre and the familiar but actually quite amazing equal weighting of video presence and live presence are thus highlighted.

Theatre can also create 'virtual spaces' with its own means, as for example in the works of Helena Waldmann who in the 1990s attracted attention through a series of inventive theatrical 'viewing arrangements'. In the performance of *Wodka konkav*, the audience is seated opposite a wall and below several large, concave mirrors. When the performance starts, dancing bodies, who are not directly physically visible, appear in the mirrors, multiplied by them and partially distorted. In the multiple indirect reflection they look so similar that the spectators are long in doubt – some until the very end – about whether they are dealing with one body somehow doubled through the mirrors, two bodies, or more. Moreover, one can only see the images of the bodies – obviously dancing behind the wall – as they are mirrored at an angle from above, in addition to the multiple reflections there are also peculiar contractions, fragmentations, optical deformations that also unite with psychedelic bodiless figures of light. Added to this spectacle that removes the living body from view while simultaneously thematizing the gaze onto the body one hears from the loudspeakers a text by the Russian author Venedikt Jerofejev (spoken by the actor Thomas Thieme) which revolves exclusively around vodka and drunkenness. When at the end the two dancers – there really are two and they are twins! – step out in front of the wall for a 'curtain call' their presence seems the most natural thing – and yet they had been there, present in such a multiply fractured and refracted way that the question about representation becomes labyrinthine: what does presence consist of? What presents itself to the audience if not a presence that crosses itself out? This seems to be the case, but what can be experienced here is rather this: presence is the effect not simply of perception but of the *desire* to see. The withdrawal calls to mind what the perception of the 'present' body had actually also been: the hallucination of an absent other body, an imago equally invested with desire and rivalry and thus open to all variants of deadly conflicts and of Eros' promises of happiness.

Moreover, it shows what the perception of the present body is also: not the perception of presence but the *consciousness* of presence, neither in need of sensuous confirmation, nor ultimately capable of it. It is obvious that this kind of theatre, even more so than traditional theatre productions, defies reproduction through film or television. Not because of the beauty of the live presence but because the (technically reproduced) image would level the layers and divisions between physical, imaginary and mental presence on which everything depends here.

Electronic images as a relief

One question media theatre poses for the spectator is this: why is it the image that fascinates us more? What constitutes the magic attraction that seduces the gaze to follow the image when given the choice between devouring something real or something imaginary? One possible answer is that the image is removed from real life, there is something liberating about the appearance of the image, which gives pleasure to the gaze. The gaze liberates desire from the bothersome 'other circumstance' of real, really producing bodies and transports it to a dream vision.

> Television, video cassettes, video tape recorders/players, video games, and personal computers all form an encompassing electronic representational system whose various forms 'interface' to constitute an alternative and absolute world that uniquely *incorporates* the spectator/user in a spatially decentered, weakly temporalized, and quasi-disembodied state . . . Indeed, the electronic is phenomenologically experienced not as a discrete, intentional, and bodily centered *projection* in space but rather as a simultaneous, *dispersed*, and insubstantial *transmission* across a network . . . Living in a schematized and intertextual meta-world far removed from all reference to a 'real' world liberates the spectator/user from what might be termed the latter's moral and physical gravity. The postmodern and electronic 'instant', in its break from the temporal structures of retension and pretension, constitutes a form of presence (one abstracted from the continuity that gives meaning to the system past/present/future) and changes the nature of the space it occupies . . . In an important sense, electronic space *disembodies* . . . electronic 'presence' has neither a point of view nor a field of vision.[18]

In the face of such a seductive superiority of the virtual image world of cyborg, internet, virtual reality, etc., the question is: where can a practice that refuses such a 'relief' find a foothold? How can the scaled down model of the theatre situation turn the nature of seeing itself into the object of conscious perception? How can the disposition of the viewing subject as it experiences itself everywhere in media technology become visible itself? Paradoxically the answer is: in another version of the virtual itself.

Theatre-bodies cannot be captured by any video, because they are only 'there' in the 'between-the-bodies' of live performance. In this insecurity and forlornness, they store memory: they actualize (and appeal to) corporeal experience. And they store future, for what they remind us of is desire as something unfulfilled and unfulfillable. This is where the alternative to the electronic images resides: art as a theatrical process that actually preserves the virtual dimension, the dimension of desire and not knowing. Theatre is first of all anthropological, the name for a *behaviour* (playing, showing oneself, playing roles, gathering, spectating as a virtual or real form of participation), secondly it is a *situation*, and only then, last of all, is it *representation*. Media images are – in the first and in the last place – nothing but representation. The image as representation gives us a lot, to be sure: especially the feeling of being always on the track of something else. We are hunters in search of the lost treasure. Always 'in the picture', we are on the scent of a secret – but in doing so at any moment already 'content at the end' because we are satisfied by the image. The reason for this is that the electronic image lures through emptiness. Emptiness offers no resistance. Nothing can block us. Nothing stagnates. The electronic image is an idol (not simply an icon). The body or face in video is enough – for itself and for us. By contrast, an air of (productive) disappointment always surrounds the presence of real bodies. It is reminiscent of the air of mourning that, according to Hegel, surrounds the ancient Greek sculptures of gods: their all too complete and perfect presence allows for no transcendence of materiality to a more spiritual interiority. Similarly, one can say of the theatre: after the body there is nothing else. We have arrived. Nothing can be or become more present. Within any fascination with the live body there remains this invariably only desired 'rest' that we cannot get access to, a beyond the frame, a background. The gaze remains before the visibility of the real body like Kafka's man 'before the law'. There is nothing but this one gate and we cannot get through it because the object of desire is always elsewhere, (in the) background, never a presence as a form of being. In this way, the body in theatre is a signifier (not the object) of desire. The electronic image, by contrast, is pure foreground. It evokes a fulfilled, superficially fulfilled kind of seeing. Since no aim or desire enters consciousness as the background of the image, there can be no lack. The electronic image *lacks lack*, and is consequently leading only to – the next image, in which again nothing 'disturbs' or prevents us from enjoying the plenitude of the image.

'Representability', fate

A figure enters the stage. It interests us because the frame of the stage, of the staging, of the action, and of the visual constellation of the scene exhibits it. The peculiar suspense that accompanies its viewing is the curiosity about an impending explanation (that fails to occur). The restless suspense only lasts as long as there is still a remnant of this open question. The figure in its presence is nevertheless – absent. Shall we say: virtual? It remains *theatrical* only in the rhythm and to the degree of a certain not-knowing that keeps the perception in its searching motion. It is the dimension of not-knowing in theatrical perception (every figure is an oracle) that accounts for its constitutive virtuality. Theatre is real virtuality. For the theatrical gaze the body on stage turns into an 'image' in another sense of the word – not into an electronic image as it has been discussed here but into an 'image' in the sense of the term used by Max Imdahl. He postulates in a 'radical conjecture', as Bernhard Waldenfels stresses, the 'possibility of a withdrawal of reality in seeing itself' and calls image (in the emphatic sense) an occasion when a seeing takes place that leads to the invisible with seeing eyes:

> But perhaps the image is also a form of representation for something else, namely the illustrative model for a reality that withdraws forever from any immediate, as well as final, grasp – a reality to which it, as something visible, refers, and which itself has no appearance.[19]

Thus understood, the 'image' is about 'the experience of an insurmountable powerlessness to dispose' over reality. This insight helps us to analyse more precisely the *withdrawal of representation* in theatre that makes sure the spectator's seeing is not deceived by the illusion of the availability of the visible (an illusion inherent to the electronic image). Inherent to the curious gaze in theatre is the expectation that it will 'at one point' see the other. But this gaze does not reach for ever more distant unreal spaces but circles inside itself, pointing inwards, towards the clarification and visibility of the figure that nevertheless remains an enigma. Therefore this gaze is accompanied by a sense of lack instead of fulfilment. Naturally, this hope cannot be fulfilled because plenitude only persists in the question, in the curiosity, in the expectation, the non-appearance, the memory, not in the 'present' reality of the object. The figure of the other in theatre always has a reality only of *arrival*, not presence. In the light of the virtual objective – the 'representation' in its plenitude – we may call this essence of the theatrical figure its '*representability*' (*Darstellbarkeit*). Compared to this, the electronic images, which bridge the emptiness, fulfil the wish and deny the border, are realizations of *representation* (*Darstellung*). This requires some further explanation.

Walter Benjamin's essay on translation defines 'translatability' as the inherently necessary determination of certain texts. They imply translatability even if they were never actually going to be adequately translated. In the same text, Benjamin writes about the 'unforgettableness' of events, which can be called unforgettable even if all people had forgotten them but if it was in their essence not to be forgotten. According to Benjamin, they would still be the object of a memory, which he interprets as God's memory. In a similar sense, 'representability' can be thought of as an essential dimension of theatre. What ancient tragedy already articulated was the thought that there must be some coherence inhering in a human's life, a *Gestalt* that remains inaccessible to his/her own knowledge, however. This coherence is representable and visible only from a totally different perspective unattainable for the mortal human, namely that of the 'gods'. This inner logic is there, despite the fact that the discourse of ancient tragedy does not deny the accidental, chance nature that humans share with all other creatures and circumstances but rather highlights it in an extreme manner. Despite the human being's subjection to Chaos and Tyche, ancient tragedy insists that *representability* in this sense should be thought of as an inherent quality of its existence as a speaking creature. Namely in this sense: life never attains such representation but in being articulated theatrically its 'representability' appears. This truth about life is not 'given' at any moment, at any 'date', because it corresponds to its nature, to use Benjamin's words, to be represented in a *different* sphere. The mediated pictures, by contrast, are *nothing but data* (the given). In theatre, the actor is the interference (*Bildstörung*, literally 'picture trouble'). Electronic pictures, by contrast, evoke the image of fulfilment, the phantasm of 'immediate contact' with the desired. In theatre, what is perceived is not 'given' but only giving. It is arriving, an event that is an advent, and it depends upon the answer from chorus and audience in what Heiner Müller called an 'incandescent circuit'. In this circuit, the signifiers are only ever 'taken on' and all involved are called upon to pass them on: from the represented they come to the performer, from the performer to the visitors, and from these back to the performer. 'Representability' is inherent in this temporal process, remaining in irreconcilable tension with all fixed representations, which it traverses.

It may appear strange to introduce at this point the perhaps oldest theatre trick, namely what we are used to calling *fate*. Yet, it may actually be helpful to state for the theatre that *fate is another word for representability*. The electronic image, understood as the sphere of representation, is essentially a perpetual affirmation of 'fatelessness'. Representability as an experience that is simultaneously aesthetic and ethical is the manifestation of fate, the main theme of tragic theatre. However, while the dramatic theatre inspired by the ancient model relegated fate to the frame of a narration, the course of a fable, in postdramatic theatre it is articulated not through a plot but through the appearance of the body: fate here speaks through the gesture, not through myth. Aristotle (and in his wake almost the entire Western theory of the theatre) demands that tragedy has to be a whole with beginning, middle and end. Of course this was a paradoxical concept, since in reality – even in narrated reality – such a 'beginning', i.e. something that according to Aristotle has no presuppositions, simply does not exist; and neither does an 'end', i.e. something that has no consequences. What Aristotle articulates here, however, in his only seemingly self-evident formula, is nothing but the abstract formula for the *law of all representation*. The whole with beginning, middle, and end is the *frame*. It is to no avail, however, that each representation tries – and must try – to assert such framing. Fate (or representability) transcends the frame – in the same sense as human life transcends the biological life through the plethora and self-reflecting multiplication and intensification of images of it. Representability, the inner logic of theatrical reality, thus by no means contradicts the insight that human reality can only be dealt with under the premise that it remains unrepresentable.

The mediated image does know the possibility of representation in the sense of a mathematization that is in principle limitless. The question of a constitutive representability that always remains virtual does not come up here. The medium closes into a circuit of mathematical assumptions, existent givens, plain evidences. Representation is here a euphemism for information. Lyotard declared in 1979 in *The Postmodern Condition* that under the conditions of a generalized communication technology anything that cannot take the form of information would be excluded from the knowledge of society. This fate could hit theatre, for 'theatre' – in the emphatic and ideal sense that has been discussed here – actually works precisely the other way round, transferring all information into something else, namely into virtuality. It turns even representation into representability. What the spectators really see in front of them is already transformed into the mere sign, indication of an indeterminate possibility, thus at the same time leaving the sphere of beholding, transforming each perceived form into an index for one that is being missed. 'Theatre' transforms even the most simple representation of death into an unthinkable virtuality. Conversely, the electronic image allows and demands to see even the most impossible things. There is no void of another efficacy here, only evident reality. We are perhaps, quite possibly, already on the way to the images, our eyes meeting nothing but variations of the ideal of fatelessness, the Word Perfect of virtual communication. We do not know, for this fate, too, does not appear in any possible representation but will only have been. As Heiner Müller says: 'Nothing is the way it stays'.

Epilogue

The political

This study of postdramatic theatre does not aim to trace the new theatrical modes of creation to sociologically determined causes and circumstances. For one thing, such deductions normally fall short, even in the case of subject matter to which scholars have more of a historical distance. They can be trusted even less when it comes to the confusing and 'unsurveyable' present (Habermas) in which highly contradictory – but therefore no less ambitious – large-scale analyses of the state of the world are chasing each other. Nevertheless, in a reality brimming with social and political conflicts, civil wars, oppression, growing poverty and social injustice, it seems appropriate to conclude with a few general reflections on the way in which one could theorize the relationship of postdramatic theatre to the political. Issues that we call 'political' have to do with social power. For a long time issues of power have been conceived in the domain of law, with its borderline phenomena of revolution, anarchy, state of emergency (*Ausnahmezustand*) and war. In spite of the noticeable tendency towards a juridification of all areas of life, however, 'power' is increasingly organized as a micro-physics, as a web, in which even the leading political elite – not to mention single individuals – hardly have any real power over economico-political processes any more. Therefore, political conflicts increasingly elude intuitive perception and cognition and consequently scenic representation. There are hardly any visible representatives of legal positions confronting each other as political opponents any more. What still attains an intuitable quality, by contrast, is the momentary *suspension* of normative, legal and political modes of behaviour, i.e. the plainly *non*-political terror, anarchy, madness, despair, laughter, revolt, antisocial behaviour – and inherent in it the already latently posited fanatical or fundamentalist negation of immanently secular, rationally founded criteria of action in general. Since Machiavelli, however, the modern demarcation of the political as an autonomous plane of argumentation has been based exactly on the immanence of these criteria.

Intercultural theatre

Some see the political dimension of theatre in furthering 'intercultural' understanding. This possibility cannot be denied outright. But haven't advocates of
intercultural theatre like Pavis, Schechner and Peter Brook been vehemently
criticized by Indian authors for keeping silent about the disrespectful and superficial appropriation often lurking in intercultural activities, i.e. the cultural
imperialist exploitation of the other culture?[1] Brook's famous *Mahabharata*, as
well as Lee Breuer's *The Gospel at Colonus* (which combined Greek-European
theatre traditions with Afro-American and Christian traditions) met not only
with approval but also with harsh criticism as examples of a patriarchal treatment of an oppressed culture by a dominant culture. An underlying ambiguity
continues to exist in all intercultural communication as long as cultural forms of
expression are always at the same time part of a politically dominant culture or
of an oppressed culture, so that it is not a 'communication' of equals that occurs
between the two cultures. Instead of hanging on to an idealizing vision of a 'new
kind of transcultural communicative synthesis through performance', it seems
more honest to join Andrzej Wirth in simply diagnosing the utilization of the
most diverse cultural patterns and emblems throughout the international theatre
landscape without hoping for a new theatrical *ersatz* site of a political public
sphere. To use Wirth's terms, we are dealing here more with an 'iconophilia'
than with interculturalism.[2]

The term 'interculturalism' should in any case provoke more political scepticism than is usually the case. It is true that it is preferable to the even more
questionable term of 'multiculturalism' that tends to favour the mutual isolation
of cultures from each other and the aggressive self-affirmation of cultural group
identities more than the urban ideal of mutual influence and interaction. But
here, too, questions should be raised: for it is not just 'cultures' as such that
meet but concrete artists, art forms and theatre productions. The inter-artistic
exchange, moreover, does not take place in the sense of a cultural 'representation': it is not as a representative of African culture that Wole Soyinka adapts a
text by Brecht as a representative of European culture. Quite apart from the
question of what 'the' African (or European or German) culture would be
anyway, it generally holds true that most artists also view their 'own' culture
from a certain distance, occupying very often a dissident, deviant and marginal
position within it.[3] A good example for intercultural theatre with all its chances
and problems was a play with the baroque title *The Aboriginal Protesters Confront
the Proclamation of the Australian Republic on 26 January 2001 with the Theatre Production 'The Mission' by Heiner Müller*. The project premiered in Sydney in early 1996
and could be seen in Weimar in the same year. The idea by Gerhard Fischer (a
German Studies specialist resident in Australia) had been realized after several
years of difficult preparations: to stage a text – written on Fischer's initiative –
by the Aborigine author Mudrooroo that shows how the intention of an Aborigine group of actors to stage Heiner Müller's important postcolonial play *The
Mission* leads to increasingly violent political conflicts. There is too much of a

rift between the political consciousness of the players and the deeply sceptical vision of the European author, who after all always proclaimed his political sympathy with the 'third world'. Müller's play with the subtitle *Memory of a Revolution* revolves around the story of three emissaries from revolutionary France who arrive in Jamaica in 1794 with the 'mission' to stir up a revolt of the blacks against their English colonizers. The play ends with treason and the failure of the revolution but raises the question of the ongoing oppression of races and classes all the more adamantly. The staging by Noel Tovey became a political theatre event in Sydney precisely because of the demonstration of the unbridgeable distance between the author and the theatre practitioners. Mudrooroo's adaptation shows how the theatre group at the end votes unanimously against a performance of the Müller text (which none the less has been shown practically in its entirety in the course of the rehearsals performed in the play). Another example was the performance piece *Borderama* (1995) by Guillermo Gómez-Peña and Robert Sifuentes, who have developed their own performance style from their experience of the borderland between the USA and Mexico in order to find an expression for the 'intercultural' experience of oppression and marginalization. In this work, radio art, hip hop, cable television, film and literature are combined. Migration, border crossings, criminalization, racism and xenophobia are addressed in a theatre form that moves with surprising ease between talk show, sports, cinema parodies and harangues, demonstrations, cabaret, night club atmosphere and aggressive pop.[4] Gómez-Peña and Coco Fusco had previously caused an international stir with the tour of their provocative performance *Two Undiscovered Amerindians Visit . . .* (also known as *The Couple in the Cage*) in 1992.[5] Posing in a cage as 'natives' from a 'newly discovered' island they intended to protest 500 years of the exhibition of colonized people, a history Fusco calls 'the other history of intercultural performance'.[6] To their shock and surprise, many spectators missed the irony and believed the performers to be real undiscovered natives.

Representation, measure and transgression

As a reaction to the difficulty of developing adequate forms of a political theatre, we find a widespread and questionable return to a deceptively *immediate morality* that is believed to be valid independently of the ambiguities of the political world. In theatre, such moralism favours the return of the idea of the 'theatre considered as a moral institution' (Schiller) – which is always going to suffer, however, from not being able really to believe in itself. On the other hand, there is one thing theatre can do: artistically deconstruct the space of political discourse as such – in as much as the latter erects the thesis, opinion, order, law and organically conceived wholeness of the political body – and to show its latently authoritarian constitution. This happens through the dismantling of discursive certainties of the political, the unmasking of rhetoric, the opening of the field of a non-thetical presentation (in the sense of Julia Kristeva). If we do not want to write off the political dimension of theatre altogether, we have to start with the diagnosis that the question of a political theatre changes radically under the conditions of contemporary information society. That politically oppressed people are shown on stage does not make theatre political. And if the political in its sensational aspects merely procures entertainment value, then theatre may well be political – but only in the bad sense of an (at least unconscious) affirmation of existing political conditions. It is not through the direct thematization of the political that theatre becomes political but through the implicit substance and critical value of its *mode of representation*.

The political, Julia Kristeva emphasizes, is that which sets the measure. The political is subject to the law of the law. It cannot help but posit an order, a rule, a power that is applicable to all, a common measure.[7] The socio-symbolic law is the common measure; the political is the sphere of its confirmation, affirmation, protection, adaptation to the changeable course of things, abolition or modification. Hence, there is an insurmountable rift between the political, which sets the rules, and art, which constitutes, we might say, always an *exception*: the exception to every rule, the affirmation of the irregular even within the rule itself. Theatre as aesthetic behaviour is unthinkable without the infringement of prescriptions, without *transgression*. Pitted against this statement is an argument that is quasi-omnipresent especially in the American debate: namely, that the present was defined by 'the breakdown of the old structural opposition of the cultural and the economic in the simultaneous commodification of the former and the symbolization of the latter'.[8] If this diagnosis were accurate, then the obvious thesis would be that no 'avant-garde' implying a politics of transgression is possible any more because 'the transgressive politics of avant-gardism presupposes cultural limits which are no longer relevant to the seemingly limitless horizon of multinational capitalism'.[9] According to this thesis, there could no longer be a 'transgressive' but only a 'resistant' politics of the arts.[10] Apart from the fact that on closer inspection of what the terms 'transgressive' and 'resistant' mean in the American debate the difference would perhaps diminish, we should just like to make the case here for the counterthesis that the transgressive moment is in our understanding essential for all art, not just political art. Art privileges – even in the 'création collective' – the individual *par excellence*, the singular, that which remains unquantifiable in relation to even the best of laws – given that the domain of the law is always the attempt to *calculate* even the unpredictable. In art, it is always Brecht's Fatzer who speaks:

> You, however, you calculate to the last fraction
> What remains to be done by me, and put it on the account.
> But I don't do it! Count!
> Count on Fatzer's ten pence perseverance
> And Fatzer's daily vagary!
> Estimate my abyss
> Take five for the unforeseen

Keep of everything there is of me
Only what is useful to you.
The rest is Fatzer.[11]

Theatre itself would hardly have come about without the hybrid act that an
individual broke free from the collective, into the unknown, aspiring to an unthinkable possibility; it would hardly have happened without the courage to
transgress borders, all borders of the collective. There is no theatre without self-
dramatization, exaggeration, overdressing, without demanding attention for this
one, personal body – its voice, its movement, its presence and what it has to say.
Certainly, at the origin of theatre as a social practice there is also the instrumen-
talizing and rational self-staging of shamans, chiefs and rulers who manifest their
elevated position *vis-à-vis* the collective through heightened gesture and costume:
theatre as an effect of power. Yet, at the same time, theatre is a practice in and
with signifying material, which does not create orders of power but introduces
chaos and novelty into the ordered, ordering perception. As an opening of the
logo-centric procedure (in which the dominant mode is conceptual identification) in favour of a practice that does not fear the suspension and interruption of
the designating function, theatre can be political. This thesis includes the merely
apparent paradox that theatre is political precisely to the degree in which it
interrupts the categories of the political itself, deposing of them instead of betting
on new laws (no matter how well-intended).

Afformance art?

This seems an appropriate moment for a certain consideration in terms of philosophy of language and at the same time of political theory, which puts the
question of the political theatre into yet another perspective. As long as we view
the political about theatre as a counterforce that is itself political – as a counter-
position and -action and not as a *non-action* and interruption of the law – we are
putting the wrong kind of game on the agenda. While acting with linguistic signs
has been defined by speech act theory as performative, theatre is not a performative act in the full sense of the word. It is – even if this may seem paradoxical
– only pretending to perform. Theatre is not even a thesis but a form of articulation that partially eludes the thetical and the active in general. We could borrow
here the term of the *afformative*, which Werner Hamacher coined in a different
context,[12] and call theatre *afformance art*, in order to allude to the somehow non-
performative in the proximity of performance. While the real political actors
rarely know what they are ultimately bringing about with their actions, they can
at least have a – perhaps false – sense of certainty that what they are doing at
least *is* a doing. While they may not know what it means, they feed the –
perhaps charitable but questionable – illusion that their acting is at all 'meaningful' or important in some way or another. Not so the theatre, which does not
even produce an object, is deceptive as an action, and deceives even when the
illusion is openly disturbed or destroyed. Theatre can only ever be ambiguously

'real' – even when it tries to escape deceptive appearance and draws close to the real. It permeates all representation with the uncertainty of whether something is represented; every act with the uncertainty of whether it was one; every thesis, every position, every work, every meaning with a wavering and potential cancellation. Perhaps theatre can never know whether it really 'does' something, whether it effects something and on top of it means something. Apart from the profitable and ridiculous mass entertainment of the musical, it therefore 'does' less and less. It produces increasingly less meaning because in proximity of the zero-point (in 'fun', in stasis, in the silence of the gazes) something might happen: a now. Doubtful performative – afformance art.

Time and again, especially when the discussion turns to the (impossible) unambiguous differentiation between theatre and performance, the idea comes up that we can oppose performance as a 'real' action to the theatre as the realm of fiction, the actions 'as if', where we can understand something and where the boundaries are clear. Some scholars go as far as to say that performance can be compared to the *terrorist act*.[13] After all, both take place in real, historical time, the performers act as themselves and simultaneously take on symbolic significance, and so on. Even if one could concede some illuminating structural similarities between terrorism and performance, one difference remains decisive: the latter does not happen as a *means* to another (political) end; as a performance it is in this sense precisely 'afformative', namely not simply a performative act. By contrast, what is at issue in the terrorist action is a political or other *determination of aims* (however one may judge these). The terrorist act is intentional, is performative through and through, an act and a postulate in the realm of the logic of means and ends.

Drama and society

Although the question as to the political character of the aesthetic concerns the arts in general and *all* forms of theatre, the relations between a postdramatic aesthetic and the possible political dimensions of theatre immediately come to mind. They resonate in the obvious question: is there a political theatre without narration? Without a fable in Brecht's sense? What might political theatre after and without Brecht be? Does theatre, as many people believe, rely on the fable as a vehicle for the representation of the world? If the artistic work of the theatre belongs to those 'ways of worldmaking' (Nelson Goodman) that are most likely still to contain some potential for reflection, it could seem paradoxical that theatre would simply relinquish drama as one of the strong points that is quasi-sanctified by tradition. Would this not be its real 'gap in the market'? After all, forms and genres always offer also the possibility of communication about collective, not just private experience – artistic forms *are* congealed collective patterns of experience. How can a 'theatrum mundi' function without the possibilities of dramatic fictionalization with its whole wealth of chances for play between fictive (but somehow quasi-real) dramatis personae and real actors? One could indeed be afraid that the disintegration of the established canon of forms could lead to the desolation of whole landscapes of the interrogation of human experience. But lo and behold: the panorama of postdramatic theatre shows that this worry is unfounded; that the new theatre can more plausibly bring the essence and specific chance of theatre to life. To the degree in which it does not represent a fictive figure (in its imaginary eternity, e.g. Hamlet) but instead exposes the body of a performer in its temporality, the themes of the oldest theatre traditions reappear, albeit certainly in a new light: enigma, death, decline, parting, old age, guilt, sacrifice, tragedy and Eros. Death may be performed as an amicably accompanied exit in the real time of the stage, not a fictive tragedy but rather a scenic gesture 'imagined as death', but henceforth the simple gesture carries within it the whole weight of the basic 'everyday' experience of saying goodbye. Postdramatic theatre has come closer to the trivial and banal, the simplicity of an encounter, a look or a shared situation. With this, however, theatre also articulates a possible answer to the tedium of the daily flood of artificial formulas of intensification. The inflationary dramatizations of daily sensations that anaesthetize the sensorium have become unbearable. What is at stake is not a heightening but a deepening of a condition, a situation. In political terms: what is at stake is also the fate of the errors of the dramatic imagination.

Several decades ago, Althusser's essay on Bertolazzi and Brecht[14] made clear how a political theatre can be constituted: namely, in such a way that it lets the dramatic phantasmagoria of the subject come apart at the unbudging wall of 'another' time of the social. What is experienced and/or stylized as 'drama' is nothing but the hopelessly deceptive 'perspectivation' of occurrences as action. Occurrences are interpreted as a 'doing': that was Nietzsche's formula for mythification. This shift also characterizes the individual's (by nature) illusory perception of reality, the 'eternal' ideology of a spontaneously anthropomorphizing perception. Thus, the experience of a split between two times – the time of the subject and the time of the historical process – is the core of political theatre, as Althusser points out, and this in fact hits the nerve of the problem of politics as a subject for theatre. Althusser could show in Brecht's work how the epic theatre assumes the alterity of two times: one is the undialectical, massive time of social and historical processes that is unknowable and inaccessible to the individual, the other the illusory time pattern of subjective experience – melodrama. In this sense, the politics of a theatre that turns the illusions of the subject and the contrasting heterogeneous reality of social processes into an experience for the spectator – as a relation of lacking relations, as discrepancy and 'alterity' – is still possible today.

In present society, almost any form has come to seem more suitable for articulating reality than the action of a causal logic with its inherent attribution of events to the decisions of individuals. Drama and society cannot come together. If dramatic theatre loses ground so 'dramatically', however, this may indicate that the form of experience that corresponds to this art form is retreating in reality itself. Within the scope of this study, we cannot tackle, never mind solve, the question as to the reasons for the retreat of dramatic imagination or for the fact that it is no longer taken for granted. We can only offer a few reflections on this topic. A first thesis could be: while the drama of modern times was based on a human being that constituted itself through interpersonal rapport, the postdramatic theatre assumes a human being for whom even the most conflictuous situations will no longer appear as drama. The representational form 'drama' is available but grasps at nothing when it is meant to articulate experienced reality (beyond the melodramatic illusions). Certainly, one can still recognize a 'dramatic form' in this or that moment (e.g. 'fights' between powerful rulers), but it soon becomes obvious that the real issues are only decided in power blocs, not by protagonists who in reality are interchangeable in what Hegel called the 'prose of civic life'. In addition, the theatre seems to *relinquish the idea of a beginning, middle and end*, since we feel more at home with the thought that the catastrophe (or the amusement) could consist in all things continuing in the same way as they used to. Scientific theories of a rhythmically expanding and contracting universe, chaos and game theory, have further de-dramatized reality.

Another reflection on the disappearance of the dramatic impulse can be tied in with Richard Schechner's theses. He emphasizes that the model 'drama' – understood in Turner's sense as the shape and model of 'social drama' with its sequence of a rupture of the social norm, crisis, reconciliation ('redressive action') and reintegration, i.e. re-establishment of the social continuum – is ultimately based on an overarching social cohesion. The sequential structure of 'performance' – in the comprehensive sense assumed by the theory of cultural performance in theatre anthropology – consists of the phases of gathering, actual performance and disbanding. Within this precisely fixed frame, it offers the image of the staging of a conflict that is surrounded by a space of solidarity and is made possible by it in the first place. This view[15] can be developed in such a way that the presence of drama could indicate precisely a society's capacity to uphold its inner coherence. If it disposes of a frame of solidarity, the latter makes it possible repeatedly to thematize evident and more hidden conflictuous dynamics in the form of wrenching conflicts. Thus, the depth, extent, precision and consequence of the thematization of the conflict indicate the state of the social 'glue', the solidarity or at least the deeper symbolic unity of the society – *how much drama it can afford*, so to speak. Viewed in this light, it would be a fact worth thinking about that drama is increasingly becoming the core of a more or less banal mass entertainment where it is flattened into mere 'action', while it is simultaneously disappearing from the more complex forms of innovative theatre.

Whether or not the processes of crisis and reconciliation and the ritualizations connected to them, as analysed by Bateson, Goffman and Turner, are accurate anthropological and sociological descriptions of the social processes has to remain undecided here. The dwindling of the dramatic space of imagination in the consciousness of society and of the artists seems, at any rate, indisputable and proves that something about this model is no longer in tune with our experience. The dwindling of the dramatic impulse has to be stated – no matter whether it is due to the fact that it has been exhausted and as reconciliation only ever stays 'the same'; whether it assumes a mode of 'action' that we no longer recognize anywhere; or whether it paints an obsolete image of social and personal conflict. If we were to give in to the temptation of regarding post-dramatic theatre as an expression of contemporary social structures – for just a moment and despite all reservations – then a rather gloomy picture would result. We could hardly suppress the suspicion that society can no longer afford the complex and profound representation of wrenching conflicts, representations that 'go to the substance' of issues. It deludes itself with the illusory comedy of a society that allegedly no longer has such inherent conflicts. The theatre aesthetics inadvertently even reflects some of this. A certain paralysis of public discourse about the basic principles of society is striking. There is no current issue that is not 'verbalized' *ad nauseam* in endless commentaries, special broadcasts, talk shows, polls and interviews – but we find hardly a sign of society's capacity to 'dramatize' the uncertainty of its really founding and fundamental issues and principles, which are after all deeply shaken. Postdramatic theatre is also theatre in an age of omitted images of conflict.

Theatre and the 'Society of the Spectacle'

It is apparent that the decline of the dramatic is by no means synonymous with the decline of the theatrical. On the contrary: theatricalization permeates the entire social life, starting with the individual attempts to produce or feign a *public self* – the cult of self-presentation and self-revelation through fashion signs or other marks designed to attest to the model of a self (albeit mostly borrowed) *vis-à-vis* a certain group, as well as *vis-à-vis* the anonymous crowd. Alongside the external construction of the individual there are the self-presentations of group- and generation-specific identities that represent themselves as theatrically organized appearances, for want of distinct linguistic discourses, programmes, ideologies or utopias. If we add advertising, the self-staging of the business world and the theatricality of mediated self-presentation in politics, it seems that we are witnessing the perfection of what Guy Debord described as emerging in his *Society of the Spectacle*. It is a fundamental fact of today's Western societies that all human experiences (life, eroticism, happiness, recognition) are tied to *commodities* or more precisely their consumption and possession (and not to a discourse). This corresponds exactly to the civilization of images that can only ever refer to the next image and call up other images. The totality of the spectacle is the 'theatricalization' of all areas of social life.

As society seems to be freeing itself more and more from needs and wants through perpetual economic growth, it enters into a more or less total dependence on precisely this growth, or rather on the political means to secure it.[16] For this mechanism, however, the *definition of the citizen as spectator* is indispensable – a definition that is gaining more and more plausibility in the society of the media anyway. In an essay devoted to the media effects in the political sphere, Samuel Weber writes:

If we remain spectators/viewers, if we stay where we are – in front of the television – the catastrophes will always stay outside, will always be 'objects' for a 'subject' – this is the implicit promise of the medium. But this comforting promise coincides with an equally clear, if unspoken threat: Stay where you are! If you move, there may be an intervention, whether humanitarian or not.[17]

One realizes here that the separation of the event from the perception of the event, precisely through the mediation of the news about it, leads to an erosion of the act of communication. The consciousness of being connected to others and thus being answerable and bound to them 'in the language', in the medium of communication itself recedes in favour of communication as (an exchange of) information. Speaking as such is in principle an accountable speaking. (The statement 'I love you' is not a piece of information but an act, an engagement.) Media, by contrast, transform the giving of signs into information and through habit and repetition dissolve the consciousness and even the sense for the fact that the act of sending signs ultimately involves sender and receiver in a shared situation connected through the medium of language. This is the real reason why fiction and reality merge, as is often deplored. Not because people mistake that in one case they are dealing with something invented and in the other with news, but because of the manner in which the signifying process divides the thing and the sign, the reference and the situation of the production of the signs. The uncontrollable degree of reality of the images, on the one hand, delocalizes the events disseminated through the medium and, on the other hand, simultaneously promotes 'communities of values' among the viewers who are receiving the images isolated in their homes. Thus the continual presentation of bodies that are abused, injured, killed through isolated (real or fictive) catastrophes creates a radical distance for passive viewing: the bond between perception and action, receiving message and 'answerability', is dissolved. We find ourselves *in* a spectacle in which we can only *look on* – bad traditional theatre. Under these conditions, postdramatic theatre tries to withdraw from the reproduction of 'images' into which all spectacles ultimately solidify. It becomes 'calm' and 'static', offering images without reference and handing over the domain of the dramatic to the images of violence and conflict in the media, unless it incorporates these in order to parody them.

Politics of perception, aesthetics of responsibility

It is not a new insight that theatre is reliant on indirectness and deceleration, on a reflecting immersion in political topics. Its political engagement does not consist in the topics but in the forms of perception. This insight presupposes the overcoming of what Peter von Becker once called the 'Lessing-Schiller-Brecht-68-syndrom' in German theatre.[18] At the same time, we have to avoid facile assertions along the lines that the political is only a superficial aspect of art – or inversely, that all art is 'somehow' political. For whether the political is considered as altogether absent from theatre or as a quite general ingredient of it anyway – in both cases it is regarded as no longer interesting. Yet theatre is an art of the social *par excellence*. Its analysis, therefore, cannot settle for a de-politicization because its practice is objectively politically co-determined. The politics of theatre, however, is to be sought in the manner of its *sign usage*. The politics of theatre is a *politics of perception*. To define it we have to remember that the mode of perception in theatre cannot be separated from the existence of theatre in a world of media which massively shapes all perception. The rapidly transmitted and seemingly 'true to life' image suggests the real which in truth it first softens, mellows and weakens. Produced far from its reception and received far from its origin, it imprints indifference onto everything shown. We enter into (mediated) contact with everything, and simultaneously experience ourselves as radically detached from the plethora of facts and fictions we are being informed about. While the media perpetually dramatize all political conflicts, the glut of information, combined with the factual disintegration of clearly discernible political frontlines of the events, produces within the omnipresence of the electronic image a *disjointedness* between representation and represented, between image and reception of the image. Denied in vain by the media with their insistent gestures of appeal, this disjointedness is incessantly confirmed by the technology of the mediated circulation of signs. We have the impression that individuals are reporting to us, but in fact it is collectives, who for their part represent nothing but *functions of the medium* instead of availing themselves of it. What happens from moment to moment is the erasure of the trace, the avoidance of the self-referencing of the sign. Consequently a 'bisection' of language occurs. On the one hand, the medium releases the senders from all connection with the emitted message and, on the other hand, it occults the viewers' perception of the fact that participation in language also makes them, the receivers, responsible for the message. In a fairytale-like manner, the technical tricks and conventional dramaturgies assert the fantasy of omnipotence inherent to mediated inscription – as a defence mechanism against the fear of the producers and consumers of images alike, a fantasy that creates the illusion of being able to preside quite calmly over all realities – even the most inconceivable – without being affected by them oneself. The more unlimited the horror of the image, the more unreal its constitution. Horror rhymes with cosiness. The 'uncanny', by contrast, which Freud found in the merging of signs and signified, remains excluded.

It would be absurd to expect theatre to oppose an effective alternative to the massive superiority of these structures. But the question can be shifted from the problem of a political thesis or antithesis onto the level of sign usage itself. The basic structure of perception mediated by media is such that there is no experience of a connection among the individual images received but above all no connection between the receiving and sending of signs; there is no experience of a relation between address and answer. Theatre can respond to this only with a *politics of perception*, which could at the same time be called an *aesthetic of responsibility (or response-ability)*. Instead of the deceptively comforting duality of here and there, inside and outside, it can move the *mutual implication of actors and spectators in the theatrical production of images* into the centre and thus make visible the broken thread between personal experience and perception. Such an experience would be not only aesthetic but therein at the same time ethico-political. All else, even the most perfected political demonstration, would not escape Baudrillard's diagnosis that we are dealing only with circulating simulacra.

Aesthetics of risk

It should be evident by now that, for a politics of perception in the theatre, it is not the thesis (or antithesis) that counts, not the political statement or engagement (both of which belong in the domain of real politics not represented politics), but rather a basic disrespect for tenability or positive affirmation. Such politics will, in other words, include the transgression of taboos. Theatre is dealing with it all the time.[19] If one defines the taboo as a socially anchored form of affective reaction that rejects ('abjects') certain realities, forms of behaviour or images as 'untouchable', disgusting or unacceptable prior to any rational judgment, then the often stated observation that the taboo has virtually disappeared in the course of the rationalization, de-mythologization and disenchantment of the world is pertinent to our theme. Instead of an extended analysis, we risk the following simplification: there is nothing, or nearly nothing, in contemporary society that cannot be rationally discussed. But what if such rationalization also anaesthetizes the equally urgently needed human reflexes, which at a crucial moment could be the condition for a quick, timely reaction? Is it not already the case that disregarding spontaneous impulses (e.g. with respect to the environment, animals, a cold social climate) in favour of economic instrumental rationality leads to disasters that are as obvious as they are unstoppable? In light of this observation of the progressive breakdown of immediate affective reaction, we have to realize the growing importance of a certain cultivation of affects, the 'training' of an emotionality that is not under the tutelage of rational preconsiderations. 'Enlightenment' and education by themselves are not enough. (Even in the eighteenth century enlightenment (*Aufklärung*) was accompanied by the equally powerful current of 'sensibility' (*Empfindsamkeit*)). It will increasingly become an important task for 'theatrical' practices in the widest sense to create playful situations in which affects are released and played out.

That the capacity to achieve a certain emotional 'training' is important to theatre was a notion even of the baroque. Opitz defined it as the task of tragedy to prepare the spectators better for their own 'afflictions' by exercising and thus reinforcing 'constantia', stoic strength of endurance. Lessing, and with him the 'Enlightenment', considered theatre as a school for training pity or empathy (*Mitleid*). Even Brecht accorded to the theatre – which he did not intend to surrender to the 'old' emotions – the task of elevating feelings 'to a higher level', promoting feelings such as the love of justice and outrage at injustice. In the age of rationalization, of the ideal of calculation and of the generalized rationality of the market, it falls to the theatre to deal with extremes of affect by means of an *aesthetics of risk*, extremes which always also contain the possibility of offending by breaking taboos. This is given when the spectators are confronted with the problem of having to react to what is happening in their presence, that is as soon as the safe distance is no longer given, which the aesthetic distance between stage and auditorium seemed to safeguard. Precisely this reality of the theatre, that it can play with the border, predestines it for acts and actions in which not an 'ethical' reality or a thesis is formulated but in which a situation develops that confronts the spectators with abysmal fear, shame and even mounting aggression. Once more, we can clearly see here that theatre does not attain its political, ethical reality by way of information, theses and messages; in short: by way of its content in the traditional sense. On the contrary: it is part of its constitution to hurt feelings, to produce shock and disorientation, which point the spectators to their own presence precisely through 'amoral', 'asocial' and seemingly 'cynical' events. In doing so, it deprives us neither of the humour and shock of cognition, nor of the pain nor the fun for which alone we gather in the theatre.

Notes

Introduction

1 The book has already been translated into French (2002), Japanese (2002), Slovenian (2003), Croatian (2003), Polish (2004) and Persian/Farsi (2005). Italian, Spanish and Portugese translations are in preparation. The book has just appeared in its third edition in German.

2 See, for example, D. Barnett, 'Text as Material? The Category of "Performativity" in Three Postdramatic German Theatre-Texts', in C. Duttlinger, L. Ruprecht (eds and intro.) and A. Webber, *Performance and Performativity in German Cultural Studies*, Bern: Peter Lang; 2003, pp. 137–57; J. Kalb, 'Samuel Beckett, Heiner Müller and Post-Dramatic Theater', in *Samuel Beckett Today/Aujourd'hui: An Annual Bilingual Review/Revue Annuelle Bilingue*, vol. 11, 2002, pp. 74–83; L. Kruger, 'Making Sense of Sensation: Enlightenment, Embodiment, and the End(s) of Modern Drama', in *Modern Drama*, vol. 43, no. 4, 2000, pp. 543–63; M. Wessendorf, 'The Postdramatic Theatre of Richard Maxwell', unpublished manuscript (2003) available online at http://www2.hawaii.edu/~wessendo/Maxwell.htm. Furthermore, the International Federation for Theatre Research (IFTR/FIRT) has had a working group on (post)dramatic text in theatrical context for some time now and *Theatre Research International* recently devoted an entire issue to a special focus on postdramatic theatre. See *Theatre Research International*, vol. 29, no. 1, March 2004.

3 'The "post-" of "postmodern" does not signify a movement of *comeback*, *flashback* or *feedback*, that is, not a movement of repetition but a procedure in "ana-": a procedure of analysis, anamnesis, anagogy, and anamorphosis that elaborates an "initial forgetting"' J.-F. Lyotard, *The Postmodern Explained: Correspondence 1982–1985*, trans. by D. Barry *et al.*, afterword by W. Godzich, Minneapolis: University of Minnesota Press, 1993. I am indebted to Michal Kobialka whose recent conference paper 'Tadeusz Kantor's Practice: A Postmodern Notebook' at the Centre for Performance Research's 'Towards Tomorrow' conference (April 2005) reminded me of this passage.

4 P. Szondi, *Theory of the Modern Drama*, ed. and trans. by M. Hays, foreword by J. Schulte-Sasse, Minneapolis: University of Minnesota Press, 1987 (originally published in German in 1956). See also Wessendorf, 'The Postdramatic Theatre of Richard Maxwell', for the connections between Lehmann's and Szondi's theories.

5 Szondi, *Theory of Modern Drama*, pp. 4–5.

6 Ibid., p. 7.

7 Wessendorf, 'The Postdramatic Theatre of Richard Maxwell'.

8 In his foreword to the English translation, J. Schulte-Sasse expresses a similar critique of Szondi, arguing that 'neither Szondi's reconstruction of the history of drama nor his Hegelian notion of the form–content relationship leave space for a dramatic form based on a semiotic understanding of theatrical practice'. He goes on to suggest that Brecht's *Lehrstücktheorie* could be considered as an 'illustration of twentieth-

century tendencies to develop a critical semiotic understanding of theatrical practice'. See Schulte-Sasse in Szondi, *Theory of Modern Drama*, p. xv.

9 The first Department of Performance Studies was founded in 1980 at Tisch School of the Arts, New York University. For an in-depth discussion of the complexity of the institutional development in the USA see S. Jackson, *Professing Performance: Theatre in the Academy from Philology to Performativity*, Cambridge: Cambridge University Press, 2004.

10 Thank you to Clare Grant, John Baylis, Nigel Kellaway and Chris Ryan, all ex-Sydney Front members, for helping me recall the details of this performance in an amusing email exchange. Margaret Hamilton has just written the first PhD thesis on postdramatic theatre in Australia.

11 See for example, E. Diamond, *Unmaking Mimesis: Essays on Feminism and the Theatre*, London and New York: Routledge, 1997; Geraldine Harris, *Staging Femininities: Performance and Performativity*, Manchester: Manchester University Press, 1999; Petra Kuppers, *Disability and Performance: Bodies on the Edge*, London and New York: Routledge, 2003.

12 Malgorzata Sugiera, 'Beyond Drama: Writing for Postdramatic Theatre', in *Theatre Research International*, vol. 29, no. 1, March 2004, p. 26.

13 For Roland Barthes' distinction between 'readerly' texts and 'writerly' texts see R. Barthes, *S/Z*, trans. by R. Miller, New York: Hill and Wang, 1974, p. 4.

14 The concept of the 'performative' can be traced back to J. L. Austin's posthumously published, *How To Do Things with Words*, Cambridge, MA: Harvard University Press, 1975 (original 1962).

15 For histories of this development see, for example, S. Shepherd and M. Wallis, *Drama/Theatre/Performance*, London and New York: Routledge, 2004, chapter 1, pp. 7–14, and S. Jackson, *Professing Performance*.

16 For discussions of the work of these companies in relation to The Wooster Group see the essays by J. Bleha, E. Fordyce, J. Callens and D. Mufson in J. Callens (ed.), *The Wooster Group and Its Traditions*, Brussels: P.I.E.–Peter Lang, 2004.

17 See the company website, http://www.stanscafe.co.uk/helpfulthings/faq.html #impact_a

18 Company website, http://www.stanscafe.co.uk/thecarrierfrequency/index.html

19 Company website, http://www.imitatingthedog.co.uk/projects/ark.asp

20 'A Decade of Forced Entertainment', in T. Etchells, *Certain Fragments: Contemporary Performance and Forced Entertainment*, London and New York: Routledge, 1999, p. 40.

21 On Forced Entertainment's exploration of mapping strategies see also A. Schleper, 'Off the Route Strategies and Approaches to the Appropriation of Space', in J. Helmer and F. Malzacher (eds), *'Not Even a Game Anymore': The Theatre of Forced Entertainment*, Berlin: Alexander Verlag: 2004, pp. 185–202.

22 Etchells, *Certain Fragments*, p. 30.

23 Etchells, 'On Performance Writing', in ibid., p. 98.

24 See, for example, A. Furse, 'Those Who Can Do Teach', in M. M. Delgado and C. Svich (eds.), *Theatre in Crisis? Performance Manifestos for a New Century*, Manchester and New York: Manchester University Press, 2002, pp. 64–73.

25 See G. Siegmund, 'Voice Masks: Subjectivity, America, and the Voice in the Theatre of The Wooster Group', in Callens, *The Wooster Group*, pp. 167–87, here p. 176.

26 J. Parker-Starbuck, 'Framing the Fragments: The Wooster Group's Use of Technology', in ibid., pp. 217–28, here p. 219.

27 T. Etchells, 'On Performance and Technology', in Etchells, *Certain Fragments*, p. 95.

28 Company website, http://www.uninvited-guests.net/etour/tour_about.htm

29 See company website http://www.uninvited-guests.net/promo/default.htm

30 Etchells, *Certain Fragments*, p. 22.

31 Programme notes for the Forced Entertainment Symposium held at Lancaster University, October 2004.

32 H.-T. Lehmann, 'Shakespeare's Grin. Remarks on World Theatre with Forced Entertainment', in Helmer and Malzacher, *'Not Even a Game Anymore'*, p. 104.

33 Ibid., p. 105.

34 For a companion to the performance that documents and reflects on the process see *Frakcija Performing Arts Magazine*, special issue 32, Zagreb, 2004.

35 Company website, http://www.stationhouseopera.com/PastProjects/maresnest.html

36 P. Auslander, *Liveness: Performance in a Mediatized Culture*, London and New York: Routledge, 1999.

37 Ibid., pp. 23–38.

38 See J.-F. Lyotard, *The Postmodern Condition: A Report on Knowledge*, trans. by G. Bennington and B. Massumi, foreword by F. Jameson, Minneapolis: University of Minnesota Press, 1984.

39 For an in-depth discussion see N. Kaye, *Postmodernism and Performance*, London: Macmillan, 1994.

40 J. Birringer, *Theatre, Theory, Postmodernism*, Bloomington and Indianapolis: Indiana University Press, 1991, p. 43.

41 Kaye, *Postmodernism and Performance*, especially the chapter 'From Postmodern Style to Performance'.

42 Wessendorf, 'The Postdramatic Theatre of Richard Maxwell'.

43 M. McGuire, 'Forced Entertainment on Politics and Pleasure', *Variant*, vol. 5, available online at http://www.variant.randomstate.org/5texts/Michelle-McGuire.html

Prologue

1 G. Poschmann, *Der nicht mehr dramatische Theatertext: Aktuelle Bühnenstücke und ihre dramatische Analyse*, Tübingen: Niemeyer, 1997, p. 177. (Unless otherwise indicated, all quotations in this book have been translated by K. Jürs-Munby.)

2 Ibid., p. 178.

3 Ibid., p. 204ff.

4 Ibid.

5 See the useful anthology of politico-philosophical texts on the theatre by T. Murray (ed.), *Mimesis, Masochism and Mime: Politics of Theatricality in Contemporary French Thought*, Ann Arbor: University of Michigan Press, 1977.

6 W. Floeck (ed.), *Tendenzen des Gegenwartstheaters*, Tübingen: Francke, 1998.

7 H.-T. Lehmann, *Theater und Mythos: Die Konstitution des Subjekts im Diskurs der antiken Tragödie*. Stuttgart: Metzler, 1991.

8 R. Schechner, *Performance Theory*, New York: Taylor and Francis, 1988, p. 21.

9 Ibid., p. 22.

10 H. Müller, *Gesammelte Irrtümer*, Frankfurt am Main: Verlag der Autoren, 1986, p. 21.

11 H.-T. Lehmann, 'Theater der Blicke: Zu Heiner Müller's "Bildbeschreibung"', in U. Profitlich (ed.), *Dramatik der DDR*, Frankfurt am Main: Suhrkamp, 1987, pp. 186–202.

12 P. Pavis, 'The Classical Heritage of Modern Drama: The Case of Postmodern Theatre', in *Modern Drama*, vol. 29, 1986, p. 1. 'Avant-garde theatre', Pavis says here, 'needs classical norms to establish its own identity.'

Drama

1 P. Szondi, *Theory of the Modern Drama*, ed. and trans. by M. Hays, foreword by J. Schulte-Sasse, Minneapolis: University of Minnesota Press, 1987, p. 6.

2 A. Wirth, 'Vom Dialog zum Diskurs: Versuch einer Synthese der nachbrechtschen Theaterkonzepte', in *Theater Heute*, vol. 1, 1980, pp. 16–19.

3 Ibid.

4 Ibid., p. 19.
5 H. Müller, *Heiner Müller Material*, ed. by F. Hörnigk, Göttingen: Steidl Verlag, 1989, p. 50.
6 I introduced the opposition (and correspondence) of predramatic and postdramatic theatre in my *Theater und Mythos*, p. 2.
7 P. Stefanek, 'Lesedrama? – Überlegungen zur szenischen Transformation "bühnenfremder" Dramaturgie', in E. Fischer-Lichte (ed.), *Das Drama und seine Inszenierung: Vorträge des internationalen literatur- und theatersemiotischen Kolloquiums Frankfurt am Main 1983*, Tübingen: M. Niemeyer, 1985, pp. 133–45.
8 M. Esslin, *An Anatomy of Drama*, New York: Hill and Wang, 1977, 3rd printing 1979, p. 14.
9 See M. Kirby, *A Formalist Theatre*, Philadelphia: University of Pennsylvania Press, 1987.
10 V. Turner, *On the Edge of a Bush*, Tucson: University of Arizona Press, 1985, p. 300ff.
11 J.-F. Lyotard, "The Tooth, the Palm", in T. Murray (ed.), *Mimesis, Masochism and Mime*, pp. 282–8, here p. 282.
12 Ibid., p. 287.
13 Ibid.
14 A. Artaud, *The Theatre and Its Double*, trans. by M. C. Richards, New York: Grove Press, 1958, p. 13.
15 See T. W. Adorno, *Aesthetic Theory*, trans. by C. Lenhardt, ed. by G. Adorno and R. Tiedemann, London: Routledge and Kegan Paul, 1984, passim; and T. W. Adorno and M. Horkheimer, *Dialectic of Enlightenment*, London and New York: Verso, 1997, esp. pp. 180–3 (in 'Elements of Antisemitism') and p. 227 (in 'A Theory of Crime'), where Adorno refers to R. Caillois, *Le Mythe et l'homme*, Paris: Gallimard, 1938, p. 125ff.
16 Adorno, *Aesthetic Theory*, p. 399.
17 See Szondi, *Theory of the Modern Drama*, especially pp. 7–10, and P. Szondi, *An Essay on the Tragic*, trans. by P. Fleming, Stanford, CA: Stanford University Press, 2002.
18 H.-T. Lehmann, 'Dramatische Form und Revolution in Georg Büchner's "Dantons Tod" und Heiner Müller's "Der Auftrag"', in P. von Becker *et al.* (eds), *Dantons Tod: Die Trauerarbeit im Schönen: Ein Theater-Lesebuch*, Frankfurt am Main: Syndikat, 1980, pp. 106–21, here p. 107.
19 Schumacher, cited in Lehmann, 'Dramatische Form und Revolution', p. 106.
20 Aristotle, *Poetics*, trans. with an introduction and notes by M. Heath, London: Penguin, 1996, p. 7.
21 Ibid., p. 14.
22 Ibid., p. 12.
23 C. Menke, *Tragödie im Sittlichen: Gerechtigkeit und Freiheit nach Hegel*, Frankfurt am Main: Suhrkamp, 1996.
24 Ibid., p. 42.
25 G. W. F. Hegel, *Aesthetics: Lectures on Fine Art*, 2 vols, trans. by T. M. Knox, Oxford: Clarendon Press, 1975, here vol. 1, p. 517.
26 Ibid., vol. 2, p. 1,218.
27 Menke, *Tragödie im Sittlichen*, p. 45.
28 P. de Man, *Die Ideologie des Ästetischen*, Frankfurt am Main: Suhrkamp, 1993, p. 54.
29 G. W. F. Hegel, *Phenomenology of Spirit*, trans. by A. V. Miller with analysis of the text and foreword by J. N. Findlay, Oxford: Clarendon Press, 1977, p. 443.
30 Hegel, *Ästhetik*, *Werke*, vol. 13, Frankfurt am Main: Suhrkamp, 1986, as cited in Menke, *Tragödie im Sittlichen*, p. 51.
31 Menke, *Tragödie im Sittlichen*, p. 54f.
32 The German term *Doppelbödigkeit* is derived from the theatre, meaning literally 'having a double floor'.
33 Menke, *Tragödie im Sittlichen*, p. 51.

34   Ibid., p. 178.
35   Hegel, *Phenomenology of Spirit*, p. 444.
36   Ibid., p. 450.
37   Ibid.
38   Ibid.
39   Ibid.
40   Ibid.

Prehistories

 1   O. Eberle, *Cenalora: Leben, Glauben, Tanz und Theatre der Urvölker*, Olten: Walter, 1954.
 2   Cited according to P. Jelavich, 'Populäre Theatralik, Massenkultur und Avantgarde: Betrachtungen zum Theater der Jahrhundertwende', in H. Schmid and J. Striedter (eds), *Dramatische und theatralische Kommunikation: Beiträge zur Geschichte und Theorie des Dramas und Theaters*, Tübingen: Gunter Narr, 1992, pp. 253–61, here p. 257.
 3   A. Kluge and H. Müller, *Ich bin ein Landvermesser: Gespräche, Neue Folge*, Hamburg: Rotbuch, 1996, p. 95.
 4   W. Benjamin, *Selected Writings*, vol. 1 (1913–26), ed. by M. Bullock and M. W. Jennings, Cambridge, MA: Harvard University Press, 1996, p. 355.
 5   P. Primavesi, *Kommentar, Übersetzung, Theater in Walter Benjamin frühen Schriften*, Frankfurt am Main: Stroemfeld/Nexus, 1998, p. 291, as well as p. 270ff.
 6   See Szondi, *Theory of the Modern Drama*, chapters 3 and 4.
 7   Compare B. Dort, 'Une écriture de la représentation', in *Théâtre en Europe*, no. 10 (special issue on Pirandello), April 1986, pp. 18–21.
 8   A. Vitez in *Théâtre en Europe*, no. 13, 1987, p. 9.
 9   Apart from her German publications see E. Fischer-Lichte, *The Show and the Gaze of Theatre: A European Perspective*, Iowa City: Iowa University Press, 1997, pp. 71ff, 115ff and passim.
10   J. J. Roubine, *Théâtre et mise en scène 1880–1980*, Paris: Presses Universitaires de France, 1980, p. 54ff.
11   E. Ionesco, *Notes et contre-notes*, Paris: Gallimard, 1962, p. 159. Compare also G. Michaud, 'Ionesco: de la dérision à l'anti-monde', in J. Jacquot (ed.), *Le Théâtre moderne*, vol. 2, Paris: CNRS, 1973, pp. 37–43, especially p. 39.
12   M. Esslin, *The Theatre of the Absurd*, New York: Anchor Books, 1961, pp. xvii–xviii.
13   Ibid., p. xix.
14   Ibid., p. xxi.
15   Poschmann, *Der nicht mehr dramatische Theatertext*, p.183.
16   H. Weinrich, *Tempus: Besprochene und erzählte Welt*, Stuttgart: Kohlhammer, 1971.
17   P. Iden, 'Am Ende der Neuigkeiten: Am Ende des Neuen?', in 'Theater 1980', Jahrbuch (Annual) of *Theater Heute*, 1980, pp. 126–8, here p. 126.
18   Ibid., p. 127.
19   M. Pfister, *The Theory and Analysis of Drama*, trans. by J. Halliday, Cambridge: Cambridge University Press, 1988 [1977], p. 249.
20   For the analysis of the latter see Lyotard, *The Postmodern Condition*.
21   Kirby, *A Formalist Theatre*, p. 99.
22   P. Szondi, *Das lyrische Drama*, Frankfurt am Main: Suhrkamp, 1975, p. 360.
23   Compare M. Watanabe, 'Quelqu'un arrive', in *Théâtre en Europe*, no 13, 1987, pp. 26–30, as well as S. Mallarmé, *Œuvres complètes*, Paris: Pleiade, 1970, p. 1,167.
24   '[D]rame monopersonnel, offrant la même structure que le rêve.' See Watanabe, 'Quelqu'un arrive', p. 30.
25   D. Plassard, *L'Acteur en effigie: figures de l'homme artificiel dans le théâtre des avantgardes historiques. Allemagne, France, Italie*, Lausanne: L'Age d'Homme, 1992, p. 38.
26   M. Borie, *Le Fantôme ou le théâtre qui doute*, Paris: Actes Sud, 1997.
27   'Quelque chose d'Hamlet est mort pour nous, le jour où nous l'avons vu mourir sur

la scène. Le spectre d'un acteur l'a détrôné, et nous ne pouvons plus écarter l'usurpateur de nos rêves.' As cited in Plassard, *L'Acteur en effigie*, p. 35.

28 H.-P. Bayerdörfer, 'Maeterlincks Impulse für die Entwicklung der Theatertheorie', in D. Kafitz (ed.), *Drama und Theater der Jahrhundertwende*, Tübingen: Francke, 1991, p. 125.

29 As cited in Szondi, *Das lyrische Drama*, p.19.

30 Ibid.

31 Ibid., p. 352.

32 Ibid.

33 Ibid., p. 143ff.

34 Ibid., p. 144.

35 O. Panizza, 'Der Klassizismus und das Eindringen des Variété', in *Die Gesellschaft*, October 1896, pp. 1,252–74.

36 As cited in Jelavich, 'Populäre Theatralik, Massenkultur und Avantgarde', p. 255.

37 For this whole section compare also H. B. Segel, *Turn of the Century Cabaret*, New York: Columbia University Press, 1987; Centre National de la Recherche Scientifique, *Du Cirque au Théâtre*, Lausanne: L'Age d'Homme, 1983.

38 As cited in E. Fuchs, *The Death of Character: Perspectives on Theatre after Modernism*, Indianapolis: Indiana University Press, 1996, p. 93.

39 Ibid., p. 102.

40 B. Marranca, *Ecologies of Theatre*, Baltimore, MD: Johns Hopkins University Press, 1996, p. 18.

41 A. van Crugten, *S. I. Witkiewicz: aux sources d'un théâtre nouveau*, Lausanne: L'Age d'Homme, 1971, p. 114ff.

42 Ibid., p. 281.

43 Ibid., pp. 290 and 357.

44 Ibid., p. 116.

45 E. Almhofer, *Performance Art: Die Kunst zu Leben*, Vienna, Cologne, Graz: Böhlau, 1986, p. 15.

46 D. G. Zinder, *The Surrealist Connection*, Ann Arbor: University of Michigan Press, 1976.

47 L. Aragon, 'Lettre ouverte à André Breton: sur Le Regard du Sourd, l'art, la science et la liberté', in *Les Lettres françaises*, Paris, no. 1,388, 2–8 June 1971, pp. 3, 15.

Panorama of postdramatic theatre

1 B. Brecht, 'A Short Organum for the Theatre', in *Brecht on Theatre: The Development of an Aesthetic*, ed. and trans. by John Willet, London: Methuen, 1974 [1964], p. 183.

2 Cited according to W. G. Müller, 'Das Ich im Dialog mit sich selbst: Bemerkungen zur Struktur des dramatischen Monologs von Shakespeare bis zu Samuel Beckett', in *Deutsche Vierteljahresschrift für Literaturwissenschaft und Geistesgeschichte*, vol. 56, no. 2, Stuttgart, 1982, pp. 314–33, here p. 333.

3 J. Mukařovský, *Kapitel aus der Ästhetik*, Frankfurt am Main: Suhrkamp, 1970, p. 32ff.

4 Schechner, *Performance Theory*.

5 See J. Jacquot, *Le Théâtre moderne depuis la deuxième guerre mondiale*, Paris: CNRS, 1973, p. 78.

6 Jean Genet, 'L'Étrange mot d'urbanisme', in *Œuvres complètes*, vol. 4, Paris: Gallimard, 1968, p. 9ff.

7 'Le dialogue avec les mort est ce qui ce donne à l'œuvre d'art sa véritable dimension.' Borie, *Le Fantôme*, p. 272.

8 Ibid.

9 Compare Lehmann, *Theater und Mythos*, where the terms predramatic and postdramatic were introduced.

10 T. S. Eliot, 'A Dialogue on Dramatic Poetry', in *Selected Essays*, London, Faber and Faber, 1932, p. 35.

11 R. Steinweg (ed.), *Brechts Modell der Lehrstücke: Zeugnisse, Diskussion, Erfahrungen*, Frankfurt am Main: Suhrkamp, 1976, p. 105.

12 T. Kantor, 'The Zero Theatre' (1963), in T. Kantor, *A Journey through Other Spaces: Essays and Manifestos, 1944–1990*, ed. and trans. by M. Kobialka with a critical study of Tadeusz Kantor's Theatre by M. Kobialka, Berkeley, Los Angeles and London: University of California Press, 1993, pp. 63–4. See also in the same volume Kantor's manifesto 'The Autonomous Theatre' (1956/63), pp. 42–50.

13 Ibid., p. 59.

14 Ibid., p. 63.

15 Ibid., p. 60.

16 Ibid., p. 145.

17 Borie, *Le Fantôme*, p. 258.

18 Kantor, *A Journey through Other Spaces*, p.124.

19 Georg Hensel, in *Frankfurter Allgemeine Zeitung*, 15 June 1995. For an extensive description and analysis of the performances in English see M. Kobialka's 'Critical Study of Tadeusz Kantor's Theatre', in Kantor, *A Journey through Other Spaces*, pp. 269–86.

20 Ibid.

21 See Kantor, 'Annexed Reality' (1963), in ibid. pp. 71–6, and 'Reality of the Lowest Rank' (1980), in ibid. pp. 117–24.

22 T. Kantor, *Theater des Todes, Die tote Klasse, Wielopole-Wielopole*, ed. by W. Fenn, Institut für Moderne Kunst Nürnberg, Zirndorf: Verlag für moderne Kunst, 1983, p. 115.

23 Ibid., p. 114.

24 Kantor, *A Journey through Other Spaces*, p. 113.

25 Ibid., pp. 113–14.

26 Kantor, *Theater des Todes*, p. 257.

27 *Frankfurter Allgemeine Zeitung*, 21 August 1989.

28 From the Greek 'isotonos', equally stretched, of equal tension or tone. In science used to describe liquids of the same osmotic pressure or concentration of molecules.

29 See C. Asman, 'Theater und Agon/Agon und Theater: Walter Benjamin und Florens Christian Rang', in *Modern Language Notes*, vol. 107, no. 3, 1992, pp. 606–24; also, on the whole complex of the agon-discussion, Primavesi, *Kommentar*, p. 254ff.

30 See G. Banu, *Klaus Michael Grüber: . . . il faut que le théâtre passe à travers les larmes . . .*, Paris : Editions du Regard, 1993.

31 See Hans-Thies Lehmann, 'Antiquité et modernité par delà le drame', in Banu, *Klaus Michael Grüber*, pp. 201–6.

32 F. Wille 'Zwielicht der Freiheit', in *Theater Heute*, no. 9, 1995, pp. 4–7; published text in ibid., pp. 50–5.

33 Schechner, *Performance Theory*, p. 185.

34 B. Waldenfels, *Sinnesschwellen: Studien zur Phänomenologie des Fremden 3*, Frankfurt am Main: Suhrkamp, 1999, p. 138.

35 Birgit Verwiebe, '"Wo die Kunst endigt und die Wahrheit beginnt": Lichtmagie und Verwandlung im 19. Jahrhundert', in U. Brandes (ed.), *Sehsucht: Über die Veränderung visueller Wahrnehmung*, Göttingen: Steidl Verlag, 1995, p. 90.

36 Ibid., p. 85

37 Stephan Oettermann, 'Das Panorama: Ein Massenmedium', in ibid., p. 80.

38 Fuchs, *The Death of Character*, p. 106.

39 Ibid., p. 107.

40 Immanuel Kant, *Critique of Judgment*, trans. by J. C. Meredith, Oxford: Clarendon Press, 1952, pp. 175–6 (par. 49).

41 Ibid., pp. 177–8.

42 *TAT-Zeitung* [Journal of Theater am Turm], Frankfurt am Main, February 1991.

43 See M. Foucault, *The Order of Things*, London: Routledge, 2001.

44 H. Goebbels and H.-T. Lehmann, 'Gespräch', in W. Storch (ed.), *Das szenische Auge*, Berlin: Institut für Auslandsbeziehungen, 1996, p. 76ff.

45 Compare Primavesi, *Kommentar*.

46 See Lyotard, *The Postmodern Condition*, 1984.

47 E. Varopoulou, 'Musikalisierung der Theaterzeichen', lecture at the first International Summer Academy in Frankfurt am Main, August 1998, unpublished manuscript.

48 Ibid.

49 Ibid.

50 Ibid.

51 'Gespräch mit Paul Koek', brochure of Theater der Welt 1996, translated from English by Bettina Funcke.

52 Varopoulou, 'Musikalisierung'.

53 S. Mallarmé, *Œuvres complètes*, p. 304 (emphasis by the author).

54 R. Kloepfer, 'Das Theater der Sinn-Erfüllung: DOUBLE & PARADISE vom Serapionstheater (Wien) als Beispiel einer totalen Inszenierung', in E. Fischer-Lichte (ed.), *Das Drama und seine Inszenierung*, Tübingen: Niemeyer, 1985, pp. 199–218.

55 Renate Lorenz, 'Jan Fabres "Die Macht der theatralischen Torheiten" und das Problem der Aufführungsanalyse', diploma thesis, Giessen, 1988.

56 Waldenfels, *Sinnesschwellen*, p. 112ff. (emphasis by the author).

57 Schechner, *Performance Theory*, p. 170.

58 Jan Mukařovský, *Kapitel aus der Ästhetik*, Frankfurt am Main: Suhrkamp, 1970. p. 12.

59 Ibid., p. 103 (emphasis by the author).

60 E. Fischer-Lichte, *The Semiotics of Theatre*, trans. by J. Gaines and D. L. Jones, Bloomington: Indiana University Press, 1992, p. 141.

61 S. Böhnisch, 'Gewalt auf der Bühne – Kritik eines Paradigmas', in J. Berg, H.-O. Hügel and H. Kurzenberger (eds), *Authentizität als Darstellung*, Hildesheim: Universität Hildesheim, 1997, p. 122–31, here p. 127.

62 'Gesucht: die Lücke im Ablauf' – a quote from Heiner Müller's 'Description of a Picture'.

63 H.-G. Gadamer, *Truth and Method*, trans. and ed. by G. Barden and J. Cumming, New York: Crossroad, 1986, p. 269.

64 G. Berreby (ed.), *Documents relatifs à la fondation de l'Internationale Situationniste*, Paris: Editions Allia, 1985, p. 616. Guy Debord wrote in the founding manifesto of the Situationist International: 'Notre idée centrale est celle de *la construction de situations*, c'est à dire la construction concrète d'ambiances momentanées de la vie, et leur transformation en une qualité passionelle supérieure.'

65 J. Ritter and K. Gründer (eds), *Historisches Wörterbuch der Philosophie*, Basel: Schwabe Verlag, 1995, vol. 9, column 936.

66 Susanne K. Langer, *Feeling and Form*, New York: Charles Scribner's Sons, 1953, p. 318.

67 Public interview on 5 June 1991, Vienna.

68 K. Herkenrath, 'Jan Lauwers "Antonius und Cleopatra": Eine nachepische Theaterkonzeption', diploma thesis, Giessen, 1993.

69 See G. Siegmund's review of the performance in June 1997 at the Künstlerhaus Mousonturm in Frankfurt am Main, in *Frankfurter Allgemeine Zeitung*, 8 June 1997.

70 *Goethe – Schiller: Briefwechsel*, Hamburg: Fischer Bücherei, 1961, p. 271.

71 Ibid.

72 T. W. Adorno, *Minima Moralia: Reflections from a Damaged Life*, trans. by E. F. N. Jephcott, London: New Left Books, 1974, p. 142.

73 Ibid.

74 J.-P. Sarrazac, *L'Avenir du drame: écritures dramatiques contemporaines*, Lausanne: Circé, 1981, p. 178: 'Recours à un hyper-naturalisme – c'est-à-dire à un naturalisme sophistiqué et, comme on dit, "au second degré" . . . Le public est convié à la consommation exotique des tranches de vie faisandées.'

75 Ibid., p. 179.
76 Ibid., p. 175ff.
77 G. Genette, *Palimpsestes*, Paris : Editions du Seuil, 1982.
78 See (as for the whole paragraph) S. Strehler, 'Popmimen in der Bühnenburg', in *spex*, no. 11, 1998, pp. 80–2.
79 Ibid.
80 A. Haas (ed.), *TheaterAngelusNovus. AntikenMaterial VI. Tod des Hektor* in *Maske und Kothurn*, vol. 36, nos 1–4, 1990; A. Haas, J. Szeiler and B. Wallburg (eds), *Menschen-Material 1 – Die Massnahme: Eine Theaterarbeit mit Josef Szeiler*, Berlin: Basis Druck, 1991; A. Haas (ed.), *HamletMaschine. TokyoMaterial*, Berlin, 1991.
81 Esslin, *Anatomy of Drama*, p. 93.
82 R. Wilson, as cited in H. Keller, *Robert Wilson: Regie im Theater*, Frankfurt am Main: Fischer, 1997, p. 105.
83 J. Kott, *Shakespeare heute*, Berlin: Alexander Verlag, 1989, p. 292.
84 Pfister, *Theory and Analysis of Drama*, p. 248.
85 Ibid., pp. 248–9.
86 Pfister makes a distinction between monologue (a long speech of reasonable length) and soliloquy (a kind of talking to oneself). See Pfister, ibid., p. 127. In our context, which is concerned not with the differentiations of the analysis of dramatic texts but with theatre, we use only the term monologue (without discussing the cogency of the distinction monologue/soliloquy as represented by Pfister) in order to characterize the speaking outside of addressing an interlocutor in the play.
87 Ibid., p. 136.
88 Ibid., p. 132.
89 Ibid., p. 134.
90 H. C. Angermeyer, *Zuschauer im Drama: Brecht, Dürrenmatt, Handke*, Frankfurt am Main: Athenäum Verlag, 1971, p. 119.
91 Einar Schleef, *Droge Faust Parzival*, Frankfurt am Main: Suhrkamp, 1997, p. 10.
92 Ibid., p. 10ff.
93 Ibid., p. 7.
94 The term was coined by Herbert Blau. See H. Blau, *Take Up the Bodies: Theatre at the Vanishing Point*, Chicago: University of Illinois Press, 1982.

Performance

1 R. Goldberg, *Performance Art: From Futurism to the Present*, New York: Harry Abrams, 1988, p. 194ff.
2 Kirby, *A Formalist Theatre*, p. 3ff.
3 K. Barck, 'Materialität, Materialismus, *performance*', in H. U. Gumbrecht and K. L. Pfeiffer (eds), *Materialität der Kommunikation*, Frankfurt am Main: Suhrkamp, 1995, pp. 121–38, here p. 133.
4 W. Matzat, *Dramenstruktur und Zuschauerrolle*, Munich: Fink, 1982, p. 54.
5 See Almhofer, *Performance Art*, p. 44.
6 Rachel Rosenthal, cited in Fischer-Lichte, *The Show and the Gaze*, p. 256ff. See also Fischer-Lichte's discussion of the topic, ibid.
7 Goldberg, *Performance Art*, p. 172.
8 J. L. Schroeder, *Identität, Überschreitung, Verwandlung: Happenings, Aktionen und Performances von bildenden Künstlern*, Münster: LIT Verlag, 1990, p. 210ff.
9 R. Schechner, *Between Theatre and Anthropology*, Philadelphia: University of Pennsylvania Press, 1985, p. 146.
10 Ibid.
11 H. U. Gumbrecht, 'Die Schönheit des Mannschafssports: American Football – im Stadion und im Fernsehen', in G. Vattimo and W. Welsch (eds), *Medien-Welten-*

Wirklichkeiten, Munich: Fink Verlag, 1998, p. 208. See also H. U. Gumbrecht's recent book, *Production of Presence. What Meaning Cannot Convey*, Stanford, CA: Stanford University Press, 2004.

12 Ibid.
13 Ibid., p. 211.
14 Ibid., p. 214.
15 K. H. Bohrer, *Das absolute Präsens*, Frankfurt am Main: Suhrkamp, 1994, p. 7. See also the translated essay collection K. H. Bohrer, *Suddenness: On the Moment of Aesthetic Appearance*, trans. by R. Crowley, New York: Columbia University Press, 1994.
16 Ibid., p. 40ff.
17 Ibid., p. 41.
18 Ibid.
19 Ibid., p. 62.
20 Ibid., p. 181.
21 Kluge and Müller, *Ich bin ein Landvermesser*, p. 95.
22 B. Brecht, 'Everything New is Better than Everything Old', trans. by C. Middleton, in B. Brecht, *Poems 1913–1956*, ed. by J. Willet and R. Manheim with the co-operation of E. Fried, London: Methuen, 2000, p. 160.

Aspects

1 B. Dort, *La Représentation émancipée*, Arles: Actes Sud, 1988, p. 173.
2 D. Polaczek about Corsetti's *Beschreibung eines Kampfes (Description of a Struggle)*, in *Frankfurter Allgemeine Zeitung*, 3 February 1992.
3 Compare J.-J. Roubine, *Théâtre et mise en scène 1880–1980*, Paris: Presses Universitaires de France, 1980, p. 107.
4 For further details on this performance see S. Seym, *Das Théâtre du Soleil: Ariane Mnouchkines Ästhetik des Theaters*, Stuttgart: Metzler, 1992, esp. pp. 91–100.
5 Aston and Savona differentiate (1) 'Time present: the location of the spectator in the "here and now" of the fictional universe', (2) 'Chronological time: the linear time sequence of the story (fabula)', (3) 'Plot time: the structuring or ordering of events from the chronological time (2) in order to shape the "here and now" of (1)', and (4) 'Performance time: the spectator in the theatre is aware there is a finite period of time for events to take their course'. See E. Aston and G. Savona, *Theatre as Sign System: A Semiotics of Text and Performance*, London: Routledge, 1991, pp. 27–9. While the first three categories in this differentiation concern dramatic theatre, the fourth category of 'performance time' seems too narrowly conceived and would have to be subdivided into the time/rhythm of the actual staging and the time of the whole performance text as a theatre-going event.
6 H. Blumenberg, *Lebenszeit und Weltzeit*, Frankfurt am Main: Suhrkamp, 1986, p. 223.
7 See L. Althusser, 'The "Piccolo Teatro": Bertolazzi and Brecht', in L. Althusser, *For Marx*, trans. by B. Brewster, London: Verso, 1986.
8 See G. Deleuze, *Difference and Repetition*, trans. by P. Patton, New York: Columbia University Press, 1994.
9 For a comprehensive discussion of the critical potential of repetition in art see ibid.
10 B. Brecht, *Werke*, vol. 22, 1, *Berliner und Frankfurter Ausgabe*, ed. by W. Hecht and I. Gellert *et al.*, Frankfurt am Main: Suhrkamp, 1993, p. 2.
11 Aristotle, *Poetics*, p. 14.
12 P. Corneille, 'Discours sur les trois unités', in *Ôeuvres complètes*, Paris: Editions du Seuil, 1963, p. 844. Compare this to the central importance of the concept of 'dérègulation' in the poetics of modernism since Arthur Rimbaud who elevates the 'dérègulation de tous les sens' to a programmatic status for poetry.
13 Ibid., p. 845: 'moins on se charge d'actions passées, plus on a l'auditeur [not the

'spectateur'!] propice par le peu de gêne qu'on lui donne, en lui rendant toutes les choses présentes, sans demander aucune réflexion à sa mémoire que pour ce qu'il a vu'.

14 V. Novarina, *Le Théâtre des paroles*, Paris: Éditions P.O.L., 1988, pp. 22 and 24: 'L'acteur n'est pas un interprète parce que le corps n'est pas un instrument.' And: 'L'acteur n'exécute pas mais s'exécute, interprète pas mais se pénètre, raisonne pas mais fait tout son corps résonner. Construit pas son personnage mais s'décompose le corps civil maintenu en ordre, se suicide. C'est pas d'la composition d'personnage, c'est de la décomposition d'l'homme qui se fait sur la planche.'

15 G. Agamben, 'Noten zur Geste', in J. G. Lauer (ed.), *Postmoderne und Politik*, Tübingen: Edition Diskord, 1992, pp. 97–107, all quotes p. 99.

16 *Heiner Müller Material*, ed. Hörnigk, p. 50.

17 Fischer-Lichte, *The Semiotics of Theatre*, p. 9ff.

18 V. Sobchack, 'The Scene of the Screen: Envisioning Cinematic and Electronic "Presence"', in R. Stam and T. Miller (eds), *Film and Theory: An Anthology*, Malden, MA, and Oxford: Blackwell Publishers, 2000, pp. 67–84, here pp. 78–80.

19 See the quotes from and discussion of Imdahl's theses in Waldenfels, *Sinnesschwellen*, 1999, p. 139.

Epilogue

1 R. Barucha and G. Dasgupta, '*The Mahabharata*: Peter Brook's "Orientalism"', in *Performing Arts Journal*, vol. x, no. 3 (1987), pp. 9–16.

2 A. Wirth, 'Interkulturalität und Ikonophilia im neuen Theater', in S. Bauschinger and S. L. Cocalis (eds), *Vom Wort zum Bild: Das neue Theater in Deutschland und den USA*, Bern: Francke, 1992, pp. 233–43.

3 Compare A. P. Nganang, *Interkulturalität und Bearbeitung: Untersuchung zu Soyinka und Brecht* (dissertation, Frankfurt am Main 1998), Munich: Iudicium, 1998.

4 For a more comprehensive documentation and discussion of this borderland performance work see G. Gómez-Peña's recent book *Dangerous Border Crossers: The Artist Talks Back*, New York: Routledge, 2000.

5 Compare Fischer-Lichte, *The Show and the Gaze of Theatre*, p. 223ff.

6 See C. Fusco, 'The Other History of Intercultural Performance', in *Drama Review*, vol. 38, no. 1, Spring 1994, pp. 143–66.

7 J. Kristeva, 'Politique de la littérature', in *Polylogue*, Paris, 1977, pp. 13–21.

8 H. Foster, *Recodings: Art, Spectacle, Cultural Politics*, Port Townsend, WA: Bay Press, 1985, p. 145.

9 Ibid.

10 See also P. Auslander, *Presence and Resistance: Postmodernism and Cultural Politics in Contemporary American Performance*, Ann Arbor: University of Michigan Press, 1994.

11 Brecht, *Werke*, vol. 10, p. 495.

12 W. Hamacher, 'Afformative, Strike: Benjamin's "Critique of Violence"', trans. by D. Hollander, in A. Benjamin and P. Osborne (eds), *Walter Benjamin's Philosophy: Destruction and Experience*, London and New York: Routledge, 1994, pp. 110–38.

13 A. J. Sabbatini, 'Terrorism, Perform', in *High Performance*, vol. 9, no. 2, 1986, pp. 29–33.

14 Althusser, 'The "Piccolo Teatro": Bertolazzi and Brecht', pp. 129–51.

15 Schechner, *Performance Theory*, p. 166ff.

16 G. Debord, *The Society of the Spectacle*, trans. by Donald Nicholson-Smith, New York: Zone Books, 1994, p. 40.

17 S. Weber, 'Humanitäre Intervention im Zeitalter der Medien: Zur Frage einer heterogenen Politik', in H.-P. Jäck and H. Pfeil (eds), *Eingriffe im Zeitalter der Medien* (*Politik des Anderen*, vol. 1), Bornheim and Rostock: Hanseatischer Fachverlag für

Wirtschaft, 1995, pp. 5-27, here p. 26. *Politik des Anderen*, vol. 1, Frankfurt am Main, 1995, pp. 5–27, here p. 26.
18 P. von Becker, in *Theater heute*, vol. 1, 1990, p. 1.
19 Compare H.-T. Lehmann, 'L'esthétique du risque', in *L'Art du théâtre*, no. 7, autumn 1987, pp. 35–44.

Bibliography

Adorno, T. W., *Minima Moralia: Reflections from a Damaged Life*, trans. by E. F. N. Jephcott, London: New Left Books, 1974.

——, *Aesthetic Theory*, trans. by C. Lenhardt, ed. by G. Adorno and R. Tiedemann, London: Routledge and Kegan Paul, 1984.

Adorno, T. W. and Horkheimer, M., *Dialectic of Enlightenment*, London and New York: Verso, 1997.

Agamben, G., 'Noten zur Geste', in J. G. Lauer, *Postmoderne und Politik*, Tübingen: Edition Diskord, 1992, pp. 97–107.

Almhofer, E., *Performance Art: Die Kunst zu Leben*, Vienna, Cologne and Graz: Böhlau, 1986.

Althusser, L., 'The "Piccolo Teatro": Bertolazzi and Brecht', in L. Althusser, *For Marx*, trans. by B. Brewster, London: Verso, 1986, pp. 129–51.

Angermeyer, H. C., *Zuschauer im Drama: Brecht, Dürrenmatt, Handke*, Frankfurt am Main: Athenäum Verlag, 1971.

Aragon, L., 'Lettre ouverte à André Breton: sur Le Regard du Sourd, l'art, la science et la liberté', in *Les Lettres françaises*, Paris, vol. 1, 388, 2–8 June 1971.

Aristotle, *Poetics*, trans. with an introduction and notes by M. Heath, London: Penguin, 1996.

Artaud, A., *The Theatre and Its Double*, trans. by M. C. Richards, New York: Grove Press, 1958.

Asman, C., 'Theater und Agon/Agon und Theater: Walter Benjamin und Florens Christian Rang', in *Modern Language Notes*, vol. 107, no. 3, 1992, pp. 606–24.

Aston, E. and Savona, G., *Theatre as Sign System: A Semiotics of Text and Performance*, London: Routledge, 1991.

Auslander, P., *Presence and Resistance: Postmodernism and Cultural Politics in Contemporary American Performance*, Ann Arbor: University of Michigan Press, 1994.

——, *From Acting to Performance: Essays in Modernism and Postmodernism*, London and New York: Routledge, 1997.

——, *Liveness: Performance in a Mediatized Culture*, London and New York Routledge, 1999.

Austin, J. L., *How To Do Things with Words*, Cambridge, MA: Harvard University Press, 1975 (original 1962).

Banu, G., *Klaus Michael Grüber: . . . il faut que le théâtre passe à travers les larmes . . .*, Paris: Editions du Regard, 1993.

Barck, K., 'Materialität, Materialismus, *Performance*', in H. U. Gumbrecht and K. L. Pfeiffer (eds), *Materialität der Kommunikation*, Frankfurt am Main: Suhrkamp, 1995, pp. 121–38.

Barnett, D., 'Text as Material? The Category of "Performativity" in Three Postdramatic German Theatre-Texts', in C. Duttlinger, L. Ruprecht (eds and intro.) and A. Webber, *Performance and Performativity in German Cultural Studies*, Bern: Peter Lang; 2003, pp. 137–57.

Barthes, R., *S/Z*, trans. by R. Miller, New York: Hill and Wang, 1974.

——, *The Grain of the Voice, Interviews 1962–1980*, Berkeley: University of California Press, 1992.

——, *Camera Lucida: Reflections on Photography*, London: Vintage, 1993.

Barucha, R. and Dasgupta, G., '*The Mahabharata*: Peter Brook's "Orientalism"', in *Performing Arts Journal*, vol. 10, no. 3, 1987, pp. 9–16.

Bayerdörfer, H.-P., 'Maeterlincks Impulse für die Entwicklung der Theatertheorie', in D. Kafitz (ed.), *Drama und Theater der Jahrhundertwende*, Tübingen: Francke, 1991, pp. 121–38.

Benjamin, W., *Illuminations*, trans. by H. Zohn (ed.) and with an introduction by H. Ahrendt, New York: Schocken Books, 1968.

——, *Selected Writings*, vol. 1 (1913–26), ed. by M. Bullock and M. W. Jennings, Cambridge, MA: Harvard University Press, 1996.

Berreby, G. (ed.), *Documents relatifs à la fondation de l'internationale Situationniste*, Paris: Editions Allia, 1985.

Birringer, Johannes, 'Postmodern Performance and Technology', in *Performing Arts Journal*, 26/27, vol. 11, no. 2/3, 1985, pp. 221–33.

——, *Theatre, Theory, Postmodernism*, Bloomington and Indianapolis: Indiana University Press, 1991.

Blau, H., *Take Up the Bodies: Theatre at the Vanishing Point*, Chicago: University of Illinois Press, 1982.

Blumenberg, H., *Lebenszeit und Weltzeit*, Frankfurt am Main: Suhrkamp, 1986.

Boehm, G. (ed.), *Was ist ein Bild*, Munich: Fink 1994.

Böhnisch, S., 'Gewalt auf der Bühne – Kritik eines Paradigmas', in J. Berg, H.-O. Hügel and H. Kurzenberger (eds), *Authentizität als Darstellung*, Hildesheim: Universität Hildesheim, 1997, pp. 122–31.

Bohrer, K. H., *Das absolute Präsens*, Frankfurt am Main: Suhrkamp, 1994.

——, *Suddenness: On the Moment of Aesthetic Appearance*, trans. by R. Crowley, New York: Columbia University Press, 1994.

Borie, M., *Le Fantôme ou le théâtre qui doute*, Paris: Actes Sud, 1997.

Brecht, B., *Brecht on Theatre: The Development of an Aesthetic*, ed. and trans. by. J. Willet, London: Methuen, 1974 [1964].

——, *Werke, Berliner und Frankfurter Ausgabe*, ed. by W. Hecht, J. Knopf, W. Mittenzwei and K.-D. Müller, Frankfurt am Main: Suhrkamp, 1989 onwards.

——, *Poems 1913–1956*, ed. by J. Willet and R. Manheim with the cooperation of E. Fried, London: Methuen, 2000.

Brendel, L., *Computers as Theatre*, Boston, MA: Addison-Wesley, 1993.

Brook, P., *The Shifting Point: Theatre, Film, Opera 1946–1987*, New York: Harper and Row, 1987.

Cadava, E., Connor, P., and Nancy, J.-L. (eds), *Who Comes after the Subject?*, London and New York: Routledge, 1991.

Caillois, R., *Le Mythe et l'homme*, Paris: Gallimard, 1938.

Callens, J. (ed.), *The Wooster Group and Its Traditions*, Brussels: P.I.E.–Peter Lang, 2004.

Case, S.-E. and Reinelt, J. (eds), *The Performance of Power*, Iowa City: University of Iowa Press, 1991.

Castellucci, C. and Castelluci, R., *Il Teatro della Societas Raffaello Sanzio: dal teatro iconoclasta alla super-icona*, Milan: Ubulibri, 1992.

Centre National de la Recherche Scientifique, *Du Cirque au Théâtre*, Lausanne: L'Age d'Homme, 1983.

Corneille, P., 'Discours sur les trois unités', in *Ôeuvres complètes*, vol. 3, Paris: Editions du Seuil, 1963, pp. 174–90.

Crugten, A. van, *S. I. Witkiewicz: aux sources d'un théâtre nouveau*, Lausanne: L'Age d'Homme, 1971.

Debord, G., *The Society of the Spectacle*, trans. by Donald Nicholson-Smith, New York: Zone Books, 1994.

Deleuze, G., *Cinema 2: The Time-Image*, trans. by H. Tomlinson and R. Galeta, London: Athlone Press, 1989.

——, *Difference and Repetition*, trans. by P. Patton, New York: Columbia University Press, 1994.

Diamond, E. (ed.), *Performance and Cultural Politics*, London and New York: Routledge, 1996.

——, *Unmaking Mimesis: Essays on Feminism and the Theatre*, London and New York: Routledge, 1997.

Dort, B., 'Une écriture de la représentation', in *Théâtre en Europe*, vol. 10, Paris: Actes Sud, April 1986, pp. 18–21.

——, *La Représentation émancipée*, Arles: Actes Sud, 1988.

Dotzler, B. J. and Müller, E. (eds), *Wahrnehmung und Geschichte – Markierungen zur Aisthesis materialis*, Berlin: Akademic-Verlag, 1995.

Eberle, O., *Cenalora: Leben, Glauben, Tanz und Theatre der Urvölker*, Olten: Walter, 1954.

Eisenstein, S. M., *Film Form*, New York: Harcourt, 1969.

Eliot, T. S., 'A Dialogue on Dramatic Poetry', in *Selected Essays*, London: Faber and Faber, 1932, pp. 432–58.

Esslin, M., *The Theatre of the Absurd*, New York: Anchor Books, 1961.

——, *An Anatomy of Drama*, New York: Hill and Wang, 1977, 3rd edition 1979.

Etchells, T., *Certain Fragments: Contemporary Performance and Forced Entertainment*, London and New York: Routledge, 1999.

Finter, H., 'Experimental Theatre and Semiology of Theatre: The Theatricalization of Voice', in *Modern Drama*, vol. 24, no. 4, December 1983, Toronto, pp. 501–17.

Fischer-Lichte, E., *Das Drama und seine Inszenierung: Vorträge des internationalen literatur- und theatersemiotischen Kolloquiums Frankfurt am Main*, Tübingen: Niemeyer, 1985.

——, *The Semiotics of Theater*, trans. by J. Gaines and D. L. Jones, Bloomington: Indiana University Press, 1992.

——, *The Show and the Gaze of Theatre: A European Perspective*, Iowa City: Iowa University Press, 1997.

Floeck, W. (ed.), *Tendenzen des Gegenwartstheaters*, Tübingen: Francke, 1998.

Foster, H., *The Anti-Aesthetic: Essays on Postmodern Culture*, Seattle: New Press, 1983.

——, *Recodings: Art, Spectacle, Cultural Politics*, Port Townsend, WA: Bay Press, 1985.

Foucault, M., *The Order of Things*, London: Routledge, 2001.

Fuchs, E., *The Death of Character: Perspectives on Theatre after Modernism*, Indianapolis: Indiana University Press, 1996.

Furse, A., 'Those Who Can Do Teach', in M. M. Delgado and C. Svich (eds.), *Theatre in Crisis? Performance Manifestos for a New Century*, Manchester and New York: Manchester University Press, 2002, pp. 64–73.

Fusco, C., 'The Other History of Intercultural Performance', in *Drama Review*, vol. 38, no. 1, Spring 1994, pp. 143–66.

Gadamer, H.-G., *Truth and Method*, trans. and ed. by G. Barden and J. Cumming, New York: Crossroad, 1986.

Genet, J., 'L'étrange mot d'urbanisme', in *Œuvres complètes*, vol. 4, Paris: Gallimard, 1968, pp. 8–18.

Genette, G., *Palimpsestes*, Paris: Editions du Seuil, 1982.

Goebbels, H. and Lehmann, H.-T., 'Gespräch', in W. Storch (ed.), *Das szenische Auge*, Berlin: Institut für Auslandsbeziehungen (IFA), 1996.

Goethe – Schiller: Briefwechsel, Hamburg: Fischer Bücherei, 1961.

Goldberg, R., *Performance Art: From Futurism to the Present*, New York: Harry Abrams, 1988.

Gómez-Peña. G., *Dangerous Border Crossers: The Artist Talks Back*, New York: Routledge, 2000.

Gray, C., *The Great Experiment: Russian Art 1863–1922*, London: Thames and Hudson, 1962.

Grotowski, J., *Towards a Poor Theatre*, ed. by E. Barba, preface by P. Brook, London: Methuen, 1975.

Gumbrecht, H. U., 'Die Schönheit des Mannschafssports: American Football – im Stadion und im Fernsehen', in G. Vattimo and W. Welsch (eds), *Medien–Welten–Wirklichkeiten*, Munich: Fink Verlag, 1998.

——, *Production of Presence: What Meaning Cannot Convey*, Stanford, CA: Stanford University Press, 2004.

Gumbrecht, H. U. and Pfeiffer, K. L. (eds), *Materialität der Kommunikation*, Frankfurt am Main: Suhrkamp, 1988.

Haas, A. (ed.), *TheaterAngelusNovus. AntikenMaterial VI. Tod des Hektor* in *Maske und Kothurn*, vol. 36, nos 1–4, 1990.

——, *HamletMaschine: Tokyo Material.*, Berlin: Alexander, 1991.

Haas, A., Szeiler, J. and Wallburg, B. (eds), *MenschenMaterial: Eine Theaterarbeit mit Josef Szeiler*, Berlin: Basis Druck: 1991.

Hamacher, W., 'Afformative, Strike: Benjamin's "Critique of Violence"', trans. by D. Hollander, in A. Benjamin and P. Osborne (eds), *Walter Benjamin's Philosophy: Destruction and Experience*, London and New York: Routledge, 1994, pp. 110–38.

Harris, Geraldine, *Staging Femininities: Performance and Performativity*, Manchester: Manchester University Press, 1999.

Hegel, G. W. F., *Aesthetics: Lectures on Fine Art*, 2 vols, trans. by T. M. Knox, Oxford: Clarendon Press, 1975.

——, *Phenomenology of Spirit*, trans. by A. V. Miller with analysis of the text and foreword by J. N. Findlay, Oxford: Clarendon Press, 1977.

Hensel, G., *Theater der siebziger Jahre*, Stuttgart: Deutsche Verlags-Austalt, 1980.

Herkenrath, K., 'Jan Lauwers "Antonius und Cleopatra": Eine nachepische Theaterkonzeption', diploma thesis, Giessen, 1993.

Hoghe, R., *Pina Bausch: Tanztheatergeschichten*, Frankfurt am Main: Suhrkamp, 1986.

Iden, P., 'Am Ende der Neuigkeiten: Am Ende des Neuen?', in 'Theater 1980', Jahrbuch (Annual) of *Theater Heute*, 1980, pp. 126–8.

Innes, C., *Avant Garde Theatre*, London and New York: Routledge, 1993.

Ionesco, E., *Notes et contre-notes*, Paris: Gallimard, 1962.

Jackson, S., *Professing Performance: Theatre in the Academy from Philology to Performativity*, Cambridge: Cambridge University Press, 2004.

Jacquot, J., *Le Théâtre moderne: depuis la deuxième guerre mondiale*, Paris: CNRS, 1973.

Jelavich, P., 'Populäre Theatralik, Massenkultur und Avantgarde: Betrachtungen zum Theater der Jahrhundertwende', in H. Schmid and J. Striedter (eds), *Dramatische und theatralische Kommunikation: Beiträge zur Geschichte und Theorie des Dramas und Theaters*, Tübingen: Gunter Narr, 1992, pp. 253–61.

Kalb, J., 'Samuel Beckett, Heiner Müller and Post-Dramatic Theater', in *Samuel Beckett Today/Aujourd'hui: An Annual Bilingual Review/Revue Annuelle Bilingue*, vol. 11, 2002, pp. 74–83.

Kant, I., *Critique of Judgement*, trans. by J. C. Meredith, Oxford: Clarendon Press, 1952.

Kantor, T., *Theater des Todes, Die tote Klasse, Wielopole-Wielopole*, ed. by W. Fenn, Institut für Moderne Kunst Nürnberg, Zirndorf: Verlag für moderne Kunst, 1983.

——, *A Journey through Other Spaces: Essays and Manifestos, 1944–1990*, ed. and trans. by M. Kobialka with a critical study of Tadeusz Kantor's theatre by M. Kobialka, Berkeley, Los Angeles and London: University of California Press, 1993.

Kaye, N., *Postmodernism and Performance*, London: Macmillan, 1994.

Keller, H., *Robert Wilson: Regie im Theater*, Frankfurt am Main: Fischer, 1997.

Kirby, M., *A Formalist Theatre*, Philadelphia: University of Pennsylvania Press, 1987.

Kittler, F., *Gramophone, Film, Typewriter*, trans. by G. Winthrop Young, Stanford, CA: Stanford University Press, 1999.

Kloepfer, R., 'Das Theater der Sinn-Erfüllung: DOUBLE & PARADISE vom Serapionstheater (Wien) als Beispiel einer totalen Inszenierung', in E. Fischer-Lichte (ed.), *Das Drama und seine Inszenierung*, Tübingen: Niemeyer, 1985, pp. 199–218.

Kluge, A. and Müller, H., *Ich bin ein Landvermesser: Gespräche, Neue Folge*, Hamburg: Rotbuch, 1996.

Kostelanetz, R., *The Theatre of Mixed Means*, London: Pitman, 1970.

Kott, J., *Shakespeare heute*, Berlin: Alexander Verlag, 1989.

Kristeva, J., *Polylogue*, Paris, 1977.

——, *Revolution in Poetic Language*, New York: Columbia University Press, 1984.

Kruger, L., 'Making Sense of Sensation: Enlightenment, Embodiment, and the End(s) of Modern Drama', in *Modern Drama*, vol. 43, no. 4, 2000, pp. 543–63.

Kuppers, Petra, *Disability and Performance: Bodies on the Edge*, London and New York: Routledge, 2003.

Lacan, J., *Four Fundamental Concepts of Psychoanalysis*, New York: Norton, 1988.

Langer, S. K., *Feeling and Form*, New York: Charles Scribner's Sons, 1953.

Lehmann, H.-T., 'Dramatische Form und Revolution in Georg Büchner's "Dantons Tod" und Heiner Müller's "Der Auftrag"', in P. von Becker *et al.* (eds), *Dantons Tod: Die Trauerarbeit im Schönen: Ein Theater-Lesebuch*, Frankfurt am Main: Syndikat, 1980, pp. 106–21.

——, 'L'esthétique du risque', in *L'Art du théâtre*, no. 7, autumn 1987, pp. 35–44.

——, 'Theater der Blicke: Zu Heiner Müller's "Bildbeschreibung"', in U. Profitlich (ed.), *Dramatik der DDR*, Frankfurt am Main: Suhrkamp, 1987, pp. 186–202.

——, 'Robert Wilson: Szenograph/Fussnote zur *Hamletmaschine*' in *Parkett*, no. 16, 1988, pp. 30–41.

——, *Theater und Mythos: Die Konstitution des Subjekts im Diskurs der antiken Tragödie*, Stuttgart: Metzler, 1991.

——, 'Antiquité et modernité par delà le drame', in G. Banu, *Klaus Michael Grüber: . . . il faut que le théâtre passe à travers les larmes . . .*, Paris: Editions du Regard 1993, pp. 201–6.

Lorenz, R., 'Jan Fabres "Die Macht der theatralischen Torheiten" und das Problem der Aufführungsanalyse', diploma thesis, Giessen, 1988.

Lyotard, J.-F., 'The Tooth, the Palm', in T. Murray (ed.), *Mimesis, Masochism and Mime: Politics of Theatricality in Contemporary French Thought*, Ann Arbor: University of Michigan Press, 1977, pp. 282–8.

——, *Essays zu einer affirmativen Ästhetik*, Berlin: Merve, 1982.

——, *The Postmodern Condition: A Report on Knowledge*, trans. by G. Bennington and B. Massumi, foreword by F. Jameson, Minneapolis: University of Minnesota Press, 1984.

——, *The Postmodern Explained: Correspondence 1982–1985*, trans. by D. Barry *et al.*, afterword by W. Godzich, Minneapolis: University of Minnesota Press, 1993.

McGuire, M., 'Forced Entertainment on Politics and Pleasure', *Variant*, vol. 5, available online at http://www.variant.randomstate.org/5texts/Michelle-McGuire.html.

Mallarmé, S., *Œuvres complètes*, Paris: Pleiade, 1970.

Man, P. de, *Die Ideologie des Ästetischen*, Frankfurt am Main: Suhrkamp, 1993.

Marranca, B., 'The Forest as Archive: Wilson and Interculturalism', in *Performing Arts Journal*, vol. 11, no 3/vol. 12, no. 1 (*PAJ* 33/34) 1989, pp. 36–44.

——, *Ecologies of Theatre*, Baltimore, MD: Johns Hopkins University Press, 1996.

Matejka, L. (ed.), *Sign, Sound, and Meaning*, Ann Arbor: University of Michigan Press, 1976.

Matzat, W., *Dramenstruktur und Zuschauerrolle*, Munich: Fink, 1982.

Menke, C., 'The Dissolution of the Beautiful: Hegel's Theory of Drama', in *L'Esprit créateur*, vol. 35, no. 3, Lexington, 1995, pp. 19–36.

——, *Tragödie im Sittlichen: Gerechtigkeit und Freiheit nach Hegel*, Frankfurt am Main: Suhrkamp, 1996.

Michaud, G., 'Ionesco: de la dérision à l'anti-monde', in J. Jacquot (ed.), *Le Théâtre moderne*, vol. 2, Paris: CNRS, 1973, pp. 37–43.

Mukařovský, J., *Kapitel aus der Ästhetik*, Frankfurt am Main: Suhrkamp, 1970.

Müller, H., *Gesammelte Irrtümer*, Frankfurt am Main: Verlag der Autoren, 1986.

——, *Heiner Müller Material*, ed. by F. Hörnigk, Göttingen: Steidl Verlag, 1989.

——, *Jenseits der Nation*, Berlin: Rotbuch, 1991.

——, *Krieg ohne Schlacht, Leben in zwei Diktaturen: Eine Autobiographie*, Cologne, 1994.

Müller, W. G., 'Das Ich im Dialog mit sich selbst: Bemerkungen zur Struktur des dramatischen Monologs von Shakespeare bis zu Samuel Beckett', in *Deutsche Vierteljahresschrift für Literaturwissenschaft und Geistesgeschichte*, vol. 56, no. 2, Stuttgart, 1982, pp. 314–33.

Murray, T. (ed.), *Mimesis, Masochism and Mime: Politics of Theatricality in Contemporary French Thought*, Ann Arbor: University of Michigan Press, 1977.

Nganang, A. P., *Interkulturalität und Bearbeitung: Untersuchung zu Soyinka und Brecht*, (dissertation, Frankfurt am Main 1998), Munich: Iudicium, 1998.

Novarina, V., *Le Théâtre des paroles*, Paris: Éditions P.O.L, 1989.

Oettermann, S., 'Das Panorama: Ein Massenmedium', in U. Brandes (ed.), *Sehsucht: Über die Veränderung visueller Wahrnehmung*, Göttingen: Steidl Verlag, 1995.

Panizza, O., 'Der Klassizismus und das Eindringen des Variété', in *Die Gesellschaft*, October 1896, pp. 1,252–74.

Pavis, P., 'The Classical Heritage of Modern Drama: The Case of Postmodern Theatre', in *Modern Drama*, vol. 29, 1986, pp. 1–22.

——, *Dictionary of the Theatre: Terms, Concepts and Analysis*, trans. by Christine Shantz, Toronto: University of Toronto Press, 1998.

Pfister, M., *The Theory and Analysis of Drama*, trans. by J. Halliday, Cambridge: Cambridge University Press, 1988 [1977].

Plassard, D., *L'Acteur en effigie: figures de l'homme artificiel dans le théâtre des avantgardes historiques. Allemagne, France, Italie*, Lausanne: L'Age d'Homme, 1992.

Ponte di Pino, O., *Il nuovo teatro italiano 1975–1988*, Florence: La Casa Usher, 1988.

Poschmann, G., *Der nicht mehr dramatische Theatertext: Aktuelle Bühnenstücke und ihre dramatische Analyse*, Tübingen: Niemeyer, 1997.

Preikschat, W., *Video: Die Poesie der neuen Medien*, Basel: Beltz, 1987.

Primavesi, P., *Kommentar, Übersetzung, Theater in Walter Benjamin frühen Schriften*, Frankfurt am Main: Stroemfeld/Nexus, 1998.

Reaney, M., 'Virtual Reality on Stage', in *VR World*, vol. 3, no. 3, May/June 1995, pp. 28–31.

Redmond, J. (ed.), *Drama and Symbolism*, Cambridge: Cambridge University Press, 1982.

Ritter, J. and Gründer, K. (eds), *Historisches Wörterbuch der Philosophie*, Basel: Schwabe Verlag, 1995, vol. 9, column 936.

Rokem, F., *Theatrical Space in Ibsen, Chekhov and Strindberg: Public Forms of Privacy*, Ann Arbor: University of Michigan Press, 1986.

Roose-Evans, J., *Experimental Theatre: From Stanislavsky to Peter Brook*, New York: Universe Books, 1984.

Rötzer, F. (ed.), *Digitaler Schein: Ästhetik der elektronischen Medien*, Frankfurt am Main: Suhrkamp, 1991.

Roubine, J. J., *Théâtre et mise en scène 1880–1980*, Paris: Presses Universitaires de France, 1980.

Sabbatini, A. J., 'Terrorism, Perform', in *High Performance*, vol. 9, no. 2, 1986, pp. 29–33.

Sarrazac, J.-P., *L'Avenir du drame: écritures dramatiques contemporaines*, Lausanne: Circé, 1981.

Savran, D, *The Wooster Group: Breaking the Rules*, New York: Theatre Communications Group, 1988.

——, 'Revolution . . . History . . . Theatre: The Politics of The Wooster Group's Second

Trilogy' in S.-E. Case and J. Reinelt (eds), *The Performance of Power*, Iowa City: University of Iowa Press, 1991, pp. 41–55.

Schechner, R., *Between Theater and Anthropology*, Philadelphia: University of Pennsylvania Press, 1985.

——, *The End of Humanism*, New York: Theatre Communications Group, 1987.

——, *Performance Theory*, New York: Taylor and Francis, 1988.

Schleef, E., *Droge Faust Parzival*, Frankfurt am Main: Suhrkamp, 1997.

Schleper, A., 'Off the Route Strategies and Approaches to the Appropriation of Space', in J. Helmer and F. Malzacher (eds), *'Not Even a Game Anymore': The Theatre of Forced Entertainment*, Berlin: Alexander Verlag: 2004, pp. 185–202.

Schroeder, J. L., *Identität, Überschreitung, Verwandlung: Happenings, Aktionen und Performances von bildenden Künstlern*, Münster: LIT Verlag, 1990.

Segel, H. B., *Turn of the Century Cabaret*, New York: Columbia University Press, 1987.

Seym, S., *Das Théâtre du Soleil: Ariane Mnouchkines Ästhetik des Theaters*, Stuttgart: Metzler, 1992.

Shank, T., *American Alternative Theatre*, London: Macmillan, 1982.

Shepherd, S. and Wallis, M., *Drama/Theatre/Performance*, London and New York: Routledge, 2004.

Siegmund, G., *Theater und Gedächtnis: Semiotische und psychoanalytische Studien zur Funktion des Dramas*, Tübingen: Narr, 1996.

——, 'Voice Masks: Subjectivity, America, and the Voice in the Theatre of The Wooster Group', in J. Callens (ed.), *The Wooster Group and Its Traditions*, Brussels: P.I.E.–Peter Lang, 2004, pp. 167–87.

Sobchak, V., 'The Scene of the Screen: Envisioning Cinematic and Electronic "Presence"', in R. Stam and T. Miller (eds), *Film and Theory: An Anthology*, Malden, MA, and Oxford: Blackwell Publishers, 2000, pp. 67–84.

Southern, R., *The Seven Ages of the Theatre*, London: Faber and Faber, 1968.

Stefanek, P., 'Lesedrama? – Überlegungen zur szenischen Transformation "bühnenfremder" Dramaturgie', in E. Fischer-Lichte (ed.), *Das Drama und seine Inszenierung: Vorträge des internationalen literatur- und theatersemiotischen Kolloquiums Frankfurt am Main 1983*, Tübingen: M. Niemeyer, 1985, pp. 133–45.

Stein, G., *Look at Me Now and Here I Am: Writings and Lectures 1909–45*, ed. by P. Meyerowitz, London: Penguin: 1984.

Steiner, G., *After Babel: Aspects of Language and Translation*, Oxford: Oxford University Press, 1975.

Steinweg, R. (ed.), *Brechts Modell der Lehrstücke: Zeugnisse, Diskussion, Erfahrungen*, Frankfurt am Main: Suhrkamp, 1976.

Storch, W., *Das szenische Auge*, Berlin: Institut für Auslandsbeziehungen, 1996.

Strehler, S., 'Popmimen in der Bühnenburg', in *spex*, vol. 11, 1998, pp. 80–2.

Sugiera, Malgorzata, 'Beyond Drama: Writing for Postdramatic Theatre', in *Theatre Research International*, vol. 29, no. 1, March 2004, p. 26.

Szondi, P., *Das lyrische Drama*, Frankfurt am Main: Suhrkamp, 1975.

——, *Theory of the Modern Drama*, ed. and trans. by M. Hays, foreword by J. Schulte-Sasse, Minneapolis: University of Minnesota Press, 1987.

——, *An Essay on the Tragic*, trans. by P. Fleming, Stanford, CA: Stanford University Press, 2002.

Theater der Welt in Dresden 1996: 20 Interviews – Regisseure und Künstler im Gespräch.

Theaterschrift, Heft 3, *Grenzverletzungen: Über Risiko, Gewalt & innere Notwendigkeit*, ed. by M. Van Kerkhoven, Brussels: Kaaitheater, 1993.

Theaterschrift, Heft 5/6, *Über Dramaturgie*, ed. by M. Van Kerkhoven, Brussels: Kaaitheater, January 1994.

Toepfer, K., *Theatre, Aristocracy and Pornocracy*, New York: Performing Arts Journal Publications, 1991.

Turner, V., *From Ritual to Theatre: The Human Seriousness of Play*, New York: Performing Arts Journal Publications, 1982.

——, *On the Edge of a Bush*, Tucson: University of Arizona Press, 1985.

Valentini, V., 'In Search of Lost Stories: Italian Performance in the Mid-80s', in *Tulane Drama Review*, vol. 32, no. 3 (119), Fall 1988, pp. 109–25.

Varopoulou, E., 'Musikalisierung der Theaterzeichen', lecture at the first International Summer Academy in Frankfurt am Main, August 1998, unpublished manuscript.

Vattimo, G. and Welsch, W., *Medien–Welten–Wirklichkeiten*, Munich: Fink Verlag, 1998.

Verwiebe, B., '"Wo die Kunst endigt und die Wahrheit beginnt": Lichtmagie und Verwandlung im 19. Jahrhundert', in U. Brandes (ed.), *Sehsucht: Über die Veränderung visueller Wahrnehmung*, Göttingen: Steidl Verlag, 1995.

Waldenfels, B., *Sinnesschwellen: Studien zur Phänomenologie des Fremden 3*, Frankfurt am Main: Suhrkamp, 1999.

Watanabe, M., 'Quelqu'un arrive', in *Théâtre en Europe*, vol. 13, 1987, pp. 26–30.

Weber, S., 'Humanitäre Intervention im Zeitalter der Medien: Zur Frage einer heterogenen Politik', in H.-P. Jäck and H. Pfeil (eds), *Eingriffe im Zeitalter der Medien* (Politik des Anderen, vol. 1), Bornheim and Rostock: Hanseatischer Fachverlag für Wirtschaft, 1995, pp. 5–27.

Weinrich, H., *Tempus: Besprochene und erzählte Welt*, Stuttgart: Kohlhammer, 1971.

Wessendorf, M., 'The Postdramatic Theatre of Richard Maxwell', unpublished manuscript (2003) available online at http://www2.hawaii.edu/~wessendo/Maxwell.htm.

Wiener Festwochen 1990, Big Motion: Theater der Gegenwart, public interviews, ed. by Brigitte Furle.

Wille, F., 'Zwielicht der Freiheit', in *Theater Heute*, no. 9, 1995, pp. 4–7.

Wirth, A., 'Vom Dialog zum Diskurs: Versuch einer Synthese der nachbrechtschen Theaterkonzepte', in *Theater Heute*, vol. 1, 1980, pp. 16–19.

——, 'Interculturalism and Iconophilia in the New Theatre', in *Performing Arts Journal*, vol. 33/34, 1989, pp. 176–83.

——, 'Interkulturalität und Ikonophilia im neuen Theater', in S. Bauschinger and S. L. Cocalis (eds), *Vom Wort zum Bild: Das neue Theater in Deutschland und den USA*, Bern: Francke, 1992.

Zinder, D. G., *The Surrealist Connection*, Ann Arbor: University of Michigan Press, 1976.

Index